ASK
YOUR
SPIRIT

Also by Christine Lang

The Body Whisperer

Praise for

ASK YOUR SPIRIT

"*Ask Your Spirit* is a critical reference guide to self-discovery, offering transformative tools for navigating life's complexities with grace and insight."

Jack Canfield, coauthor of the #1 *New York Times* bestselling *Chicken Soup for the Soul®* series and *The Success Principles™*, and a featured teacher in *The Secret*

"Reading this book felt like sitting down with a wise and loving mentor. The insights here will change the way you see yourself and your journey."

Marci Shimoff, #1 *New York Times* bestselling author of *Happy for No Reason* and *Chicken Soup for the Woman's Soul*

"This book is a game-changer! Filled with outstanding examples of the healing potential of asking your spirit for advice, it will empower you to uncover solutions to your most pressing challenges."

Suzanne Giesemann, author of *The Awakened Way*

"What a gift Christine has given the world! A step-by-step tutorial in creating powerful communication with your spirit. As a longtime client of Christine's, I've experienced firsthand the power of receiving direct specific guidance from the nonphysical part of you who knows everything you want and how to heal it, release it, and manifest it. Lots of case studies for divine inspiration. A book that should be in everyone's library."

Sheri Salata, author of *The Beautiful No* and former executive producer of *The Oprah Winfrey Show*

"*Ask Your Spirit* unlocks the gateway to your deepest wisdom, offering clarity and connection to navigate life's journey with purpose and grace and helping you connect with your own Spirit for total wellness of body, mind, and heart."

Sadhvi Bhagawati Saraswati, spiritual leader, social activist, and bestselling author of *Hollywood to the Himalayas: A Journey of Healing and Transformation*

"*Ask Your Spirit* delivers clear, simple steps on how to meditate and connect with your inner guidance. It then delivers an abundance of potent exercises and examples of how you can access your deepest wisdom to experience a more insightful, satisfying life."

Thomas Fitzgerald, MD, medical director of Southlake Psychiatry, Davidson, North Carolina

"As a nurse practitioner in a cardiac recovery unit, I know that it's essential to be able to ask 'why?' *Ask Your Spirit* provides clear steps on how to acquire answers from your spirit and heal everything from your worst symptoms to your important relationships. It's rare to find teachings that are so comprehensive but not overwhelming."

Katie Dziedzic, nurse practitioner

ASK YOUR SPIRIT

Receiving Life-Changing
Answers from Your
Elevated Intelligence

Christine Lang

balance

NEW YORK   BOSTON

Copyright © 2025 by Christine Lang

Cover design by Jim Datz. Cover image by Shutterstock.
Cover copyright © 2025 by Hachette Book Group, Inc.

Balance
Hachette Book Group
1290 Avenue of the Americas
New York, NY 10104
GCP-Balance.com
@GCPBalance

First Edition: May 2025

Balance is an imprint of Grand Central Publishing. The Balance name and logo are registered trademarks of Hachette Book Group, Inc.

The publisher is not responsible for websites (or their content) that are not owned by the publisher.

The Hachette Speakers Bureau provides a wide range of authors for speaking events. To find out more, go to hachettespeakersbureau.com or email HachetteSpeakers@hbgusa.com.

Balance books may be purchased in bulk for business, educational, or promotional use. For information, please contact your local bookseller or the Hachette Book Group Special Markets Department at special.markets@hbgusa.com.

Print book interior design by Six Red Marbles.

Library of Congress Control Number: 2025931486

ISBNs: 978-1-5387-7391-8 (trade paperback); 978-1-5387-7392-5 (ebook)

Printed in the United States of America

LSC-C

Printing 1, 2025

CONTENTS

THE ANSWERS BELONG TO YOU

"I don't believe you," the woman said forcefully, her hand trembling slightly as she gripped the microphone. She was standing in the audience with her shoulders squared off for battle, and she was glaring at me. "You say that our spirit wants to answer our questions, but my spirit must hate me. Either that or she's quit!"

Nervous laughter rippled through the audience; they felt sympathy for the woman's situation, but their focus remained glued on me. I'd been a medical intuitive for over twenty-five years, conversing with clients and their spirits to discover the underlying reasons for people's struggles in health, work, and relationships. My job is to be the translator for each person's spirit, providing answers and reassurance. But at this moment I have two hundred people staring at me, waiting for me to immediately transform this woman's anger and confusion into clarity.

The woman named Sharon continued, sharing that she'd been a nurse for twenty years and was good at it. But she'd had to leave her job last year and go on disability because of adrenal fatigue despite "doing all the right things" to heal herself.

As she continued, the tension in her voice escalated along with the volume. "I see the best doctors! I eat a ridiculously clean diet! I see the best alternative medicine practitioners, and I take about a million supplements! I sit in meditation like you talk about, and I've asked my spirit how to heal my adrenals so I can go back to work. But I hear nothing back from her! So here I am—still tired and on disability with no answers! So please explain: How exactly is my spirit trying to help me?"

Once again, the audience's focus pivoted from her back toward me on the stage, ready for my explanation.

Gently I offered, "Perhaps it's not that she won't answer your question. Maybe we just need to ask the question in a different way. May I connect my energy to yours and speak with your spirit?"

Sharon threw up her hands. "Go ahead! Maybe she'll actually talk to you."

I closed my eyes and focused my energy so that I could hear her spirit, and then relayed the message I heard.

"Your spirit tells me that she's trying to answer your questions, but that you're missing what she's saying because you're not on the same page about the goals to be pursued."

For a second, I thought that Sharon was going to throw the microphone at me. She actually stomped her right foot as she said, "Are you kidding me? My spirit doesn't think that I should be well? See, I told you she hates me!"

I took a slow breath and released it, hoping that Sharon would do the same. Then I continued, "Your spirit is the wisest part of you, so she's always trying to help. Sometimes when we don't get answers it's because our questions are framed in such a way that our spirit can't answer them accurately and simultaneously take care of us. In this case, your spirit doesn't want you to resume your old life, but that's not because she hates you."

Sharon's shoulders slumped forward. "I just don't understand," she said in a small, tired voice.

"I know," I said sympathetically, "and I want to clear this up for you. Your spirit says that your childhood prepared you to take care of others—does that feel true for you?"

Sharon paused for a moment. "Yeah, I guess that's true. My mom was an alcoholic, and my dad was away a lot. I was the oldest, so it fell on me to hold things together so that all of us kids were okay. But how is that relevant?"

I held up my hand. "Bear with me here. I've learned that such questions usually lead to good insights."

Sharon nodded for me to continue, so I shared the next message from her spirit. "I'm hearing that your mom and dad both praised you for this caretaking work, and it became a very big piece of your identity. And that what you value *most* in yourself is how much you do for others."

"So, what's wrong with that?" Sharon demanded, edging back toward her earlier agitation.

"It's not that it's wrong," I continued, "but it's out of balance, and your spirit says that it's not serving you anymore. Your spirit asks this question: 'What qualities do you value in yourself *that aren't about helping others?*' "

The audience waited silently as Sharon thought. Tears began to roll down her face and she quietly admitted, "I can't think of anything...I really can't."

I continued softly. "Your spirit says that as you've lost track of your other valuable qualities, you leaned more and more into this behavior of helping others, even when it was to your own detriment. You frequently did more than your share of work at the hospital, you lent money to friends and never asked for repayment, and you became more and more miserable in your life. The adrenal fatigue is the *physical manifestation* of how you were allowing other people's needs to drain you. Not being able to work was a gift that helped you break a pattern that had become very unhealthy for you. It wasn't that you were doing anything wrong! You weren't successful because your desired outcome of going back to work wouldn't have served you."

Sharon was silent for a very long time. "Oh...wow," she said eventually.

I pressed on. "With your permission, I'd like to ask your spirit how she recommends that you *heal completely*, not just what will enable you to get you back to work as a nurse."

"Yes, please!" Sharon nodded eagerly.

Sharon's spirit gave me a visual of an orchid plant, so I asked her, "Do you enjoy working with plants?"

Sharon's eyes opened wide, and a smile lit up her face. She exclaimed, "Yes! I raise rare orchids! I've even started a blog about it while I've been at home. It's really crazy how many people are following it!"

"Your spirit says that working with plants has been helping you heal because they don't require much energy output from you. And that when you write about them in your blog, you're sharing your experiences and feelings along with tips on plant care. Your followers value you and your writing because of what they learn and feel from you, not because you're actually doing things for them. Can you feel the energetic difference between that sort of work and your nursing work?"

"Yes..." Sharon said hesitatingly. "But the orchids and the blog are just a hobby, not a real job."

I smiled. "Your spirit is telling me that she encourages you to follow this passion because she believes that you can make a career out of this hobby of yours. And if not, this time at home has given you a new model of how you want your next job to feel—less draining and more inspired."

[Follow-up: Sharon is now "retired" from nursing and supports herself as an orchid breeder and expert blogger. Her adrenal fatigue has completely healed.]

WHY YOU NEED TO INVEST IN YOUR ELEVATED INTELLIGENCE

If you've picked up this book, I'm assuming that you—like Sharon—may be navigating through some challenges and are wondering why you cannot find the right answers. Most of my clients consider themselves to be "on a path" in some way. They come to me because they have unanswered questions about their health, career, and relationships. They're frequently feeling lost or disconnected from themselves in some way.

In their quest for answers, they've done at least one (and maybe all) of these things:

- Read books that are considered self-help, spiritual, or holistic

- Consulted with alternative health-care providers (chiropractors, naturopaths, acupuncturists, etc.)
- Tried meditation
- Tried listening to their "gut"
- Listened to podcasts geared toward personal growth or self-healing
- Researched natural healing methods online
- Attended online classes focused on creating financial abundance, attracting love, or developing healing abilities

And yet they're still not receiving the answers they seek. Like them, you're likely feeling frustrated because you have SO many unanswered questions.

I want to help you get answers. Answers about how your body got this way (and how to fix it), why the unhealthy parts of your relationships seem to be on repeat, and why your money issues persist despite your hard work. I promise that your spirit wants to answer all of your questions—you just need to learn how to ask the *right* questions and how to listen in a slightly different way.

I've worked with more than twelve thousand clients, and each of them was dedicated to their pursuit of useful solutions. The problem was never a lack of effort; it was the ineffective process that they had for asking questions, as well as the infrequency with which they were practicing connecting to the part of themselves that was seeking solutions. Most people attempt to engage with the spirit world (be it God, the Universe, angels, guides, or one's spirit) when they're in crisis—physically or emotionally. By this point, they're in such a state of desperation that their efforts are akin to you frantically searching the internet to look up a strange new symptom: your results will be spotty at best, and any relief will be short-lived.

The solution is twofold. The right questions, coupled with a regular practice of engagement with one's spirit, will get you functioning from what I call your elevated intelligence. Think of it like your own internal Chat GPT.

When you engage in frequent conversations with your spirit, your conscious mind becomes connected to and influenced by your spirit's wisdom. Because your spirit, your inner wisdom, has knowledge far beyond the scope of ordinary logic and memory, you are then operating from your elevated intelligence. This is the key to sustaining the equilibrium we're all searching for, and I'm here to get you operating from this system.

We now realize that the key to getting productive answers from AI technology is knowing the right prompts, or questions, to ask. Similarly, reaping the benefits of your elevated intelligence involves asking the right questions and connecting fully with this aspect of your intelligence on a daily basis. This is the key. We must be actively engaging with our spirit, even when we don't think we need to (or don't have a specific question), in order to operate from our elevated intelligence.

People who are exceptional at their jobs, from the renowned brain surgeon to the superbly accurate plumber, are tapping into their elevated intelligence, but they may be calling it by different names. They may say that they are "in the zone," receiving "divine inspiration," or even that they have "amazing gut instincts." But I believe that they're each aligned with their inner wisdom—their spirit—and are being given directions that make them gloriously successful. These individuals have lives that look a bit magical and effortless, and their self-confidence can be felt when you're near them.

This is the "edge" that I want to give you—the ability to be guided by your spirit's wisdom at all times, not just when you're desperate for relief. When you incorporate your elevated intelligence into your daily life, your decisions become more accurate, your insights are more profound, and your healing processes become amplified.

Your spirit knows why that supplement or medication didn't work and who the best practitioner is for you to work with. Your spirit also knows which old wounds are prompting you to repeat patterns in your relationships and which beliefs you hold about money are blocking your abundance. Your spirit is eager to help you reach your highest potential, and your elevated intelligence offers you the best therapist, coach, and limitless source for answers.

So who is your spirit? I describe it as your higher self, your deepest wisdom, your own inner divinity. It is the very wise, compassionate, subtle voice that whispers within all of us. Your spirit is always seeking to promote your expansion and development. Imagine a radio station that plays twenty-four hours a day and offers brilliant counsel just for you. The trick is finding that station on your radio. This book is meant to help you turn up the volume, "tune in" to your own personal channel, and actively engage in its dialogue. I want to support you becoming self-reliant on your journey, fostering independence and self-empowerment rather than creating a dependency on external sources. This personalized, ongoing conversation with your elevated intelligence is akin to having your spirit on speed dial.

HOW I BEGAN WORKING WITH MY ELEVATED INTELLIGENCE

My journey of connection with my own spirit began, as so many people's journeys begin, with persistent physical symptoms that I desperately wanted to get rid of. Since my second year of law school, I'd battled constant allergies and was tired of being labeled as the "constantly sick lawyer" by my colleagues in the legal department of one of the United States' biggest banks.

Traditional remedies delivered unwanted side effects, prompting me to explore alternative healing modalities, including homeopathy, herbs, and energy healing. When I noticed that my allergies increased when I felt stressed, I began a regular meditation practice. I learned Reiki and soon began offering my friends healing energy treatments. Before each session, I would meditate to center myself and often received intuitive "nudges" about my friends' symptoms. I'd encounter words or visuals that provided valuable insights into their physical conditions or the situations they were navigating in their lives. While my friends were amazed by these "psychic messages," a few questioned their origin. Unsure of how to respond, I felt compelled to seek answers of my own.

Sitting in my meditation chair, I raised my energy up above my head and asked, "Who am I speaking with?" A loving voice answered, "Welcome Home!" Tears streamed down my face as I felt a rush of loving energy wash over me. Then the same voice introduced herself as my spirit, and she said, "Get ready! This is who you came here to be. It's time—time to learn." Many hours of daily meditation followed, during which my spirit "trained me," answering my thousands of questions and revealing the connections between physical symptoms and emotional imbalances.

My spirit told me that I wasn't actually allergic to dust; instead, I was "allergic" to how I spoke to myself. During law school my self-talk had become so toxic that I had triggered an immune response. Over the next two years, I healed myself completely of allergies *and* radically transformed how I spoke to myself. More importantly, I had opened up a channel of communication with the wisest teacher I'd ever met.

As word spread about my abilities, friends and strangers requested healing sessions, leading to the birth of my medical intuitive practice. For the past twenty-eight years I've been helping people receive messages from their spirits so they could heal and transform their lives. There's a reason why so many doctors and psychologists refer their patients to me. Once I help someone tap into their elevated intelligence, their life is forever improved.

You may also have annoying, frustrating, painful, or even debilitating issues that affect how you live your life. I've come to see our most painful experiences—both the physical and the emotional ones—as indicators of changes that are needed in our lives. They are a message *to* you *from* your wisest self.

I've learned that there is ALWAYS a reason—for everything that happens. Sometimes the answers seem confusing while we're in the midst of a situation, but as events unfold, your spirit can help you see the perfect orchestration of your life's journey. There is a persistent peacefulness that permeates your life once you experience evidence that the Universe isn't just random, or worse, that God is indifferent.

I've also learned this: Your spirit wants a direct line of

communication with you. You don't have to have my level of abilities to get answers from your spirit. Once you create a connection with your spirit and a practice of asking questions and listening, there's an endless number of ways that you can receive information. Your spirit may send you visuals, feelings, a meaningful song on the radio, or an "odd coincidence" at the perfect time.

Communicating with your spirit regularly will dramatically increase your intuition—that gut feeling or hunch that leads you to the next perfect step for you. You're already getting these "divine nudges" or clues—you had one to pick up this book. I want to turn up the frequency of them exponentially. When your conscious mind begins partnering regularly with your intuition—that's when you're working from your elevated intelligence!

Once you have your spirit's assistance, I promise that your life will make sense in ways you can't even imagine. I think of my spirit as a wise consultant, coach, and therapist who's available to meet with me 24/7 and offer concrete, practical answers.

HOW THIS BOOK IS STRUCTURED

Getting answers doesn't mean that you can avoid every uncomfortable lesson in your life. It means you can spend less time feeling confused and alone. My elevated intelligence has consistently given me and my thousands of clients increased clarity and reduced our emotional suffering.

Here's how this book will help you get the most powerful answers to all of your questions.

First, I'll teach you my style of meditation, one that creates an opening for conversations with your spirit. In the next chapters we'll cover my approach to asking your spirit questions. Understanding why I phrase questions the way that I do will prepare you to get the most complete and helpful answers. And I'll offer you different ways to double-check the answers you receive so that you can build your confidence in this new way of gathering information.

Once you understand how to communicate with your spirit, we'll jump into the most common areas (your health, relationships, and work) that you may want to ask your spirit about and walk you through the best ways to approach asking questions on each topic. And throughout I'll use client stories to demonstrate the various ways that your spirit can send you messages and why. I think of this section of the book as your Relationship Manual, where you'll acquire the tools you'll need to have a powerful, productive relationship with your spirit.

In the Relationship Manual portion of the book, I'll begin by teaching you how to ask your spirit questions about your physical symptoms. As soon as you have a clear enough understanding of why we get symptoms, you'll be able to frame your questions in ways that will yield helpful answers. Then we'll focus on the topic that has preoccupied human hearts and minds for centuries: relationships. Once you're feeling more optimistic about transforming your relationships, we'll cover the subject that fills so many of our waking hours: work. I want to describe how both your work and your relationships function energetically and how they can either leave you energized or flustered and depleted.

In total, this Relationship Manual can function as a

"spiritual toolkit" that you can use when facing different challenges. All you need to do is return to the chapter that addresses your current dilemma, and you'll be provided with practices, exercises, stories, and the right kinds of questions to help you access your elevated intelligence.

In my two and a half decades of conversing with people's spirits, I've learned that context is critically important. The more you understand about the spirit world, the more skillful you become at asking the most powerful questions. And as my understanding has deepened, my spirit has offered me more detailed answers to my questions. I want to provide you with enough foundational information on the topics of healing, relationships, and money so that you can ask your spirit targeted, effective questions.

Since my early childhood, I've often heard the complaint "You ask too many questions!" For nearly three decades I've been pummeling the spirit world with questions, and never once have I been told to stop asking. Instead, my spirit and various guides have patiently answered my questions, and they have politely told me when they were unable to answer an inquiry because my frame of reference was not large enough to grasp the true answer (and they could not boil it down to something simple enough for me to comprehend).

While I'm still learning from the spirit world daily, what I currently understand has increased my effectiveness and feelings of competency, resulting in a life that feels *so much easier* than before I partnered with my spirit! It's my hope that this information will also reassure, empower, and inspire you.

My ultimate goal is for you to develop a powerful relationship with your spirit wherein your questions are answered, guidance is obtained, and your worries are reassured. Because your spirit is the key to accessing your elevated intelligence, it's the most skillful guide to help you see your blocks, develop your natural gifts, and get "unstuck." Throughout this book you'll discover, as I have, that investing in a relationship with your spirit pays big dividends. Let's begin!

PART I

MEETING YOUR SPIRIT

CHAPTER 1

THE PREP WORK FOR SPIRIT CONNECTION

Tomorrow morning when you walk into your kitchen, imagine that there's a small, furry alien sitting on your counter. You realize that she's friendly and you reach out to stroke her soft lavender coat. She makes a purring noise and leans on you, and you're instantly charmed by her sweet personality. Then you realize that even though she's the size of your small dog, she's *way* smarter than your beloved Fido. She begins trying to communicate with you, and over the next few months you patiently learn to speak—and listen—in a way that she teaches you.

I don't mean to imply that your spirit is a fuzzy purple alien. But I'm asking you to embrace a new way of communicating that is vastly different from what you're used to. Since you were an infant, you've focused on understanding the physical world by absorbing external information through your five senses. Now I'm asking you to learn to listen to words/sounds/images that may appear to come from within you.

Every human (and animal) has both a soul and a conscious mind. Some people call this the ego or ego-mind, but for simplicity I'll often refer to it as simply the mind. Your spirit is composed of both your mind and your soul—I think of it as the overlap or blending of the two. I'm often asked what the exact percentage split is for the two. For the sake of not getting too into the weeds, my spirit says that our spirits are composed of roughly 80 percent soul and 20 percent ego-mind.

Because your soul's perspective is so vast, it can be difficult for your mind to relate to the knowledge and goals of your soul. But your spirit contains a blend of your mind's preferences and your soul's priorities, which makes your spirit a much wiser version of you than just your mind alone.

When you receive information from your spirit, this is frequently referred to as intuition. Merriam-Webster defines intuition as cognition or knowing without the use of rational thought. You may describe this as "a knowing" or "a gut feeling"—you may know something but not be able to explain how you know it.

This concept of a person getting information from their spirit in different forms is often described as their "abilities," and they're often categorized as the following:

Clairaudient: This refers to hearing messages from the spirit world and is my strongest method of knowing things that I have no logical way of knowing. The voice I hear sounds similar to my own voice, just more patient and less urgent than the way I usually talk to myself. And when I hear a client's spirit, or the spirit of someone who has died, it sounds like a softer version of that person's voice.

When my students first begin hearing their spirit, they describe hearing a "random word" pop into their head repeatedly, or a slightly different version of their own voice saying something unexpected.

Clairvoyant: This refers to "seeing" events or information that you have no logical way of knowing. When I look at a person or a photo of a person, my spirit frequently shows me a visual or a diagram of what's occurring in that person's body. I'm not literally seeing into the person's body as if I have X-ray vision; instead, I'm watching a short movie or sketch with my spirit narrating or explaining the image.

When my students first begin experiencing clairvoyance, it may start as seeing a slight haze of energy around the edges of leaves on a plant. Or it may appear as silver "glitter" that they see out of the corner of their eye. From here, the skill builds to being shown visual images. It's also common for students to be shown colors when meditating; these colors are a spirit's first steps toward creating a shorthand with you that you will continue to develop. For instance, many students describe seeing a purple light when they raise their energy above their heads. And if their energy slips down, their spirit sends a flash of blue to let them know that the energy is now vibrating at a lower rate (making it harder to receive messages from one's spirit).

Clairsentience: This refers to "feeling energy" information that doesn't necessarily make sense to your logical mind. Have you ever met someone and had a strong sense that the person wasn't safe? Or seen someone across the room and just knew that you were going to click with that person? That is clairsentience, and as you lean into the teachings and exercises in this book, those experiences will happen more frequently as you become more attuned to your spirit's nudges.

Meditation will be the crucial tool that we use to access the reservoir of knowledge that your spirit holds. The benefits of meditation extend beyond the time that you actually sit in meditation; studies show that meditators have heightened intuition for hours after they meditate. So, in addition to having conversations with your spirit, this process will increase your intuition throughout each day (which can look like any one of the abilities described above).

Meditation is a process that can feel daunting. Unfortunately, many people believe that the goal of meditation is to stop the mind from creating an endless stream of thoughts. When I first began meditating, I pursued this goal, and of course I failed because it isn't possible. Our mind is always churning out thoughts—whether we're awake or asleep. Eventually I learned that the primary goal of meditation isn't to stop all thoughts; it's *to change how you relate to your thoughts.* We typically believe each thought our mind produces without stopping to consider if it is helpful or even true. As we bring our attention to our mind's activity, we can notice each thought, decide if it's useful in the moment, and then release it like a feather floating in the air. Practicing this gentle way of relating to our thoughts begins to slow down our internal chatter. This gives us an opportunity to calmly notice the thoughts and feelings that we want to nurture.

Now I have two goals when I sit down to meditate: to spend time in a calm state of being, and to be open to receive messages from my spirit. Before I go into my style of meditation, I'd love to teach you a powerful exercise to switch into a calmer state of being. Two beautiful healing guides taught me this technique, and I've been using it with my students ever since because it's so powerful!

DIVINE CENTERING TECHNIQUE

Sit comfortably with your eyes closed. You may want to place your right hand over your heart, but that's optional. There are three sentences that you will repeat silently to yourself. Slowly repeat the first sentence multiple times until your mind and body believe you. Then move on to silently repeating the next sentence. You will know when you experience your body believing your statement because it will "downshift" in some way. People usually sigh, take a deep breath, or feel their shoulders drop. That's when you know it's time to move on to repeating the next sentence. By the time you finish repeating the third sentence, I promise that you will be calmer, more centered, and you'll have an easier time meditating! (You're likely to find this exercise so helpful that you do it whenever you feel stressed, even if you're not preparing to meditate.)

Here are the three sentences. Remember not to rush through them; wait for that feeling of downshifting before moving on to the next sentence.

1. I am safe.
2. There is no urgency.
3. I can be calm and still.

Now you're ready to meditate! You're in a relaxed, centered state, so it's easier to calmly notice the thoughts that you're having.

I call my meditation technique "Spirit Connection." It differs from the other meditation styles that I know of in two ways.

First because I gather my energy and move it to just above my head. And second because rather than quietly observing my thoughts, my goal is to ask questions and listen patiently for answers. This process is how my spirit taught me to connect to her, and I've been successfully teaching this technique for over twenty-six years. Keeping my energy and focus up above my head helps me receive visuals and auditory messages from my spirit, and I'd like to share the explanations my spirit has given as to why this works so well.

There are three access portals through which we can connect to the spirit world and receive information. The first portal is in the center of the chest, also known as the heart chakra. Through this portal we receive information about people we have emotional connections with, such as the mother who's at home but can "feel" that her child has just fallen and hurt himself at school.

The plus side to using this portal to receive messages from your spirit is that it's easy to access—we can all move our energy and focus to this area without too much effort. In exercises where you're seeking to center yourself and connect quickly to your feelings, focusing on the center of your chest can be useful.

The downside to this portal is that the impressions that come through this heart opening tend to be fleeting and mixed in with our own thoughts, emotions, and fears, so accuracy can be challenging. If you're seeking specific answers, then you'll probably want to try connecting to your spirit through a different portal.

The next portal through which we can interact with the spirit world is located in the center of our forehead. Sometimes referred to as the sixth chakra or the third eye, this is another opening through which we can connect to our spirit and other beings in the spirit world. My understanding is that this is the access point that many native cultures use when they're tapping into what I describe as Universal Knowledge—things that are true for everyone. When Indigenous medicine women sit to gather information about the best uses for a particular plant or herb, they may raise their energy to this portal and ask the Earth for information. And when Tibetan monks meditate and ask for insight about helping the world feel more peace, this is where they initially seek to focus their energy.

The plus side to using this portal to connect to the spirit world is that the information obtained here tends to be universally true. The downside is that it may not be specific enough to your particular situation. For example, if you're asking about your back pain, you may receive information about how back pain may stem from many things, including feeling unsupported, taking on too many responsibilities, or feeling a lack of personal power. This is technically accurate but leaves you to sort out which of these applies to you in this instance, and that can be confusing.

The third portal through which you can connect to the spirit world is just above your head, and it is the one I feel is the best to access your spirit. This access point is sometimes referred to as the seventh chakra or the crown chakra. When I first began meditating, I was not seeking to move my energy and focus to this area. I'd been taught to focus on the center of my forehead, described above, and I would dutifully gather my energy and try to hold it there.

But something kept nudging my energy upward to just above my head. I would pull it back down, chastise myself for losing focus, and watch with frustration as my energy seemed to float right back up above my head. Finally, I decided to just let my energy rest there, and I immediately heard a voice sigh and say "There!," which made my eyes fly open in surprise!

It turns out that I was hearing my spirit, and she'd been pulling my energy up to the access point from which it's easiest for me (and most people) to hear individual spirits. I've been teaching this format in my meditation classes ever since, as it seems to deliver the fastest, most reliable way for individuals to form a clear communication pathway with their own spirit. Here's how connecting directly to her spirit worked for one of my students as she moved her energy to the different portals.

A woman with wavy black hair and bright blue glasses was sitting in the front row of one of my meditation classes in Southern California. She was smiling widely but jiggling her foot impatiently. I'd just explained the different portals, or access points, that we can use to connect to our spirit. She piped up, "I'm willing to use *any* opening to hear my spirit—I just need to ask her why this back pain is so horrible!"

The group chuckled and nodded their understanding and support, and we began the meditation. I directed everyone to gather their energy and raise it to the center of their forehead. After six minutes, I suggested that they imagine sending the same ball of energy up higher so that it rested just above their head. After the meditation was finished, I asked if anyone would like to share their experiences, and the woman—whose name was Demi—shot her hand into the air.

"That was so powerful! When I had my energy focused in the center of my forehead, I heard this voice in my head tell me that my back pain is almost always from an imbalance in one of my relationships—usually with my wife, Olivia. Then I just had this 'knowing.' You know how you can work an algebra equation from either side, but you always get the same answer? Well, I can sit in meditation and ask about the back pain, or I can ask about my relationship issues with Olivia, but whichever approach I take I'll usually end up hearing advice about both."

I smiled at Demi and replied, "What an interesting way to describe the connection between your physical symptoms and your relationships. Was there any difference when you tried the other portals?"

Demi smiled and said, "Yes! When you had us raise our energy up higher, I heard another voice, and this one sounded more like my own voice. Just a little nicer (more chuckles from the group). That's when I heard specifics—about both things. My spirit said that Olivia's reluctance to include me in her family conversations makes me feel excluded and unsupported, and those feelings show up in my body as back pain. So when the pain appears, I can be on the lookout for ways I've accepted a lack of support. It's important that I talk to her about them, share how I'm feeling, and make specific requests for the support I want. That feels really doable, and it was awesome to get such specific advice!"

Demi's experiences highlighted how, when our energy is focused in the center of our forehead, we can draw in and receive information from the Universe that is true for everyone but nonspecific to your situation. And how if we learn to raise our energy to the access point above our heads and hold the intention to converse directly with our spirit, the information we perceive is specifically geared toward our current issues and understandings.

Teaching you how to have conversations with your spirit involves learning 1) to directly connect to your spirit and 2) to apply the Expectation Eraser—the specific steps to use before asking your spirit questions. The remainder of this chapter will teach you how to directly connect to your spirit during meditation, and the next chapter will teach you how to use the Expectation Eraser.

A DIRECT CONNECTION TO YOUR SPIRIT

When you sit down to meditate, your first goal will be to gather your energy. You'll do this by paying attention to your breathing because noticing the breath helps bring your focus into the center of your body. This is important because *your energy will follow your focus and intent*, and we want to concentrate as much of your energy in your chest as possible.

With your eyes closed, imagine watching the air as it goes in and out of your lungs. As you inhale, picture the air coming in through your nose and rolling down the back of your lungs. As you exhale, imagine the air coming up the front of your lungs and out. As your energy accumulates in the center of your chest, your torso area should feel more expanded.

Once you feel that you've gathered energy in your chest area, imagine that the energy is like damp sand or snow. Visualize packing it down into a small ball and raising this ball of energy up with each inhalation until it rests just above your head. You might feel tingling or warmth at the top of your head, or like you're sitting up straighter—both indicators that your energy is in the right place.

Now your energy is raised up high enough to perceive, or hear, your spirit. The next step is to clear some of the thoughts that your mind produces so that you can make room for feelings, images, and messages to come in from your spirit.

When your spirit speaks to you, she/he/they speaks softly and gently, so it can be tough to hear your spirit over the persistent chattering of your mind. Many meditation teachers refer to this experience of our constant random thoughts as "Monkey Mind." My spirit likes to say, "Your mind yells, while your spirit whispers."

To quiet the mind a little bit and turn down the volume of its thoughts, you'll begin ushering away each thought that pops into your awareness.

When I meditate, I use a visualization to help my mind release its thoughts without judgment.

I visualize that I'm standing either on an empty beach or in an open meadow of flowers. If I'm on the beach, then I place each thought that comes to me on the damp sand and let the next wave carry it out to sea. If I'm in a meadow, then I release each thought like a silk ribbon in the warm breeze.

Between thoughts you will get a clear space—*it is in these clear spaces that your spirit talks to you.* Sometimes it seems that my clear spaces are less than a second long, so my spirit can't possibly have enough time to send me a message! On such days I have to be patient with myself and the process and chalk that meditation session up to "practicing being open and still." But most of the time you'll experience at least a few "openings"— times when you usher away a thought and a few seconds pass before the next thought occurs. And that's all your spirit needs to send you a message in the form of a word, a visual, or a distinct feeling.

Now the trick is to keep your energy up above your head, which can be challenging; often it feels like snow in a snow globe, drifting downward. If you begin to analyze what you think your spirit just said, then you're almost certainly allowing your energy to float down to your abdomen area, as this is where our energy usually vibrates when we're thinking and problem-solving. You'll need to get into the practice of gathering it up and moving it back up above your head. To do this, I usually visualize scooping up the energy that's in my lower abdomen with my cupped hand or a small shovel and adding it to the energy that's still vibrating above my head.

That's it. The instructions are simple; doing them takes **a lot** of practice. But don't get discouraged—soon it will become second nature for you, and you'll gather your energy and move it up above your head in less than ten minutes. When I first started hearing my spirit, I had to regather my energy and start my meditation over many times in each sitting, as I'd notice that my mind had drifted, and consequently all my energy had sunk back down into my body. But it felt to me like I was wearing a path down in the woods—the pathway became smoother and faster to traverse each time I meditated. And whenever you sit to meditate in this way you'll be building your energetic endurance, a crucial part of successful conversations with your spirit.

When I first began connecting to my spirit using the direct connection approach I've given you, I'd get tired very quickly. Sometimes I would start yawning within fifteen minutes of moving my energy above my head. When I complained to my spirit about this, she gave me the analogy of lifting heavy weights above my head. If I wanted to learn to hold the weights above my head for periods of time, I would have to go in stages, adding extra time each day so that I could build up my endurance. Lifting (and holding) your energy up above your head will require you to build up your focus and your endurance, so the more often you meditate, the faster you'll become proficient at holding open this connection line with your spirit.

After thirty years of communicating with my spirit using this process, I can make that direct connection within seconds. But in the beginning, I'd sit in meditation for twenty or thirty minutes just to achieve that connection to my spirit. Everyone's mind wanders, and no one walks around focused on holding their energy above their heads. So repetition is the key ingredient here.

How do you know when you're ready to start asking your spirit questions and having a conversation? When you feel that you've developed the focus and the energetic endurance to hold your energy up above your head for fifteen to twenty minutes, you're ready! Fifteen minutes with your energy held that high may seem like a long time, but once you've done it four or five times, you'll start thinking that fifteen minutes is very attainable.

Your next challenge will be to remain open to receiving all possible answers that your spirit may offer you (even to questions that you haven't asked!). In the next chapter, you'll learn how to filter out many of your mind's assumptions so that you can receive the widest possible range of messages from your spirit.

CHAPTER 2

THE EXPECTATION ERASER

My client Alesia flopped down on the sofa in my treatment room with a frown on her face. "Is it possible that my spirit can't make up her mind?" she asked.

I smiled at her question. "It's more likely that you've asked your spirit a question and you're somehow blocking her answer."

Alesia furrowed her brows. "What? No! Why would I do that?"

"Not intentionally of course," I reassured her. "But we all have assumptions and worries that we're not aware of, and these can limit our listening so that we're really only open to hearing one or two possible answers."

Alesia leaned forward. "But I don't have a bias! I just want my daughter Anna to go to the best college for her. But we don't have the time or unlimited resources to tour fifty different schools! We created a short list. But I keep getting this feeling that there's one more college that we're supposed to go see. I sit in meditation and ask my spirit, but I just can't hear an answer from her!"

I nodded my head in understanding. "Okay, let me ask your spirit the same question since I don't have any biases or worries about which college would be best for Anna."

I connected to Alesia's spirit, who immediately suggested Vanderbilt University in Nashville, Tennessee. When I relayed this to Alesia, she gasped.

"What? Vanderbilt? But Anna said that she wants to go to a big college! And Vanderbilt is expensive! I think it's like $30,000 a semester!"

I double-checked with Alesia's spirit to make sure that I had heard her correctly, and again I was given the name of Vanderbilt University.

I told this to Alesia and then asked, "What does Anna want to study in college?"

Alesia smiled proudly. "She's a hell of a writer! She's dead set on being a speechwriter, so she wants to study political science and policy writing."

I picked up my phone and googled "best colleges for political science and speech writing." Immediately my search revealed three different lists, and Vanderbilt was in the top ten on all three lists. I flipped my phone around and showed it to Alesia, who sat back and said, "Well I'll be damned!"

Alesia suddenly looked anxious and started fidgeting. "Can my spirit tell me how we'd pay for such an expensive school?"

I smiled encouragingly. "In my experience, the spirit world doesn't set us up for unnecessary disappointment. So my guess is that either Anna will get in and be offered scholarship money, or touring Vanderbilt will give her clarity about what she's really looking for. Either way, I'd check it out."

Anna walked onto the campus at Vanderbilt and within ten minutes was teary-eyed. She looked at her mother and said, "Mom, I don't know how I know, but these are my people. I just know that I belong here."

Anna applied for early admission and was accepted and given a scholarship that covered the majority of her tuition. She is now thriving in her second year at Vanderbilt. And Alesia learned that her spirit wasn't being wishy-washy like she thought; in reality, her spirit had brilliant clarity.

Your spirit is such a deep reservoir of wisdom, and there's no end to the topics that you can ask questions about. But there's a catch—you have to be open to hearing the answers.

Having the desire to get answers doesn't guarantee that you're open enough to receiving them. Usually, our internal thoughts are biased in a particular direction, leading to something researchers call "selective listening," where we're only able to hear a version of what we expect to hear.

So while you may think that you're asking an open-ended question, like "Spirit, why do I have this back pain?," your focus may be narrowed in one direction, like "Spirit, why do I have this back pain? Is it because my husband and kids never clean up around here and I'm feeling like everyone's maid?" Our mind's thoughts and fears can narrow our focus and block us from receiving the full answers we seek.

My spirit suggests that we visualize an open chute or funnel that opens above our head as we meditate. This chute represents your receptivity—the answers that you're able to hear because you're open to those possibilities—so you want it to be as wide an opening as possible. Think soccer net rather than a catcher's mitt.

Each fear, hope, and assumption you have about what your spirit may suggest will restrict that opening of that chute until it's only open enough to receive the one or two answers that you think are the most probable. Because your spirit doesn't want to give you an incorrect or incomplete answer, and the true answer won't fit within the opening that you've left, your spirit will back away and wait for you to be open enough to receive the most accurate answer. And this is when your mind may jump in and try to provide an answer, leaving you with inaccurate information.

To help you keep your receptivity as open as possible, my spirit has created a three-step process to do before you meditate. I call this process the Expectation Eraser, as it helps you to temporarily put aside the worries, hopes, and expectations that you may have about the topic you're considering.

Here are the steps in the Expectation Eraser:

1. Think of a topic (instead of your specific question).
2. Write down your mind's thoughts about this topic.
3. Move these thoughts aside using a visualization or prayer.

Then you're ready to meditate and be open to your spirit giving you messages.

Let's go over the steps in more detail.

Step 1: In step one, you take your specific question and expand it outward to a larger topic. The broader we can make the topic, the less likely the mind is to try jumping in with its presumed answer.

For instance, if you're wondering which of two houses you should make an offer on, I recommend asking your spirit to talk to you about your next house. If you asked your spirit the specific question "Which house should I buy?," you may not get an answer if there's a third possible house that your spirit wants you to consider.

I try to ask general questions that are very open-ended to give my spirit plenty of room to reply with answers that I may not even be considering.

Here are a few open-ended questions that I use regularly:

- What would it benefit me to know?
- What can you tell me about my physical body?
- Can you help me understand why I feel so "off" or low-energy?
- What next steps are recommended for me?
- Is my body trying to tell me something? (If you think that you already know the answer to this one, then skip this question, as you'll restrict your listening too much.)
- What messages have I been blocking?

Step 2: Write down your mind's thoughts about this topic.

Once you have your chosen topic, grab a piece of paper and write down every thought you have about that topic. I want you to list all your mind's biases, anxieties, assumptions, worries, and hopes about what you'll hear. Make that list as long as you can—your goal is to cover all the possibilities your mind can generate.

I highly recommend writing them down and not just thinking about them. Writing or typing them forces your mind to acknowledge the many assumptions that you already have. A written list will always be longer than a few items listed off in your head.

Step 3: Move these thoughts aside.

This step can be done through prayer or a visualization, or a combination of both. The goal is to temporarily push aside all those thoughts that you've listed. I like to visualize them written on a whiteboard, and I erase them all. Sometimes I visualize a snowplow pushing a big pile of thoughts off to the side or a bulldozer pushing them off a cliff. I have clients who tell me they prefer to release them like a large bunch of helium balloons or bury them in a deep hole.

Some of my students tell me that they pray and ask God to hold on to the list for a while, or they ask their guardian angels to help hold back all the worries that are present on that topic. What we're seeking is a release of the heaviness or tightness we feel in our body when we think about that list of assumptions, worries, etc. Pay attention to how your body feels, and that will let you know when you've successfully moved that list aside. Most people tell me they feel lighter in their chest once they've successfully removed their "worry list."

Step 4: Meditate and connect to your spirit to receive information.

The final step is to follow the meditation instructions I offered in the last chapter. Stay alert for thoughts that are on the list you made. When one of them pops into your mind, quietly usher it away using the visual that you've chosen for your meditation (either placing the thoughts on the beach or releasing them into the breeze in the meadow).

Your spirit may send you a message in words, visuals, or with feelings. Eventually, you may receive multisensory answers at times, which will make it even easier to feel/recognize the message. But I recommend that your primary goal be simply connecting to your spirit, as this is even more important than receiving a message. This connection, once established and experienced several times, will provide powerful reassurance and comfort. How do you know if you've connected with your spirit? My students report feeling goose bumps or tingles, getting teary-eyed or actually crying (tears of relief), seeing purple or dark blue while their eyes are still closed, and sighing deeply. These signals from your spirit are meant to validate that you're on the right track, so notice how you feel emotionally as you receive them. These comforting feelings are what will bring you back to your meditation spot each day.

While it takes a lot of practice to learn to perceive messages from your spirit, once you become proficient at this form of conversation, you'll have access to unlimited volumes of information and guidance!

I find that gratitude and curiosity help us stay open to all possible answers from our spirit. When I feel irritated that I haven't yet heard a useful answer, my frustration lowers my energy back down into my body, which disconnects me from the connection with my spirit. When I'm trying to avoid this "shut down," or lowering of my energy, I start with being grateful that I've been given the opportunity to communicate with my spirit. Most people are not even aware that they can ask their spirit for guidance and receive concrete responses, so remembering the uniqueness of this connection helps me to stay patient and open.

To get the most complete answers from your spirit, notice if you're presuming that you know what will be "best" for you. Such a presumption will surely bias your listening as you strain to hear answers that match your assumptions.

You may be tempted to skip using the Expectation Eraser and jump straight to meditating. Please make a few minutes for this process before you sit and meditate; it will dramatically increase your chances of successfully receiving messages from your spirit.

For a quick review, here are the three steps in the Expectation Eraser:

1. Think of a topic (as opposed to a specific question).
2. Write down your mind's thoughts about this topic.
3. Move these thoughts aside using a visualization or prayer.

I'm very excited for you to connect with your spirit! But you may be asking yourself: "How do I know if my spirit or my mind gave me this message?" Don't worry, I've got you covered! The next chapter gives you multiple ways to check your answers for accuracy.

CHAPTER 3

CHECKING YOUR
ANSWERS

My favorite crossword puzzle app lets me know if I type in the wrong word; don't you wish you also had a way to double-check the messages you receive during your meditations? I've got some great methods to help you do just that.

While you're meditating you may receive information in the form of visuals, words, or "knowings," and you'll want to make sure that the information came from your spirit and not from your mind's random thoughts. This discernment is critical for anyone who is developing their intuition/psychic gifts. Even the most talented channelers of the spirit world occasionally make mistakes, just like you can mishear a friend when she's talking to you on the phone. The goal is not to eliminate all mistakes; it's to notice the difference in how it feels when information comes to you from your spirit versus from your mind.

Before we proceed, I want to emphasize: *You Will Make Mistakes.*

Please remember that you're learning a new method of communication. People make many mistakes when they're learning a new language. It doesn't mean you're failing or that you're not listening to your spirit—you're just in the learning process.

Toddlers make mistakes constantly when they're learning to communicate, but they happily bubble along, undaunted by their often comical errors because they're highly motivated. They're eager to be understood, to get answers to their questions, and to share their delight. And so they persevere, and I encourage you to bring this same sense of lighthearted enthusiasm for learning to communicate with your spirit.

There are three methods I use to confirm that the information I've received during meditation is from my spirit and therefore accurate/true for me. They are: 1) feeling for resonance, 2) the manta ray exercise, and 3) quick research.

METHOD 1—DOES IT RESONATE FOR YOU?

The litmus test that I encourage you to apply to every bit of information you receive is: How does it *feel*? You're aiming for the feeling of resonance or alignment; the information from your spirit should feel like TRUTH in every way—physically, mentally, and emotionally. Here are some examples of how my students say it feels when they get messages from their spirit:

"My body relaxes. I sit back slightly and exhale."

"I get a quick flush of goose bumps all over."

"I tear up when I hear the truth from my spirit. Not an ugly cry, more like a joyful recognition."

"This might sound weird, but it feels like my mind sighs. Like I've figured out a math puzzle or remembered someone's name that I'd forgotten."

"When a message comes from my spirit I feel it in my chest, like my chest is expanding open."

"It feels like relief, or less pressure on me. Even when it's not the answer that I was hoping for."

Conversely, when the message you receive has come from your mind, most people feel a slight tensing of the muscles; you may lean forward slightly or pull your shoulders up. Your thoughts may race as your mind tries to figure out the next step. Your ego-mind is like a three-year-old constantly interrupting your thoughts. My students have offered these comments:

"When the message is from my mind, I immediately start planning the next steps, and my chest contracts slightly."

"I know that a visual is just mentally generated when I have five or six thoughts right after it, like a machine gun. Then I find myself leaning forward, ready to jump into action."

"Messages from my mind always make me think, 'Well then if that's true, then what about this? And this?' There's no peaceful knowing like when I get messages from my spirit."

Personally, when I receive a message from the spirit world that resonates for me, I feel myself move into alignment as if all the layers of me are magnetized into perfect calibration. It frequently feels to me like teeth in a zipper all lining up. My spirit's truth floats gently into my head but my ego-mind thoughts zip in like an arrow. Messages from my spirit don't feel like fireworks but rather like a calm resetting of all the aspects of myself.

Even when I hear a truth that's a bit painful, it's accompanied by a feeling of softness. I describe it as the truth floating into my head gently like a cloud. Even when my spirit gives me an answer that I don't want to hear (like when she told me that a relationship was no longer healthy and needed to transform or end), it feels like a loving message gliding in peacefully.

There have been many times when I was so attached to the answer that I was hoping to hear that I blocked my spirit from communicating with me. So as soon as a message feels urgent or fear based in some way, I check to see if I've lost the connection with my spirit and my mind has jumped in to "help."

You can learn a lot from your mistakes. But it's easier when you don't sink into self-judgment each time you make one. It's only natural for your mind to want to get involved. You'll soon develop the ability to differentiate between how it feels when your spirit sends you a message versus your mind offering its latest theory.

METHOD 2—MANTA RAY EXERCISE

If you're still not sure if the answers that came to you during your meditation were from your spirit, here's a great exercise you can use to gain clarity.

Imagine a manta ray. You can do an image search if you need a reference image.

This exercise works best if you frame your question into a yes/no or an either/or format. For your first time, I suggest that you ask something you already know the answer to, like asking the manta ray if your middle name is Vanilla and then asking if it's _____ (your actual middle name). Then you'll know the feeling response that your spirit will show you for a yes and a no.

Once you have your question ready, picture a manta ray swimming close to the water's edge (they can swim in very shallow waters). As you walk alongside the manta ray, imagine merging into its body. Your breathing will become deep and slow in rhythm with the up and down movement of its winglike pectoral fins. Swim along like this for a few moments until you feel harmonious with the manta ray and the water you're swimming through. You should feel that same softening of your chest and shoulders that I described above because you've moved into alignment with your spirit.

Once you feel that harmonious feeling of being in sync with the manta ray, quietly pose the question in your mind. Notice the feeling of the manta ray's swimming. To recap, your order will be this:

- Ask if your middle name is Vanilla and feel the response.
- Get realigned with the manta ray's swimming.
- Ask if your middle name is (your actual name) and feel that response.

Frequently a "no" answer feels like resistance or a slight shuddering as if the manta ray is swimming through choppy water. And a "yes" is frequently felt as the manta ray turning and gliding through the water and out into the open sea. It feels smooth, light, and slightly exhilarating.

Now just to give you more clarity, try the exercise again and this time offer two possible answers that are *both* wrong/inaccurate. This is important because this is how you'll learn the signal that your spirit will offer you when she can't answer your question—either because both options you give her are inaccurate or because you're not allowed to have this information. (An example is when I ask a question about the future that isn't really something I need to know—I'm just curious!)

If you don't get any response/change in the manta ray's swimming, then this usually means that your question was phrased in such a way that your spirit could not answer it accurately. This happens when a small part of what you heard during your meditation was accurate/from your spirit, but then your mind jumped in and added a lot of extra details that were not accurate.

If you tried this exercise and felt in harmony with the manta ray, but you didn't get a clear response to your question, try again with a different question. Some of my students have told me that this exercise becomes how they ask their spirit for help in deciding things like which house to buy or which school to send their kids to. Just remember that your spirit may opt not to answer if she can't answer your question in a way that is accurate and helpful to you. Sometimes we're meant to feel out the two choices for ourselves without our spirit giving us the "right" answer. I don't always like that, but I've learned that my spirit simply doesn't have a strong opinion/preference on some of my decisions.

If you want to use this manta ray exercise for questions other than "Did I correctly understand this message from my spirit?," here are a few tips.

Keep your questions short. The more qualifying statements you add to your question, the greater the chances are that your spirit cannot give you a yes/no answer.

So if you want to ask about two different jobs you've been

offered, and each one has pros and cons, I recommend *not* asking it like: "Which job should I take?" Instead, ask it in this way:

- Get in sync with the manta ray.
- Ask if it's recommended that you take the first job. Feel the response.
- Get realigned with the manta ray's swimming.
- Ask if it's recommended that you take the second job.

With this information-gathering system, you probably won't get any specifics on why your spirit is recommending one job over the other—those types of details are obtained in meditation where your spirit can bring you visuals, knowings, or auditory messages. But this exercise can give you clarity about the decision your spirit recommends.

If you're asking a question about someone else, there's a chance that you may not be allowed to have the answer. For this reason, I recommend asking if you may have info on the topic before you pose your question. It means doing the exercise twice but avoids the confusion of an unclear response from your spirit.

METHOD 3—QUICK RESEARCH

The final method that you can use to explore the accuracy of the messages you receive in your meditations is to do some brief research. And I want to emphasize the word *brief.* Think less than ten minutes. It's so easy to go down a rabbit hole of researching symptoms, obscure diagnoses, etc., and I want you to avoid such trips into fearful caves of thinking. (Rarely do they ever yield any practical advice, instead usually generating lots of scary "what-ifs.")

Here are some examples of quick research from my clients:

- Susan sat in meditation and asked her spirit what she could know about her digestive issues. In response, Susan's spirit sent her a mental image of a papaya. At first, Susan assumed that her mind inserted this "random" picture into her meditation, but then she googled "Digestion & Papaya" and was immediately shown supplements made from papaya enzymes that assist with digestion. She began taking them, and her digestive issues completely resolved.

- Ryan asked his spirit in meditation about the best colleges to tour with his son. He was shown an image of a mountain lion or cougar that he'd never seen before—navy blue on a white background. He researched college logos that are navy and white cats and quickly found Penn State college, a school that his son had never considered. Father and son toured the college and it felt like a perfect fit. Ryan's son recently graduated from Penn State with honors.

- While meditating, Kati asked her spirit how she could help the daylilies in her yard that were dying. Her spirit gave her a visual of a ladybug, which made no sense to Kati. She called her local nursery and asked the saleswoman if they sold ladybugs and what they were used for. Kati learned that ladybugs are helpful to control the aphids that can infect daylilies. Upon closer inspection, Kati saw the tiny aphids and purchased a container of ladybugs to eliminate the aphids naturally.

Each of these examples highlights the small amount of research that can validate the messages you may receive in meditation. Your spirit is aware of the extent of your knowledge and will rarely suggest that you embark on hours of research to figure out the meaning behind a message that you're given. As a rule of thumb, if your "quick research" takes longer than a few minutes, or if it causes you to feel anxious or worried, please abandon it right away. It's better to repeat the meditation and ask for more information or clarity than to try to hunt down a potential explanation.

Each of these methods can help you build your confidence in the messages you receive in meditation, and simultaneously they lead to increasing your intuition by helping you spend more time in alignment with your spirit. This alignment with your spirit is valuable because it leads to being more sensitive to your spirit's nudges and clues, which can show up as feelings, coincidences, or ah-ha insights while you're going about your day. The net result is a more resilient, powerful version of you.

An important feature of your budding relationship with your spirit is *trust*. I've found that when a client doesn't understand why she's going through a difficult time, she can lose trust in her spirit, which makes it difficult to meditate and have a conversation with her. In the next chapter we're going to tackle this issue of trust so that when you're confused and suffering, you don't lose faith in your spirit and your journey.

CHAPTER 4

BUILDING TRUST

Understanding Your Spirit's Priorities

When I began communicating with my spirit, I made the assumption that since she's the wisest part of me, we must have identical goals and priorities. Boy was I wrong! In the (many) moments when I have felt unsure about my spirit's loyalty to me—and temporarily lost faith in my spirit, my spiritual journey, and the Universe in general—it was always because my spirit and I were operating from different sets of priorities. The main area where this comes up is my spirit's comfort level with pain and drama.

You're probably like me—I want to feel good as often as possible, which means avoiding discomfort and pain. My mind works diligently to avoid physical pain and emotionally painful situations. But my spirit's goal is to experience the fullest expression of my potential, even if that means going through some uncomfortable lessons. So while one of the highest priorities of my mind is "Avoid everything unpleasant!," one of my spirit's highest priorities is "Pursue growth!"

Looking back, I can see that many of my biggest periods of learning have been accompanied by a good deal of discomfort and struggle. This discomfort wasn't always physical—I've been known to spend a lot of time mentally resisting things that I don't want to accept. Like the man I thought was such a good match for me but who drank too much. Because we looked like the perfect match on paper (he was attractive, successful, and involved in a holistic healing profession), I rationalized away his behavior and purposefully didn't ask my spirit for her advice on the relationship.

The good times were fun with this man, but his tendency to disengage by drinking heavily left me feeling alone and insecure—like I wasn't interesting enough to hold his attention. And when my friends would say, "You guys are dating? That's such a perfect match!" I'd recommit to the relationship and ignore my actual experiences. I had to learn to honor how the relationship actually felt within me and pay less attention to the potential that I believed was there. This wisdom was acquired through some awkward dates and tearful evenings alone, and to be honest I would've rather just had my spirit "give me the answer" to spare me the months of heartache that led to our breakup.

During these phases of painful learning, my spirit wasn't indifferent to my suffering, but she trusted that the difficulties were leading me toward the important goal of honoring myself and what I needed in a relationship. I believe that when we learn through actual experiences instead of from our spirit just telling us the answer, the lessons become embedded within us so that we live the new truths instinctively.

Part of my own spiritual journey has been learning to trust that "the pain has a purpose" and that my difficult periods almost always generate important understandings and yield a more powerful, expanded version of myself.

The second way that my spirit's goals can show up as very different from mine is on the topic of drama. Several times I've declared to my spirit, "Look, I'm not big on drama. So let's find ways to learn and grow easily and quietly without going into all of that intense drama." Her response is always, "You DO like drama—you just don't like it when it happens to you!"

It's true—humans are fascinated by other people's drama. Which is why we go to the movies, watch television shows, and listen to stories (okay, sometimes gossip) about our neighbors, coworkers, and friends. It turns out that *the spirit world feels the same way—dramatic events are captivating.*

Our attraction to drama is why we crane our necks to look at the car accident as we drive by. There's no reason for us to look at the crash scene; there's no role for us to play in it. But it's hard to resist peeking at the drama of someone else's life. The same car accident that was curiously interesting as we drove by it immediately becomes "a terrible, dramatic event" when it happens to us.

I'm assuming that you share my aversion to your own episodes of uncomfortable drama. I remember a client angrily saying to her spirit, "I don't have time for this stupid drama in my life!" To which her spirit responded, "Is there a time that you've set aside for drama each month?" Ha! Some spirits are quite funny.

Here's an example of a client's spirit who "signed her up" for some awful experiences in order to achieve a big, wonderful goal.

I logged on to my Zoom session and saw that my client Beth was crying. Sobbing, actually. She had followed the advice I translated from her spirit a few weeks before and taken a new job. And now her new boss was sexually harassing her. "How could my spirit give me such terrible advice?" she wailed. I was asking myself the same question.

In Beth's first session she said she needed my help to avoid committing murder (not an actual homicide, although she did seem at her wit's end). The truth was that Beth was having difficulties with her work environment, and she felt that she was nearing a breaking point. She was very uncomfortable setting boundaries, so her boss and coworkers had been taking advantage of her for months, piling their work onto her desk and trusting that she'd work long hours to get it done. Beth confessed that when she wasn't fantasizing about hiring a hitman to bury her boss and coworkers under a mountain of their own paperwork, she was dreaming about quitting her job and moving to Paris to become a painter, even though she didn't have the money or the courage to pursue either fantasy.

In our first few sessions, Beth's spirit coached her on establishing healthy boundaries and enforcing them, and she was pleased with the difference it was making in her work life. Then she was offered a new job that sounded amazing, and in our next session Beth's spirit matched her excitement, so she accepted the position with the new company.

Within weeks she had sold her condo and bought a beautiful new place in Chicago. The Universe seemed to be endorsing her move, as everything was falling neatly into place. Then she started the new job. Unbelievably, her new boss was even worse than her last one and even made disgusting sexual comments when no one else was present.

Beth was devastated and cried in her next session as she asked me how her spirit could give her such horrible advice. I felt terrible and shared her confusion. Inwardly I cringed as I translated Beth's spirit, who again encouraged her to stay in the job and practice setting healthy boundaries.

For three months Beth's life was absolutely miserable, and her complaints to the human resources department seemed to have no effect. In our sessions I would ask Beth's spirit how she could get her new boss to respect her boundaries, and I would hear suggestions about how Beth should formally document each sexually inappropriate incident.

I was feeling so bad for Beth that I began interrogating her spirit as if I were a lawyer representing Beth in court.

"Why are you so comfortable with Beth's suffering?" I challenged.

"She's in no physical danger, and I'm focused on a bigger goal," Beth's spirit calmly replied.

"Ugh!" I responded. "When can we know what that goal is?"

"Soon" was the only response Beth's spirit offered.

So Beth decided to "keep the faith" and stay in the new job for one more month; if her spirit didn't offer more help or insights by then, she would quit.

Our next session was two weeks later, and this time Beth's spirit had a new suggestion.

"Write another letter to the human resources department, and this time copy the new CEO on the email. In the email, mention that you're pursuing legal advice regarding your next steps."

That was surprising advice, and Beth felt very uncomfortable escalating her situation to the new CEO, someone she'd never met and had no relationship with. We discussed it, and Beth shared her understanding of the corporate culture there in which sending an email to the CEO was "just not done." Beth meditated and prayed about it and decided that it did feel right to send the email anyway.

A week later, Beth called me, ecstatic. The new CEO was a woman, and when she read Beth's email, she decided that her first priority was to "clean house" of all employees who were potential liabilities because of inappropriate behavior. She contacted Beth and told her that she had read her HR file and that her boss had been terminated that very day. In exchange for Beth signing a legal document promising to never sue the company for her boss's behavior, the company would offer her a severance package equivalent to two years of salary!

Six weeks later, Beth messaged me from the South of France where she was studying painting and had rented a beautiful house for the year. When I connected to Beth's spirit, I could feel her grinning broadly as she said, "THIS is the bigger goal that I was working on. If I'd told Beth about the possibility of this result, she wouldn't have believed it. I needed her to 'not get in the way' of what I was trying to create for her—the realization of her big, audacious dream. And along the way it benefitted her to learn to set healthy boundaries; she's using them now as she gets settled in France and begins to sell her paintings."

I confess that during Beth's difficult journey, I was doubting her spirit's guidance. I felt guilty and wondered if I'd channeled her spirit inaccurately, mistakenly sending her in the wrong direction. When the large severance package was offered to Beth and she left for France, I promised myself that I would stop questioning the wisdom of people's spirits, and I will encourage you to do the same. I recommend that you pledge to be in partnership with your spirit. I understand that it can be difficult to "keep the faith" when we're suffering and feeling confused, but I promise you that there's always a remarkable result that your spirit is orchestrating.

Of course, if you're ever in danger, please abandon this plan to "keep the faith." It's vital to protect your own safety and make the best decisions for your own well-being. Generally, I've found that there's usually something else at play behind hardship, but that doesn't mean anyone should ignore when something doesn't feel safe.

The lesson here is that when something happens that's unpleasant for you, assume that there's a reason for it and get *curious* instead of immediately *critical*. Ask what your next best step is, and then try to trust the overall journey. Your spirit knows where you want to go today, but remember that her dreams are bigger and more complex than yours.

Being able to ask your spirit questions about why things are happening in your body and in your life doesn't mean that unpleasant things will never happen. But your spirit's answers can reassure you, help you heal, and assist you in swiftly moving through difficult times. Such conversations can change the way that you engage with your life, even when your spirit's tolerance for drama and conflict is higher than your own.

Sometimes communications from your spirit can feel more like looking through a windshield during a heavy rainstorm than receiving a clear, concise message, but don't worry. In the next chapter, I'll offer tips on deciphering your spirit's visuals and suggestions, as well as a list of messages frequently contained within common symptoms so you can build your confidence in interpreting your specific messages.

CHAPTER 5

DECODING THE MESSAGES FROM YOUR SPIRIT

"My spirit is speaking gibberish," my client Nicole complained. "She tries to give me messages during my meditations, but I feel like we're playing charades and she's a bad actress!"

Frustrations like this are not uncommon, as there can be a learning curve in understanding and interpreting the messages you receive in meditation. Even after you've used the Expectation Eraser, your mind is likely to jump in and try to "help," offering suggestions in the form of words or phrases. This can make it tricky for your spirit to finish her sentence. To get around this problem, our spirits frequently speak to us in visuals, metaphors, and analogies. When your spirit uses a metaphor to convey an idea to you, it's more difficult for your mind to interrupt because an entire idea is conveyed quickly.

Whenever you receive a message during your meditation that isn't immediately clear, start with noticing how you feel as you receive it. This is the best way to decipher the meaning behind your spirit's messages. Here are some examples of interpreting messages from the spirit world.

It was a brisk fall morning, and I was sitting in a circle of twenty-four students. They'd come for my Intuitive Energy Healing Workshop, where they would learn to both channel healing energy through their hands and communicate with their spirits during meditation. I'd just led them through a guided meditation to help them receive a message from their spirits, and as we opened our eyes, I looked around the room and saw some disappointed faces looking back at me. I asked for a volunteer—someone who wasn't sure they'd even received a message. Quite a few hands went up.

I started with Vicki, a thirty-four-year-old veterinarian with bright red glasses who explained that she'd hoped to hear a message from her spirit about the back and neck pain that she experienced each month during the monthly visits from her in-laws. She said that she'd made the connection between her in-laws visiting and her symptoms but was hoping her spirit could give her advice on resolving the pain.

"But I didn't hear one word from my spirit. I just got a weird visual that made no sense."

"What was the weird visual?" I asked.

"A big ol' draft horse pulling a heavy wagon. I mean, what? I mean I like the Budweiser horses—they're beautiful, but other than that I can't think of anything about them, or how it relates to me, so I was probably just making it up."

"Maybe not," I ventured. "May I ask: If having your in-laws visit frequently is difficult for you, why do you agree to it?"

Vicki's forehead crinkled and her shoulders drooped in defeat. "Because I want to be a good daughter-in-law and a good wife. I love my husband and he loves his family. I don't want to complain, but his mother is very critical of me."

I nodded with understanding. "Do me a favor and recall the draft horse that came to you during your meditation. Did it seem happy?"

Vicki scoffed. "Heck no! He looked like a beast of burden, you know, just plodding it out and doing what was expected of him. Ohhhh!" she said as recognition began to dawn on her.

I smiled and waited for her to continue.

"That poor horse just expected to be worked to death, like, 'This is what I'm supposed to do.' Huh! Okay, what do I do with that message?"

"What do you want to do with it?" I asked.

"I think that I need to stop assuming this is the way it has to be. I think I should ask my husband if we can set up different boundaries and expectations for their visits," she said excitedly, building momentum as she spoke. "And I need to promise myself that I'll keep asking for what I need so that I don't feel like that damn draft horse in the field every time they come, working so hard to host demanding, unhappy people!" Vicki sat back, a wide smile spreading across her face.

Satisfied that Vicki had understood her spirit's suggestion, I moved on to the next student. Daniel was in his thirties, quiet and reserved, dressed in khakis and a white shirt. He prefaced his comments by saying that he'd asked his spirit about the anxiety he'd been experiencing since moving into a new apartment building. "But all I saw was my parents' dining room," he said dejectedly. "I hope that doesn't mean that my spirit is suggesting I move back home!"

I chuckled with the rest of the group. "Probably not, but let's unpack that visual message. I'm assuming that you ushered the image away as if it was a random thought, and it came floating back, so you really felt that it was a message from your spirit?"

Daniel nodded, so I continued.

"Describe your parents' dining room to me—what it looks like and how you feel when you're in it."

"To be honest, it's kinda boring. I don't want to criticize my parents, but they spent all this money to hang wallpaper, and the wallpaper is plain beige. I mean, it almost looks like the cream-colored paint that was on the walls before."

"Why do you think your parents chose such a plain wallpaper?" I asked.

"I dunno. Probably because they never want to stand out or look too showy. They rarely talk about anything that's potentially controversial, and they used to tell us kids to keep our opinions to ourselves so that we didn't offend anyone."

I gently offered a theory. "It sounds like your parents work so hard to not make anyone uncomfortable that they may end up living lives that feel rather flat and bland."

"Totally! That's exactly right!" Daniel nodded vigorously.

"Could it be that your spirit is inviting you to notice that so you can make different choices?

Daniel sat quietly, looking rather uncomfortable, so I added, "I think your spirit is pointing out that your anxiety may be the result of you trying really hard to not offend anyone. And that your fears are preventing people from getting to know the real, authentic you. Our spirits are good at helping us see when we're suppressing some part of ourselves unnecessarily so that we can be accepted." Daniel nodded and looked relieved. "Thanks—I can really feel the truth in that."

Chloe piped up, saying, "Hey, I'd take that encouraging message over what I got from my spirit! I just heard the word 'trust.' Uh, what exactly am I supposed to trust?"

I turned to face Chloe and asked, "What symptom did you ask your spirit about?"

Chloe shook her shoulder-length red hair as she pointed to her temple. "I asked about my headaches. Lately I get them when I meditate."

I nodded. "I feel like you received more than just the word 'trust' because your spirit is showing me a picture of half a pie. Can you remember anything else that came to you?"

Chloe frowned, wrinkling her forehead. "Mmm...there were several visuals, but I didn't have enough time to usher them away and see if they came back, so I don't know if they were just my imagination."

"That's okay," I said. "Close your eyes, go back, and feel each visual now. Remember how it felt when each picture popped into your mind. I think there's one that felt different."

"Yeah, a sweet scene of a baby horse standing up on its wobbly legs. But that doesn't seem relevant..."

It was tempting to give Chloe the answer, but I knew it would be more powerful if she recognized it herself, so I suggested, "Sit with the image of the baby horse standing, and then recall hearing the word 'Trust.'"

Chloe closed her eyes for a moment and then tears began rolling down her cheeks. "My spirit said, '*Trust THIS.*' I'm like the baby horse just learning to stand! It feels wobbly but I think that my spirit is telling me that I've got this!"

"Yes!" I said as the group murmured their encouragement to Chloe, who continued.

"And when I meditate, I notice that I furrow my brows a lot like I'm squinting because I'm trying so hard! I think I need to just relax and trust this process. And if I don't get a message every time, that's okay—I'm not failing at this!"

I felt a collective exhale from the group as Chloe's message reassured all of us. It's always rewarding to observe how individual messages from someone's spirit can serve the whole group that I'm teaching.

I love it when my spirit gives me an answer that has an obvious visual or a literal sentence that answers my client's question or my own. But I've learned that when we're blocking our perception in some way, our spirit can get creative and send us all sorts of interesting metaphors and analogies. My goal is to help you decode them for yourself. Here are some tips for interpreting a metaphor or confusing visuals from your spirit.

First, focus on how you felt during the message. When our spirits speak to us using metaphors, it's nearly always presented like a short movie clip that seems unrelated to our current thinking. Rather than trying to make the unexpected clip make literal sense, notice how you felt as you watched the scene. Did you feel optimistic or worried and tired? Did you feel safe? Alone or supported?

In the examples above, I helped the students understand the meaning behind the metaphors used by their spirits, but you can do this for yourself. Tune into the emotions that you felt during the brief message, and then return to your meditation and be open to hearing more information on that particular feeling. Taking this approach will lead you to the meaning behind your spirit's clues.

The second approach that you can take is to look up your symptom in the appendix that I've provided. This appendix offers common messages that are being sent with particular symptoms. Combining the metaphors, feelings, and other clues that your spirit gave you with the suggestions given in the appendix can help you understand the "why" behind your specific symptoms. Knowing the topics that tend to get stored in each section of your body can help you narrow down the possible messages that may be contained within your symptoms.

This appendix is not the definitive answer to the messages contained within each symptom, but it's a great way to open your mind to the possible "memos" that your body is sending you. I encourage you to view your body as a road map, with certain areas relating to particular subjects. The simplest example I can offer is the throat area. This part of the body is where we tend to store stress related to speaking our truth. If you were punished as a child for telling the truth about your experiences, then you may feel hesitant to speak openly as an adult. And each time you "bite back your words" because you fear the repercussions, you store the energy of that negative emotion in your mouth and throat area. Over time your spirit may bring this to your attention by prompting your body to have symptoms such as a sore throat, laryngitis, a postnasal drip that has you clearing your throat, teeth grinding, etc.

I'm thrilled for you—you're on your way to living a very different lifestyle! Once you have an open line of communication with your spirit, much of your day-to-day confusion about your physical symptoms, career worries, and relationship issues can be resolved.

Now, we've covered a lot of topics, and I'm sure you've had a few questions pop up. A common one is: How long does each message from your spirit remain accurate? Remember the scenes from spy movies where the message self-destructs as soon as the spy reads it? Your spirit's messages are a little bit like that, so in the next chapter we'll cover the expiration date of each of the messages that you receive.

CHAPTER 6

EVERYTHING IS TEMPORARY

The Expiration Date of Your Spirit's Messages

You might be surprised (okay…maybe more like exasperated and annoyed) to learn that the messages your spirit sends may only be accurate for a short time. But as usual, the spirit world has good reasons.

Your intuitive nudges—those feelings prompting a shift or urging you to take action—are incredibly accurate for you at the moment they arise. As we continuously grow and develop a more loving sense of self, our desires and aspirations may change. What once felt appealing, like pursuing a relationship or starting a new project, may gradually lose its appeal. As we evolve, it's common for our preferences to shift on topics such as where we want to live and who we want to spend time with. This evolution often leads us to seek out new and different relationships, career paths, and living arrangements. Our spirit acts as a guide in the present moment, helping us recognize when a change in our job, relationship, or location is in alignment with our personal growth and serves our evolving selves. This means our answers might shift from one day to the next.

Just as your body may only need a medication for a period of time and then be healed enough to thrive without it, you may also outgrow some types of relationships and work arrangements. It's important not to criticize yourself for your initial choices simply because they no longer resonate. When your spirit provides guidance, remember that over time, you may evolve beyond the alignment of that suggestion. If this happens, you might start feeling like you're wearing shoes that are too small; they once felt ideal, but now they feel uncomfortable. Luckily, you now have your spirit on "speed dial" and can sit in meditation and ask for updated recommendations.

Here's how Sierra learned to trust two different messages from her spirit, even though they seemed like they were in direct conflict with each other.

I logged into a Zoom session with my client Sierra; she didn't look like herself. Her hazel eyes looked sad, and she was chewing nervously on one of her fingernails. Typically, Sierra's energy was upbeat, bright yellow, and looked almost sparkly, but today her energy looked cloudy and felt contracted and heavy. I recognized that gray, foggy-looking energy as confusion, so I asked what was troubling her.

Sierra shook her head slowly, sending her auburn curls bouncing. "I feel weird even talking to you about this—like maybe I'm being disloyal to my spirit," she confessed.

I appreciated how much she valued her partnership with her spirit, so I paused and thought carefully about my next words. "I hear you, but our spirits don't get offended; they know that we're always trying to do our best. So if you give me a little more context, then I'm sure that we can get you some clarity."

"Okay. Let me start again." Sierra took a deep breath and leaned forward toward the camera with an intense look on her face. "About six months ago I met this guy—Owen—at a friend's party. I wasn't really attracted to him, but he kept texting me cute messages, and one day during a meditation my spirit suggested that I spend some time with him and see how it felt. Turns out it felt amazing! He was sweet and kind and a great listener."

"That sounds great...so what's the problem?" I said encouragingly.

"Well, it *was* amazing..." Sierra said with hesitation. "But the last three months have been...hard. He tells me how great I am, which is nice, but then he wants my advice constantly! It seems like we're always fixing him in some way, and lately I've been getting headaches every time I hang out with him. It makes me wonder if I'm..."

"Done?" I offered.

"Yeah, I guess," she said sheepishly. Then her brown eyes opened wide. "But then I think that it's crazy to just ignore my spirit's advice to date him."

"You *did* date him," I replied.

Sierra looked anxious. "If my spirit thinks that this is the right guy for me, then I should probably stick with him. Her advice is always really accurate, so I don't want to ignore her suggestions."

"Brace yourself," I warned. "When you hear a message from your spirit, you can only count on it being accurate for about five minutes. It has a very short expiration date."

"What?" Sierra looked stunned and then angry. "Well, how's this going to work? 'Cause it's not like I can check in with my spirit every two minutes to get the latest updates!"

"Don't worry, you don't need to," I reassured her. "You just have to pay attention to how you feel. And when something feels off—emotionally or physically—then you check in and ask about it during your next meditation. It sounds like you've been feeling emotionally heavy for a while. And when that shift didn't prompt you to question the relationship, your body developed headaches as a way to get your attention."

Sierra looked doubtful. "Why can't my spirit just tell me the end date at the same time that she gives me the recommendation? Like, 'Hey, Sierra, date this guy for three months.'"

I smiled. "That would be great, and sometimes we do get messages that are that specific. But usually, the timetable depends a lot on us—on how quickly we move through things."

"Yeah, I guess that makes sense," Sierra conceded. "I remember last year when you told me that my spirit wanted me to start taking a different supplement for my skin."

"Exactly!" I said. "You'd changed so much, and your personal growth was reflected in your body, which needed different nutrients as a result. Did the new supplement work better?"

"Yeah, it actually did!" Sierra reported.

"You know that's not because it's a better product than the first one. It's because it's a better match for who you are currently."

"Okay, I get it," Sierra said with her usual grin. "If I wasn't changing and healing so fast, my spirit's suggestions would probably have had a longer expiration date!"

"Exactly!" I chuckled. "Congratulations on outgrowing another piece of your spirit's advice!"

Sierra smiled for a moment but then frowned again. "But why was Owen the right guy for a while? And what about the headaches? How do I get rid of those?"

I connected to Sierra's spirit and heard that Sierra had a habit of dating men who were less successful than her, and that this frequently resulted in them becoming her "fixer-uppers." I conveyed this to Sierra, and she grimaced.

"Crap! I guess I do tend to do that!"

I smiled to encourage her. "Well, this may be the pivotal moment where you shift that pattern. Your spirit says she suggested that you date Owen because she felt that he would highlight this trend of yours enough for you to see it clearly."

Sierra grinned again. "Well, yeah, he's made it kind of hard to miss! Why would I do something like that?"

"Your spirit says that when you were young your father left your mother, and she really struggled to raise you and your siblings alone."

Sierra nodded, so I continued. "And that by choosing men who were less successful than you, you were trying to ensure that they would need you more than you needed them. It was an attempt to avoid being left like your mother was."

Sierra nodded and blinked back tears. "My spirit's right—as usual. I didn't even realize it, but I keep picking this same kind of guy, and then I feel exhausted by them and want out of the relationship. Wow! Okay, well that pattern stops today."

Over the next few sessions, Sierra and I healed many of her childhood wounds that had been dictating her dating choices. Her spirit coached her on the kindest explanations to give to Owen when she ended their relationship. He was upset and begged her to reconsider, but once she ended the relationship her headaches never returned, which gave her confidence in not responding to his requests. She confessed to feeling "guilty" about not resuming her relationship with him. Her spirit helped her see that her guilt was an indicator of how she had taken responsibility for his daily well-being, and this understanding helped her release those feelings of guilt.

You may feel thrown by the notion that we can't predict how long your spirit's advice will be accurate. But have no fear—as you're meditating more often and connecting to your spirit, you're becoming more intuitive, and you'll feel when something has shifted for you. It's wonderful to have an open line of communication with your spirit and to know that this wisdom source will be with you every step of the way, noticing your growth and giving you updated recommendations.

I encourage you to embrace a "reframing" of the relationship that you have with your spirit. Initially, my students think of their spirit as someone separate from themselves—a smarter being with all the answers! But eventually I advocate for them to adopt the perspective that they are rebuilding their natural connection to the aspect of themselves that is their spirit. This "more truth-filled" version of them will help keep the ego-mind's constant suggestions of worries and fears in perspective.

As you engage in more conversations with your spirit, you'll begin to notice a natural integration that increases your trust in yourself. As that occurs, you won't automatically believe your ego-mind's apprehensions like you did in the past; they become more like background chatter instead of the yelling voice in your head.

The beautiful partnering that's possible with your spirit can be witnessed in Julie's story. (This is the only story I'm sharing where the names have not been changed, as Julie believes that Branden would want his story to be shared.)

On a Saturday morning a client called me in distress. Her stepson Branden had been rushed to the hospital and was currently in the intensive care unit. Julie had been studying with me for several years and was already productively communicating with her spirit. She received messages in the form of "knowings"—brief flashes of insight about how to offer healing energy to herself or her clients. Terrified for her beloved stepson, Julie was alternating between praying for help and asking her spirit for guidance on how to heal Branden.

Branden appeared to be the epitome of good health, radiating vitality and joy upon returning home from a European adventure with his wife. But he'd been having headaches for several weeks, and his doctor had diagnosed him with a pinched nerve. Then he collapsed and was rushed to the hospital where scans revealed that his brain was bleeding. Doctors took him in for immediate surgery and discovered that Branden had a glioblastoma—a rare, fatal brain tumor that grows quickly. The tumor had so badly damaged the brain stem that he never regained consciousness.

Neither Julie nor I could receive any messages about how to help Branden heal, and after the doctors discovered the fatal brain tumor, we realized that his spirit had already decided to end this lifetime.

Julie was devastated, but instead of collapsing in despair and grief, she switched her requests to her spirit. She had been asking, "How can I heal Branden?" Now she asked, "How can I be of service to Branden?" She says that the answers arrived immediately, washing over her like a gentle ocean wave. Her spirit said, "Send him energy to assist his soul in leaving the body. Then promise him that you will remain with his body, feeding energy to his organs to keep them alive for transplant purposes. You will be the custodian of his physical body once his spirit vacates it."

The message felt so clear and resonated with her entire body, so Julie immediately agreed. Branden's wife validated the message Julie heard, relaying that Branden felt strongly about organ donation and had listed himself as an organ donor on his license. Julie stayed with Branden for the next three days, sending energy to every organ in his body as well as his eyes, skin, and limbs. Her goal was to keep each part of his body in the best possible condition while the hundreds of tests were performed to determine if each organ could be used to help someone else.

After three days, Branden's hospital bed was wheeled through the "Honor Walk," where doctors, nurses, and hospital staff line the hallways from the ICU to the operating room where the organs are harvested. Representatives from hospitals all over the country arrived to collect Branden's organs, and the transplant team reported that Branden had some of the highest transplant numbers they had ever seen; at least seventy-five people received life-changing transplants due to Branden's donated body! Every organ was utilized, and his eyes gave vision back to two other people. His skin was used to help burn victims, and even his limbs were able to be used for amputees.

At the time of this writing, the medical team has no reports of rejections from a transplant recipient—also very rare. The man who received Branden's heart has already contacted Julie's family to express his deep gratitude for the life-saving transplant.

When Julie connected with her spirit the following week,

she asked what she could know about what Branden was experiencing since "crossing over." Julie's spirit said, "He's in the Rest & Recovery stage" and showed Julie an orb that represented Branden. There were angels surrounding the orb, and they were feeding energy to the orb to help it recover. There were sparks landing on the orb, and Julie's spirit said that those sparks were the prayers that loved ones sent, reaching Branden as intended. Julie said that this experience has forever changed her perception of people dying, and she's learned that "Even in a tragic situation, there can be magic." Julie now hears messages from Branden regularly, assuring her that he's at peace and still a part of their lives.

I understand that this kind of story might feel unnerving and upsetting. But as we learn to relate to ourselves (and to others) as having our own answers within, we realize that we all get to make our own life choices. Julie's acceptance of Branden's soul's choice to depart this lifetime reminds us that even in the face of tragedy, there can be profound lessons about acceptance, respect, autonomy, and the inherent sovereignty of each of us on our life paths. I hope that you will come to see yourself (and others) as the wise, calm, and knowing spirits that they truly are.

Congratulations! Your spirit is now an active partner in your evolution. Now the journey really begins. Don't look so surprised; your healing process was never about just healing one symptom or relationship. It's about upleveling all areas of your life and following your individual spiritual path. Let's help you set realistic expectations for this new relationship with your spirit.

CHAPTER 7

WHAT YOU CAN EXPECT GOING FORWARD

You might be surprised to learn that my favorite client cases are not the ones where the client walks off into the sunset free of all symptoms and with an awestruck look on her face. That makes for a great story, but I've found that frequently this process is about personal transformation as well as physical healing. So while I enjoy the cases where my clients and I quickly achieve clarity and healing, that's not typically how things unfold.

What makes this process beautiful for me is to witness how my clients are guided by their spirit once a symptom has gotten their attention. There's great benefit to your spirit continuing to use a symptom to help you track your progress as you make important changes in your life. Thus, the symptom that began as an annoyance becomes your coach.

Each situation is unique of course, but in general once you understand the message contained within your symptom, you'll feel a positive energetic shift—both emotionally and physically. This can feel like a slight release of tension or a warm feeling throughout your body as you feel the resonance of the message.

And once you begin making changes based on your

message, the symptoms typically resolve as their message has been "delivered." But before your symptoms vanish, your spirit may use them to alert you to times when you've slipped back into old patterns of imbalance. This concept reminds me of Patti's story.

One day, I opened my front door to see my client Patti wearing a puffy red down coat. Which was surprising—and confusing—because it was summer, and the outside temperature was ninety-one degrees.

"Are you okay?" I asked as she hustled past me and quickly sat down.

"Yeah, why?" she replied.

I arched my eyebrows and stared at her heavy coat. "Well, your choice of attire is...interesting for July."

Patti crossed and uncrossed her legs, trying to get comfortable. Her standard business suit had been replaced by black lounge pants and a white short-sleeved T-shirt. At my comment, she glanced down at her coat and then gave a sheepish grin. "Oh yeah, crazy right? But it was the first coat I could find, and I wasn't leaving the house with my arms bare, 'cause look!"

As she peeled off her coat, I could see that Patti's arms were covered in fiery red patches of psoriasis.

"I can't figure this out!" she wailed. "I've never had it this bad! My doctor is talking about putting me on this really pricey biologic drug, and I really don't want to do that. It's so expensive! And I'm worried about the side effects."

"When was the last time your psoriasis flared up?" I asked.

"Like this? Never! When I was in college I had my first serious boyfriend, and I was insecure about my weight. That's when it began."

I connected to Patti's spirit, who showed me that there was a link between Patti's focus on her weight and her skin condition. So I asked, "You have a boyfriend now, right?"

"Yeah, but it's not new—we've been dating for six months. And Tim's always saying that he's got a few pounds to lose, so I don't think that this psoriasis is about my fear that he'll think I'm too heavy."

Patti's spirit gave me a visual of a dartboard with a dart near the center, so I trusted that this topic was important and I pressed on. "Well, indulge me for a minute. Have you been worried about your weight lately? Before you answer, let me sit with you while you connect with your spirit and get her perspective."

Patti closed her eyes and gathered her energy, moving it up above her head with a sigh. She waited for several moments and then said, "Oh! My spirit just reminded me of something. Two weeks ago, we ran into Tim's old girlfriend at a restaurant. I know her through our industry, and I was surprised to see that she'd lost a ton of weight since last year! After seeing his ex, I kept thinking, 'How did she get her act together and lose all that weight while I'm still lugging around this extra twenty-five pounds?' I'd kinda forgotten about that night..." she said with a slight scowl.

I smiled at her. "I can feel your spirit telling us that this is the key to your psoriasis flaring up. Remember that psoriasis is an autoimmune problem. I look at autoimmune issues as the way that our spirit can tell us that we feel under attack—usually from ourselves!"

Patti grimaced. "Well, Lord knows I can be hard on myself," she said in her deep Southern drawl. "But isn't this kind of an overreaction? Can't we tell my spirit to give me a more subtle signal?"

Patti's spirit immediately responded with: "She *did* have more subtle signals. She had an upset stomach that night and throughout the next day, and then she had a herpes outbreak. Her body was registering her self-blame and criticism and demonstrating it to her."

Patti held up her hands. "Oh, I am so busted! My spirit's right. But I really should be eating better and exercising more. I know what to do; I'm just being lazy and not doing it!"

Patti's spirit spoke up quickly. "This is not about laziness. The extra weight that you carry has remained because you believe that you're stuck with it because you haven't 'earned' the weight loss."

"What does that mean?" Patti groaned. "I can't exactly just wish the pounds off, can I?"

Patti's spirit offered more details. "True, it's not as simple as just wishing it was gone. It's about understanding the beliefs you hold (below your level of awareness) that direct your body to hold on to excess weight. And realizing the subconsciously held beliefs that lead you to resist exercising or eating better. Losing weight feels like too much of an uphill climb with your current beliefs, so you hesitate to even start making those efforts."

For the next five sessions, Patti received helpful guidance from her spirit about releasing her inaccurate beliefs around weight loss and body shame. Gradually, Patti was less critical of herself regarding her weight. And each time she slipped back into her old thought patterns and began beating herself up, her skin would soon demonstrate her inflamed thinking.

Within six months Patti's skin was clear, and she had healed many of her shame-based thoughts about herself. She was gradually losing weight and was deliberately focusing on having compassion for herself. At times she would get frustrated that her psoriasis was more apparent and said that she felt like she was "being graded" on how she treated herself each day. But once her skin was fully healed and she realized how much kinder she was to herself, she understood the value of that healing journey.

I know we'd all rather just "get the message" contained within our symptoms and have them disappear. And sometimes that happens. But other times your spirit will utilize this signaling system that she now has with you to help you transform. It can be easy to feel like you're failing, or backsliding, when a symptom reappears, but the truth is that the healing process is more like an upward spiral than a straight line, and you may revisit the same topic multiple times from different angles. For this reason, it can be confusing if you look for incremental improvements that directly parallel each step-by-step change that you make.

The body has its own timetable for healing processes, and this will also dictate the speed of your symptom's resolution. Perhaps your symptoms are allergies, and you get the message that your allergies represent your failure to advocate for yourself at work. Then on Monday when you began sneezing at your desk, you remember a conversation you had with your boss. You decide to go back to his office and advocate for yourself. I would expect you to feel more at peace as you return to your desk, but it may take thirty or forty minutes for your symptoms to completely resolve. This is because our body's histamine responses have a "ramping up" and "shutting down" process, so there will be a time lag between acting on the message and the symptoms ending. This is a normal part of the physiological process.

With symptoms like a headache, it may take a while for

the vascular constriction to fully release. Or the inflammation to subside. Look for overall improvements but not a minute-by-minute linear progression of your healing.

Try to remember that while our primary goal is to feel good as soon as possible, our *spirit's goal* is to increase our awareness and heal our emotional wounds, fears, and limiting beliefs. We'll need to trust the entire process, even when we don't experience the immediate result that we're pursuing. All of my clients, when asked if they had positive transformations as a result of their symptoms (once they understood the message), have answered, "Yes!" And the reappearance of a symptom can lead you to "check in" with your spirit repeatedly, which helps you further develop your elevated intelligence.

It's amazing how healing results can begin to flow into other areas of the body. Once you start this process, you may find that you're improving your health in rather unexpected ways.

Cindi was referred to me by her dentist after she'd struggled for years with recurring gum and teeth problems. Symptoms in the mouth frequently relate to the fear of being punished when we say what is true for us, but I've learned that there are always exceptions to this pattern, so I logged on to her first online session with an open curiosity. When I saw her, my first impression was that this was a woman who didn't want to be seen. Cindi was in a poorly lit room, and she was sitting as far back from her computer as possible. Her image was so tiny on the screen that she barely showed up at all. Her light brown hair was straight and styled simply, and she wore a loose-fitting charcoal gray top and jeans. As I looked at her and felt her timid energy, my spirit gave me a visual of a small mouse in the corner of a room, looking like it might scurry off at any moment.

I connected to Cindi's spirit, and she suggested that I ask Cindi how she would describe her childhood. In a very tremulous voice, she said, "It was a pretty typical middle-class, suburban upbringing. My parents were very attentive to me and my sister, making sure that we were raised right."

I could feel that her words had been carefully chosen, so I dug a little deeper. "That's an interesting phrase: 'being raised right.' Do you mean that your parents were strict?"

Cindi immediately looked flustered and began squeezing her hands together. "Well, no, I don't think so! I mean...we definitely had rules, but all kids have rules, right?"

"Sure," I said slowly, realizing that her fear of criticizing her parents was blocking her from answering honestly. Cindi's spirit guided me to ask, "Can you give me an example of one of your parents' rules that really stands out for you?"

She hesitated but then said, "Well, we weren't allowed to speak at the dinner table."

"At all?" I asked, trying to sound neutral. She shook her head sadly.

"So what were the consequences of breaking that rule?" I asked gently.

"My little sister would get her hand slapped by my mother. But I sat next to Dad, so when I spoke up, he would hit me. Once, when I was eight, I said that my peas were cold, and he backhanded me so hard that I fell over backward in my chair."

I tried not to look horrified because I didn't want to make her more self-conscious. "That sounds like a pretty severe consequence for a child commenting on her food temperature."

Cindi peered hopefully into the camera. "It is, isn't it? I've always thought so, but I've never talked about it to anyone. My parents are very popular in their community, very involved in the church and the neighborhood, so I never wanted to say anything that would make them look bad."

I smiled as I sent her supportive energy. "I understand your carefulness, but your spirit is telling me that your parents' rules and punishments made you very afraid to speak openly. Not just with your parents but in general."

Cindi bowed her head and looked ashamed. "Yes, at work my manager always says that I need to speak up more."

I assured Cindi that her hesitancy to speak freely was an understandable reaction to being punished for saying anything that annoyed her parents. Her fear of speaking had led to her collecting a lot of negative energy in her throat and mouth, weakening those areas and predisposing her to all the dental issues.

Over the next few months, Cindi allowed her spirit to guide her in healing the trauma that she had regarding speaking, and I was delighted to hear her voice get stronger with each session. She received a promotion at work and was thrilled with the results of her healing work—until she began having new symptoms.

In her next session, Cindi told me that she was feeling rundown and was noticing that her heart was racing and she frequently had heart palpitations. She asked, "Is this new symptom trying to tell me something? I'm really worried that my heart has some big problem now."

I connected to Cindi's spirit, who immediately assured me that this symptom was a positive indicator and not a negative one.

"Cindi," I asked, "did you forget to mention to me that you take medication for your thyroid?"

"Oh—yeah! I've been taking it for so long that I forget about it."

I smiled. "Well, your spirit says that as a result of the great healing work that you've been doing, your mouth wasn't the only area to improve—your thyroid has been healing as well. Your spirit says that now your current medication levels may be too high, so I recommend you go see your endocrinologist."

"Well, that's great news." Cindi grinned and promised to make an appointment. In our next session, Cindi confirmed what her spirit had told us.

"My endocrinologist was surprised, as my dosage has been the same for so many years. He said that he doesn't know why I suddenly need less than half the dose that I've always needed! I didn't even try to explain to him that it was because of the work we've been doing."

We both smiled and agreed that it was worth a few days of worry and discomfort to get the wonderful confirmation that her thyroid had healed and was now operating almost completely on its own.

I've had clients report to me that conditions such as endometriosis, scoliosis, and osteoporosis have all "miraculously healed" while they were shifting in response to messages from their spirits about other conditions. Everything is interconnected, particularly within our bodies, so it's natural to have healing in one region of your body benefit your whole system.

Your healing isn't limited to one symptom at a time. I encourage you not to view each healing as a singular event, a project to complete like replacing your car's battery. Envision your new approach toward healing as more of a dance that you'll now engage in with your spirit's help. Your spirit is committed to helping you end sabotaging patterns and flush up inaccurate beliefs so that you can live your best life possible.

When you notice a pattern that feels like it's on repeat for you, bring it up in meditation and let your spirit help you transcend it. "Feeling stuck" comes from not being able to see the next powerful step that we should take. Your spirit's expansive viewpoint can be so helpful, and I hope you gratefully invite that wisdom-filled perspective into your consciousness.

Now that you've established this nourishing avenue for communicating with your spirit, I encourage you to embrace the idea of being in partnership with the deepest, wisest aspects of yourself—your spirit. This partnership acknowledges the desires, goals, and worries that your ego-mind has, but it also turns to the calmer, wisdom-filled part of you that is your spirit.

The rest of this book will be your "Partnership Manual"—a guide to help you partner effectively with your spirit. We will cover how to ask your spirit questions about your health, your relationships, and your career. Each chapter will cover difficulties you may face in these areas. I'll share what I've learned from the spirit world on the topic and how I suggest that you ask your spirit for guidance. Along the way I'll share tips on better understanding your spirit's priorities, as well as ways to frame questions so you receive the most helpful answers. Let's start with the topic of health issues.

PART II

YOUR RELATIONSHIP MANUAL

CHAPTER 8

HEALTH ISSUES: WHY DO HUMANS HAVE SYMPTOMS?

When I first began having conversations with my spirit, I asked her, "Why do I even have to get sick or have injuries? If we're such divine beings, then what's with these big design flaws?"

My spirit patiently responded to my aggressive interrogations by explaining that every person has physical symptoms for three primary reasons:

1. It's part of our shared experience as humans.
2. Our spirits use symptoms to bring us specific experiences.
3. The body provides a kind of "messaging center" where our spirit can leave us messages through our symptoms.

Let's dive deeper into each of these concepts.

THE SHARED HUMAN EXPERIENCE

What do you have in common with the president of France, a mail carrier in Iowa, Julia Roberts, and Shaquille O'Neal? The answer: you've all had colds, headaches, diarrhea, and other physical symptoms.

In a world where one person's reality can differ dramatically from another's, physical symptoms can be a unifying experience that help us relate to one another. If you think about the people listed above, physical symptoms may be the only thing you have in common with any of them.

Experiencing physical injuries and illness helps us to be compassionate with another person's particular discomfort. It also encourages us to reach out to one another for support—both medically (seeing a practitioner) and socially (asking a friend for help).

Despite our frustration at how our bodies experience aging, illness, and injuries, such events do indeed provide a universal experience; I'm confident that you cannot name one adult who has never had an injury or illness. And when celebrities are open about their illnesses, like Michael J. Fox and his diagnosis of Parkinson's disease or Mariah Carey's struggle with Bipolar II disorder, it also reminds us that no one is immune to health challenges.

SYMPTOMS BRING YOU SPECIFIC EXPERIENCES

There are times when your physical symptoms may be helping you have a specific experience, or they might be giving you an opportunity for a shift in your perspective. (Yeah, I rolled my eyes when I first learned about this too.) Some examples of what these opportunities might be are: to notice that you need more support from your loved ones, to find a new medical practitioner, to allow others to help you, or to get motivated to make important changes in your life.

Over the years, there have been dozens of times when my spirit told me that I couldn't help a client with a particular symptom because that symptom was there to serve a specific purpose. While this can feel frustrating to hear—for both me and my client—I've learned to trust this message from the spirit world.

Greg contacted me for help when he felt himself coming down with a cold. When Greg signed on to Zoom, his watery eyes and red nose told me that he wasn't feeling well, and the energy around his sinuses looked inflamed and signaled me to check him for bacteria and viruses. I connected to Greg's energy field and felt the presence of a virus, but when I asked his spirit for permission to kill the virus, I was told no. "What?" I thought to myself. Both Greg and I were disappointed, as I'd successfully used energy to kill a virus germ in him previously, and he'd felt better by the next day.

Greg had recently started a new job as an internal accountant for a small company, and he hated missing two days of work, but he felt miserable and stayed home to avoid infecting his new coworkers.

When Greg went back to work the following Monday, he learned that while he was home sick, his company had gone through a surprise audit by the parent company. The audit focused on a group of suspicious expenses that occurred prior to Greg being hired, and two people were fired on the spot when embezzlement was confirmed.

The entire office had been extremely tense, and Greg's spirit had kept him home for two reasons: 1) to keep him from experiencing the extreme stress that the office staff was under and 2) so that he wouldn't be associated with the internal accountants who were fired. Greg and I both understood that his cold was a "gift" from his spirit, and that's why I wasn't allowed to kill the virus.

Another example I'd like to share is from my client Brenda. The focus of her session was helping her resolve conflicts at work and at home with her two teenagers, and her spirit offered great suggestions. I believed that the session went well until a few months later when Brenda wrote to me and let me know that she'd had an emergency appendectomy two days after our session! She was understandably very upset that her spirit hadn't clued her in on what was happening in her body.

I immediately left my desk and went to sit in meditation and connect with my spirit. The conversation went something like this:

Me: What the hell? Brenda was sitting right in front of me! You couldn't clue me in as to what was impending for her? Even if we couldn't have stopped it, we could have let her know what was coming her way so that she wasn't taken by surprise at 2:00 a.m.

My Spirit: I can't give you any information on this right now.

Me: What? How is that helpful? What can I say to her?

My Spirit: You can reassure her that everything is unfolding just as it should be. Her physical body had stored a lot of upset energy in that area, which over the years had weakened the arteries providing blood supply to the appendix. It was inevitable that it would falter, as it's been in a compromised state for many months.

Me: Okaaaay, but still! You could've let me warn her so that she had faith in this work. Now she's wondering if I'm any good at my job.

My Spirit: She was given quite a lot of helpful advice from her spirit during her session and was quite impressed with your abilities. The doubt that you have now is for *you* to resolve.

Me: (grumbling) I still don't like how this went down.

My Spirit: Noted. (Which I've learned means "Oh well, I can live with you being upset.")

I replied to Brenda's email and apologized for not getting a heads-up from her spirit about her emergency surgery. I assured her that there was a reason—something that her spirit had planned, even if it would be some time before we knew the reason for her spirit's silence.

Four months later, I was delighted to see Brenda's name on my calendar and happy to meet on Zoom for her second session. She told me that while she'd been discouraged by her emergency surgery just days after our session, she now understood what was being "set up."

Because she couldn't drive right after surgery, her sister drove Brenda to the doctor's office for her post-op checkup. When the doctor came into the exam room, she was accompanied by a man that she introduced as Brian, a new intern. Brenda didn't think much of it, but she noticed that her sister and the intern kept staring at each other. Finally, her sister blurted out, "Did you go to college at UCLA?" Brian smiled with recognition and said, "That's where I know you from—we were in that physics class together!" Brenda said that it was almost uncomfortable being in the room with the two of them, as the sparks were clearly flying between them. They've been dating ever since, and Brenda's family loves him!

Now, you may be thinking: Couldn't the Universe have brought those two together in an easier way than having Brenda get her appendix out at 2:00 a.m.? I asked my spirit the same thing, and she reassured me that the events unfolded as they did for many reasons, all of which were in support of Brenda, her sister, and everyone involved, even me. "How did that support me?" I asked. My spirit's answer: "It gave you another chance to deepen your faith—in yourself and in your work with the spirit world."

My response: noted.

Not every "opportunity" that a person's spirit creates gets resolved this quickly or this clearly. Some of the journeys that come with cancer and other ailments are long and arduous, and I don't mean to minimize the fear, pain, and suffering that accompany such events. But I've worked with so many clients as they traverse such journeys, and afterward they're able to recount multiple lessons learned and blessings that they realize were sent to them along the way. I hope you will learn to do the same when physical symptoms come your way.

YOUR BODY AS A MESSAGING CENTER

One of your spirit's constant endeavors is to help you realize when you're making your life more difficult and painful than it needs to be. Your spirit's preference is to communicate with you through feelings (you may have heard the expression "Feelings are the language of the soul"). But we live in a culture that encourages us to suppress any feelings that might make others uncomfortable. So emotions that might not be well received are stuffed down to be looked at later, and typically, later never comes. And when the same feeling is ignored multiple times, our spirit may turn to symptoms to give us physical representations of our feelings.

I believe that nearly every chronic bodily issue can be traced back to a shift that occurred on the energetic level first. Because we rarely tune in to our energy during an experience, the body serves as a place where energetic imbalances can be witnessed later in a concrete, physical form.

When you bury your negative feelings, your body will store that negative energy. Where your body stores this "negative energy" is determined by how you relate to and internalize your negative emotions. For example, being upset about your current workload can show up as shoulder pain or back pain, depending on how you're thinking about/relating to the heavy workload. (More details on this in later chapters.)

Other negative emotions may be stored in that same area of the body, creating a "weakness"—a part of the body that's prone to injury or illness. At this point, your spirit may draw your attention to this weakened area with symptoms there. Or your spirit may give you generalized symptoms, such as inflammation throughout your body. This can occur when you're being asked to pay attention to your overall well-being because there are numerous upsetting emotions that you've been ignoring. There's no denying that symptoms get our attention and prompt us to tune inward and practice more self-care.

Once we understand that an internalized stressor is caus-ing or aggravating a particular symptom, we can begin to problem-solve in a way that's both fruitful in resolving the symptoms *and* helpful emotionally.

The beauty of this system—clumsy as it may feel at times—is that your spirit's goal is to help you see where you're limiting yourself by "playing it small" so that you can expand into a happier, more authentic version of yourself. As my clients have each received and acted on their spirit's guidance, their symptoms have resolved *and* their lives have improved dramatically.

A physical symptom that contained a healing message revealed itself one evening with the help of a ghost. I was lecturing to a group of 125 people in an auditorium-style classroom on a warm August night. I'd been talking about how our symptoms frequently contain messages for us when a man interrupted me and said challengingly, "Is this stuff actually real?"

I paused and turned to the man, now standing in the middle of the audience, hands on his hips. He appeared to be in his midfifties with a thin, wiry body. He wore shorts and a T-shirt that said "Running Is My Happy Hour," although he certainly didn't look happy at that moment. His wife looked embarrassed by his outburst and was gently tugging on his hand to pull him back into his seat, but he swatted her hand away.

I've learned that sometimes when people rudely challenge me it's because they're afraid to get their hopes up if I can't help them. So I skipped the niceties of an introduction and asked, "What are you hoping that I can help you with?"

The man scowled and said, "I'm Jason. My doctor already told me that I need knee surgery, so it's not like you can magically perform surgery in the air, can you?"

"No," I said slowly, "but if you'd like I can see if your spirit can help us get any messages contained within that inflamed right knee."

"How did you know it was my *right* knee?" he demanded, then glanced at his wife accusingly. She shrugged her shoulders to convey that she hadn't said anything to me (I'd never met either of them prior to that evening).

I explained my reasoning. "Well, there's a large area of red energy around your right knee, and the energy there looks like it's throbbing, which usually signifies pain."

He had no response to that, so I continued. "May I connect to your spirit and ask him what we may know about your knee pain?"

"If you think it'll do any good, sure," he said as he crossed his arms.

I connected to Jason's spirit, who told me that he works as a biotech researcher and that for months he'd been mentally blocked at work. As he put more pressure on himself to achieve results, his knee had become increasingly inflamed. I relayed this message to Jason, who suddenly seemed self-conscious about discussing himself publicly. But we were in it now, so I pressed on.

Jason paused for a moment and then said, "Well I've always pushed myself hard. So why am I having this knee pain now?"

As he asked that question, an image appeared right next to Jason, although I seemed to be the only person who saw it. It was a filmy outline of a man, and as I watched, the image filled in. It was the ghost of an older man, and his energy felt very fatherly.

The ghost said, "I'm afraid that's my fault. My son was always trying to prove himself to me, and when I died earlier this year, Jason lost the chance to impress me. Or so he thinks."

I said, "Jason, your father's spirit has just arrived and told me that he feels you are reacting to his recent death. He says that you were always hoping to impress him, and now that he's gone you may be feeling that you've missed your chance."

Jason's mouth fell open, then closed, then opened again. He whipped his head around the room, looking for his father. He finally stammered, "How...how do you know that? Who are you talking to?"

Gently, I continued. "Your father's spirit, or ghost, is here with you. He says that he wants you to know that he's always been impressed by you—both your research work and the loving care that you put into your family. And that he's truly sorry that he was never able to express his admiration while he was alive. He says that he's still watching you, and not only is he impressed but he loves you as much as you love your two children."

By this point Jason was crying, along with everyone in the room including me. The love that his father felt for him was palpable, and we were all basking in it. It's amazing how when we receive an impactful message from the spirit world, all of our defenses and reserves can drop away. I've seen it many times while helping my clients. No matter how cynical someone may be initially, when a message is delivered that feels like someone's undeniable truth, there is a powerful (usually teary-eyed) recognition of that truth.

Jason looked warmly at me and asked, "May I hug you?"

As he walked down the aisle of the small lecture hall, he stopped suddenly and stared down at his right leg. He picked it up and flexed his leg backward and forward slowly, then looked up at me.

"What did you do?"

I held up my hands in front of me. "Nothing, Jason. I promise."

"But the pain! It's gone! Look! I can put all my weight on this leg! It's unbelievable! How did you do that?"

I smiled. "I just delivered the messages that prompted you to release the blockages—emotionally and energetically. Those energetic blockages were what was causing you physical pain. I expect that the remaining swelling will be gone by tomorrow morning."

Jason shook his head disbelievingly as he approached me onstage, wrapped his arms around me, and tearfully whispered "thank you" in my ear.

A week later I received an email from Jason letting me know that he had canceled his knee surgery and was back to running. His research work was back on track as well. For Jason, the miracle occurred when he allowed himself to feel the approval that he'd been craving.

When we relate to our symptoms as prompts, asking us to consider the choices that we're making and the beliefs we're holding, everything can transform. We can shift from being at war with our symptoms to investigating their meaning with kindness and curiosity. Then we can experience powerful healing physically and emotionally, and our life is enriched every time.

CHAPTER 9

HEALTH ISSUES: WHY DO YOU HAVE THAT SYMPTOM?

So humans have symptoms, but why do you have THIS particular symptom? I know that's why you're here. Let's get you some answers!

I'm going to tell you something that may surprise you. Before you talk to your spirit about your symptoms, it's important to answer one question for yourself: "Do I need professional medical help for this?" Because if you need to see a doctor, nurse practitioner, dentist, or other medical practitioner, then that should be the first priority. Getting information on *why* your symptoms are happening should only be done once you know that you're not in an urgent medical situation physically or mentally.

You might think it's odd that I'm leading with the question of going to a medical doctor when you've come to this book for answers you can obtain for yourself. I've worked with many clients who believe that once they're on a spiritual path and conversing with their spirit, they should never again need help from a medical doctor. And I'll be honest, that has not been my experience. In this line of thinking, Western medicine becomes the bad guy, and therefore any trip to the doctor is viewed as a failure or defeat. I've heard my clients say things like:

"I try to talk to my spirit every day! She shouldn't need to send me messages through my body anymore!"

"I shouldn't have to go through this much suffering when I'm trying to do everything right. I feel like I'm being punished."

"If I'm a healer, then I should be able to fix anything that goes wrong in my body."

Remember that one of the reasons we have physical symptoms is so that we can share the common experience of illness and injury. Even if you're the most gifted healer, or you're devoutly spiritual and have long conversations with your spirit each day, your spirit has still chosen to have a human experience. Heck, the Dalai Lama has a Western-trained physician (Dr. Barry Kerzin) in addition to his traditionally trained Tibetan doctor. Being in conversation with your spirit doesn't mean that you get to bypass the human experience, so I encourage you to embrace all of the valuable resources that you have to take care of yourself medically.

The next thing I recommend is to take inventory of how you're feeling. It's normal to feel scared when we're dealing with injury or illness. But when we feel resentment at our condition, we can block our own intuition/ability to receive messages from our spirit. Watch out for thoughts that indicate mental rigidity or righteous indignation so that you can step away from the resentment and stay open to guidance from your spirit. Thoughts like "I shouldn't have to go to the doctor—I was just there last month!" or "I can't afford one more doctor visit!" are indicators that you need to lean into accepting your current situation.

Until you do, it will be difficult for you to access intuitive guidance from spirit.

Sometimes when we're sick or injured, we're too uncomfortable to sit in meditation. As an alternative, you can try doing the manta ray exercise (given in Chapter 5) and pose the question "Do I need to see a doctor for this symptom?"

Once you feel assured that you don't need to seek prompt medical attention, or if you've already seen your doctor and know that your symptoms are not in need of medical intervention (surgery or medication), then I recommend that you ask your spirit if the symptom contains a message for you or if it exists primarily to bring you an opportunity. Our goal here is to ask your spirit if this symptom is encouraging you to take action (because it contains a message that is prompting you to notice, shift, speak up, etc.) or wait and let it unfold for the experience that it can deliver. To illustrate the difference, here are some examples.

When symptoms deliver an opportunity, the experience can be very unexpected. Two years ago, Nancy experienced a virulent ear infection that left her so dizzy she was unable to walk. Little did she know that her symptoms would change the dynamics of her marriage.

Nancy is a lovely tall woman with almond-shaped eyes and long dark hair that's usually pulled back into a high ponytail. She runs a successful company that she began with $5,000 and grew to over $5 million in yearly revenue. Nancy is funny, bold, and frequently described as a force of nature by people within her industry. Her Swedish-born husband, Keith, is also successful but has a quiet, easygoing demeanor. Nancy has always prided herself on her independence and resiliency; the dark side of these traits can be her resistance to an equal partnership with Keith, as she's hesitant to ask for help for fear of appearing needy. Several times during my sessions with Nancy, her spirit had spoken to her about her fear of vulnerability, but Nancy hadn't really shifted her behavior.

When she got sick, simply taking a few steps resulted in her vomiting or crashing into furniture. She had no choice but to give up control. Surprisingly, Nancy was able to meditate and converse with her spirit during this illness. Nancy's spirit told her that there was no message for her within the symptoms and encouraged her to proceed with her doctor's medical care to heal the ear infection.

Medications eventually cleared up the infection, but Nancy was forced to heavily rely on her husband for several weeks. To her amazement, he took fantastic care of her and their two children, responding intuitively to what each of them needed. As her balance returned, Nancy resisted the urge to seize back control of the daily operations of her household, and instead she transformed her dynamic with Keith. Their relationship now has more healthy interdependence and intimacy as a result of that transformative experience, and Nancy understands the gifts that were present for her in that illness.

Sometimes your symptom(s) aren't there to deliver an opportunity but rather to get your attention and prompt you to make changes—in your actions and/or your beliefs. This is typically the case with chronic symptoms, which are frequently there to prompt us to notice an imbalance in our behavior or an inaccuracy in our thinking.

If your symptoms contain messages from your spirit, when you sit in meditation, you'll be given clues—visual cues, auditory messages, or a feeling (sometimes called "a knowing").

Hopefully you'll apply the Expectation Eraser (Chapter 2) before meditating and temporarily move aside any assumptions that you're holding about your symptom. If you're in doubt about whether a message has come from your mind or your spirit, usher it away as if it's a thought. If it's truly a message, your spirit will gently float the communication back to you or send you a slightly different version of the same message.

Now, here's an example of symptoms that contained a message.

Kierra's story gives us a whole new understanding of what can happen in our bodies when we get "pissed off." Kierra is one of the talented writers for a hit TV show that's been successful for many seasons.

One day, Kierra awoke to find that she had the classic symptoms of a bladder infection: painful urination and an urgent feeling that her bladder was full. She contacted her gynecologist who tested her urine and then prescribed an antibiotic. Three weeks later, her urine tested clear of any infections, but Kierra still had lingering symptoms. Her doctor assured her that no more medications were warranted, so Kierra sat in meditation to ask her spirit for guidance on the remaining discomfort.

Kierra was surprised when her spirit showed her a giant tug-of-war rope with her at one end and the director of the TV show at the other. She wasn't exactly sure what her spirit meant by that image, so she continued meditating. Then she heard the word "competition" and saw the face of the lead actor in the show.

Kierra had become close friends with the lead actor, Brad (not his real name), and hadn't paid much attention to the director's relationship with him. But in her meditation, her spirit showed her flashbacks of incidents when the director had questioned Kierra's writing and stage direction repeatedly, particularly when he was standing next to Brad. Kierra was already aware that the director was very controlling and that he singled her out more than the other writers, but she hadn't made the connection that the director was trying to discredit her in front of Brad.

Wondering what to do with that information, Kierra asked her spirit for suggestions. Her spirit helped her feel that having a private conversation with the director would help so that she would no longer store the frustration in her body.

Kierra utilized her great writing skills to draft a compelling script for her conversation with the director, and when she stood in front of him the next day, she eloquently pointed out his behavior and laid out new boundaries. The director seemed flummoxed by someone standing up to him and actually seemed to admire Kierra's approach. Kierra's symptoms disappeared within forty-eight hours, and her work life became much more collaborative and enjoyable.

The same symptoms (of a bladder infection) held a completely different message for Jackie. Jackie's bladder infections kept returning like unwanted houseguests, and she was determined to evict them permanently.

Jackie arrived in my office looking frazzled and uncomfortable. Her large brown eyes and tight facial expressions told me that she was in pain. She sat down and brushed her long braids off her shoulder and sighed.

"I've been attending your classes and doing your style of meditation for almost six months," she complained, "but I can't figure out why my body keeps getting these darn bladder infections! The only message I get is some visual of me crying. And the feeling that I need to be out dating—or something like that."

When I connected to Jackie's spirit, I heard that Jackie had received the message correctly, but she wasn't understanding it because it involved an old belief that she'd had since childhood.

I looked up at Jackie as I asked, "Am I hearing your spirit correctly when she says that the first boyfriend you loved passed away in a car accident?"

Jackie looked startled and confused. "Well, yeah, Marcus—he died when I was nineteen. I definitely cried a lot when it happened, but I got over that a long time ago."

I touched her arm sympathetically. "Bear with me here; there's another layer to this. Your spirit is showing me that when you were young, your grandmother was around a lot—is that right?"

Jackie nodded. "Yeah. She lived with us when I was young. She sat in front of the TV all day watching her soap operas."

I continued. "Your spirit tells me that your grandmother believed that there was only one person for each woman—something like that. Do you remember her exact words?"

"Oh yeah!" Jackie exclaimed. "Nana used to wag her finger at me and say, 'You only get one true love, Jackie...'"

Jackie's spirit gave me a thumbs-up to let me know that we were on target, so I asked, "Have you been worried that Marcus was your 'one true love?'"

Jackie's eyes opened wide with recognition. "Oh my God! I have always said that Marcus was my once-in-a-lifetime man."

I nodded. "You carry a lot of sadness within you because you've never questioned this belief that you absorbed from your grandmother when you were young. But that belief has you worried that you'll never be in love again, and so you're resistant to dating."

Jackie sat back in her chair and looked thoughtful. "So I've been walking around with this belief that 'It's over for me—I've had my one great love and that was it.'"

"Sure," I agreed. "It makes sense that if you thought you'd never fall in love again you wouldn't want to bother with dating."

Jackie hesitated and then shyly said, "So are you and my spirit telling me that I really can fall in love again?"

I grinned at her because her spirit was nodding her head enthusiastically. "Yes. I don't usually get information about people's future, but your spirit is showing me you and a man, walking on a beach, and you look very much in love with each other."

As I gave Jackie an energy treatment, she allowed herself to cry and release the sadness that she'd been carrying along with the belief that her love life had ended at the age of nineteen. The bladder infections never returned, and Jackie began dating. Last year, I received a Christmas card from Jackie with a photo of her and her husband, Carl, getting married on a beach in Jamaica.

It's so easy to get frustrated with unwanted symptoms, especially painful ones. But if you approach each one with curiosity about what it may be highlighting for you, you'll stay open to receiving the experiences and messages that each one can deliver. Your spirit wants to help you notice old limiting beliefs that you've outgrown or coping mechanisms that worked when you were younger but that no longer serve you. These limiting beliefs block you from achieving what your heart yearns to experience, so your spirit is highly motivated to help you notice them, even if that means a painful throbbing in the bladder. Utilizing your elevated intelligence on a regular basis requires you to remember that symptoms usually occur for your benefit, even if they're frequently unpleasant.

Now that you see how your thoughts affect your physical well-being, let's uncover other factors influencing your life's quality. You might be surprised to learn that your spirit is eager to discuss a wide variety of topics, with relationships often being at the forefront.

CHAPTER 10

UNDERSTANDING THE ENERGY EXCHANGE OF RELATIONSHIPS

When people are in great health and their spirit is offering advice on any topic, most turn their focus to their relationships.

Relationships have preoccupied human hearts for centuries because they're integral to our survival. There's abundant research showing a direct correlation between health and longevity and high-quality relationships. Before we start asking our spirit questions pertaining to our most valued connections, we first need to understand common relationship dysfunctions and the best questions to ask your spirit so you can successfully transform any unhealthy dynamics.

In my experience, unaddressed relationship issues nearly always lead to physical symptoms, so keeping your relationships healthy is a great investment in keeping *you* healthy—physically and emotionally. Your health and your relationships are inextricably linked. While you probably sense intuitively that the quality of your relationships is a key factor in your happiness, you may be wondering specifically how your relationships affect your health. To shed light on this, let's look at the energy exchanges that happen within all relationships.

We're all composed of energy, and science has demonstrated that all energy vibrates, even the energy within objects that appear solid. There are many types of energy waves and fields around us, but most of them aren't visible to the naked eye, so they operate below our levels of awareness. They have names like electromagnetic fields, infrared waves, microwaves, and radio waves. There's also a category of energy that Albert Einstein referred to as "subtle energies." These are energies that we know of because we can feel them in some way, but we don't yet have instruments to accurately measure and display them. Don't let the name fool you—subtle energies have a big impact on how you feel and how you function.

Ancient traditions refer to subtle energies by names like chi, qi, etheric energy, mana, life force, and prana. Subtle energies are thought to be a vital portion of the energies that fuel the biological processes within each living organism, including you.

Have you ever walked into a room and felt the tension immediately? That's subtle energy. You may not have known why it felt like you could "cut the air with a knife," but you knew that something unpleasant was happening before you walked in. We react to subtle energies every time we interact with other people; subtle energies provide us with clues and context that help us fill in the blanks when someone's words don't seem to correspond to facial expressions or body language.

When you ask your friend Crystal how she's doing and she says "fine" but there's an odd tone to her voice, you'll instantaneously scan her face and body language for clues. You'll also use your own body to feel the subtle energy coming from her body. If the energy Crystal's emitting feels relaxed and typical for her, then you'll assume that her response was accurate. But if her subtle energy feels brittle and tense, you're likely to ask follow-up questions to investigate if she really is "fine."

Each conversation that we have with another person includes an exchange of subtle energies. This exchange actually creates additional energy, which vibrates at the frequency of the interaction between the two people. This is why a hate-filled rally can be so toxic for a town; the malignant energy created by the group's exchanges can be felt long after the meeting disbands, typically resulting in an increased rate of hate crimes. This is also why in the beginning of a romantic relationship, you can stay up all night talking and not feel tired the next day. You're running off the extra energy that you and your romantic interest created between you the night before.

Every living creature draws in energy and discharges it, and the energy that each creature emits has a vibratory rate or frequency. Vibrational rates are determined by the nature of the living organism, as well as its current thoughts and emotions (if it's a sentient creature). In general, the higher you vibrate, the more optimistic and peaceful you feel. Your vibratory rate is greatly affected by the people around you and how happy they are, as well as whether your own thoughts are negative or positive. Let's look at the energies that we absorb from our environment and from our relationships.

We are all affected by the vibratory rate of the energy around us. You can use breathing as an analogy. If you're standing in a smoky room, then you will be forced to inhale smoky air. If the energy in a room feels heavy and sad, it will influence your emotional state and impact the positive or negative tendency of your thoughts. It's not that it's impossible to have a happy thought while sitting in a room full of angry people, but it's certainly more difficult than if you were sitting in a room laughing with your best friend. The energy in the places where you live and work has a big impact on your own energy and how you feel. I know that I'm a lot more optimistic while hiking out in the woods than when I'm standing in line at the DMV.

Plants discharge energy that vibrates at a frequency that feels peaceful to us, which is why being in nature tends to relax and soothe us. Babies—both human and animal—tend to vibrate at a frequency associated with feeling love, which is why we usually feel drawn to them. When you pick up a kitten or puppy and hold it, your own vibration tends to rise in response, and you'll likely find yourself smiling. This is known as the Principle of Resonance: Things in motion (in this case living beings that are vibrating) will seek to move in harmony with one another. The Principle of Resonance is also why a group of women living together for more than a few months will tend to have menstrual cycles that align.

So how does this connect directly to your relationships and ultimately your health? Imagine standing in front of your friend Chloe. As your conversation flows back and forth, you're each sending energy out and simultaneously absorbing energy from the other. In the space between you, the energy amplifies so that in a delightful conversation, you both walk away with more energy than you started with, which feels very satisfying. Let's imagine that you output twenty-five units of energy, and so does Chloe. (This is an oversimplification but bear with me.) This energy amplifies between you, and one hundred units of energy are created via the conversation. In an ideal situation, each of you would walk away with fifty units of energy, feeling pleasantly buoyed up by that exchange.

But in reality, the split is rarely even. So who gets the larger portion? The person who's the most dominant in that conversation. Who's the dominant person in each conversation? It's the person who "pulls" more energy toward herself because she feels entitled to it at that moment. This entitlement may be due to need or simply an expectation. For example, if I'm asking my friend Dana for directions to her house, I'm needing information from her, and so I'm expecting to receive more of the energy between us. And if your boss is asking you to talk him through your budget proposal, you're likely to be sending most of the energy between you toward him.

In a healthy relationship, the energy may not be evenly divided in every interaction, but overall, it's a fairly even distribution of the energy created through energy exchanges and the resulting amplification. When the scale tips away from you and the relationship leaves you feeling a bit heavy or sad, it's usually a sign that either you're consistently getting less than half of the energy created by the two of you, or your conversations are creating more negative energy than positive energy (hint: you're absorbing this negative energy). And if you feel really depleted, then it's likely that you're not getting *any* of the energy from the interaction, and thus you're left drained by spending time with that person. In the worst-case scenario, you could begin to have physical symptoms due to the energetic imbalance.

In my lectures I frequently say, "Relationships are both a mirror and a feedback loop." The people we choose to interact with can serve as a mirror for us, highlighting belief systems and attitudes that we may not be noticing within ourselves. Take a moment to reflect on who has been drawn to you lately and who you're eager to spend time with. Since the energy of the people around you will influence your own vibration, it's worth periodically stepping back and looking for patterns in the people you interact with. Are they content or disgruntled? Are they feeling empowered or a lack of personal power?

Let's take a few minutes to inventory the primary people in your life and assess the quality of the energy exchanges you tend to have with them. The people you surround yourself with provide insight into the vibrations that you're emitting and the messages you're likely telling yourself—about how hard life is, how kind people are, etc.

YOUR RELATIONSHIP ENERGY AUDIT

1. Create a list of the people that you spend most of your free time with—your favorite people and your "obligatory relationships."

2. Now write three adjectives next to each person's name. These adjectives should describe how that person's energy felt during your recent conversations. You can make a side note if this person is acting "out of character" due to illness, travel, or a big transition that they're currently going through.

3. As you recall your recent conversations with each person, assign a number to that person. A zero indicates that during your conversations you didn't feel much energy coming from the person, and a 1 means that you felt a little bit of positive energy coming toward

you. Let's assume a scale of 1–5, with a 5 being given to someone who had lots of positive energy streaming your way during conversations. Let's use negative numbers to identify conversations that felt negatively focused, with a -5 being assigned to the interactions that were the most draining, critical, or generally unpleasant.

4.   Lastly, write down how you typically felt after interacting with this person: energized, unchanged, or drained.

Here's a sample Relationship Energy Audit.

Name	Their Energy	Typical Energy	My Experience
Harper	(Currently heartbroken), Stuck, Sad	-4	Drained
Oliver	Exhausted, Spacey, Kind	+1 or 0	Unchanged
Layla	Engaged, Vulnerable, Open	+4 or +5	Energized
Mom	Attentive, Worried, Loving	+2	Energized
Sister	Ambitious, Self-Absorbed, Defiant	-2	Drained
Aunt Nora	Funny, Irreverent, Sarcastic	-2	Drained
Riley	Intense, Witty, Supportive	+3 or +4	Energized

From this audit we can see that the person's relationships with Harper, Sister, and Aunt Nora tend to be the most draining and would likely benefit from some transformation.

Look over your list, noting the sum totals you assigned to each person: Did you benefit energetically from your interactions with your friends and family? If you notice that some of your relationships are consistently depleting you, those are the ideal relationships to focus on as you read through the following chapters.

Improving your relationships protects your health, as well as your sanity! The following chapters will cover common types of relationships and ways that each of them can include unhealthy patterns. Each chapter will include questions you can ask your spirit if you want to investigate ways to resolve conflicts in your relationships and reclaim your energy.

Unresolved conflicts in one type of relationship tend to bleed over and pollute the waters of our other relationships and our health, so investing in optimizing our relationships is always time well spent. Read on to learn how to collaborate with your spirit for an energetic upgrade to all of your relationships.

The next three chapters deal with our most important relationship—the relationship that we have with ourselves! I was flustered the first time my spirit told me that most of the negative energy within my body was coming not from others, but from my own negative self-talk! In the years since, I've been diligently working on being a better friend to myself, and I wholeheartedly encourage you to invest in the relationship that you have with yourself. Being a better friend to yourself will ultimately improve every relationship that you're in—I promise.

CHAPTER 11

YOUR RELATIONSHIP WITH YOU

Forgiving Your Mistakes

How many people do you know who are great at self-forgiveness? They are the rare unicorns; most of us have a ready list of our flaws and a big pile of "shoulds" that can generate self-loathing in a second. We may bristle at even minor criticism because getting the slightest whiff that we might be "bad" in some way brings up our insecurities and past mistakes. Here's how my client Giselle learned that being reactive to her partner was more about her inability to forgive herself than the actual situation at hand.

Giselle is a beloved orthopedic surgeon who works long hours at a prestigious hospital in France. I wasn't surprised when she showed up for her online session wearing her surgical scrubs and her signature scrub cap with python snakes on it (the creature with the most bones: 1,800!). In her direct, animated style, Giselle waved hello and then launched straight into her reason for booking a session.

"Christine, I need your help with something. It's recently been brought to my attention—by my lovely wife, Sophie—that I get really defensive about my drinking. Which is weird because I don't actually drink that much. But Sophie's mom was an alcoholic, so she worries. If I have a second drink when we're out to dinner, she may raise her eyebrow at me or frown a little. And then I get really snappy and defensive."

Intrigued, I leaned forward and made eye contact with Giselle. "It sounds like both you and Sophie understand why *she* gets very anxious about alcohol. Why do you think *you* get defensive about it?"

Giselle thought for a moment and then replied, "When I asked my spirit about this during my meditation, she showed me short 'video clips' of me drinking a lot in college. And let me tell you, I was making some poor choices back then and drinking way too much. But I couldn't figure out why my spirit was showing me those snippets—it's not like I ever drink like that now! So I confess that I got frustrated and quit that meditation."

From observing Giselle's energy while she spoke, I sensed that humiliation was the real reason she had ended the conversation with her spirit. So I asked, "What's the most predominant feeling you have about that time in your life?"

Giselle looked down as she replied, "I'm embarrassed about that time period, so I've always tried to put it behind me."

"It sounds like maybe you need to forgive yourself for those college years. What specific things are you holding shame and regret about?"

She took a deep breath and exhaled slowly. "When I was in college I would drink way too much. I deliberately set out to get drunk even though I knew I'd probably do something stupid. Which was usually having sex with someone I didn't know. I'd always be embarrassed about it the next day. But the pattern continued— every weekend—all through my junior year of college."

"Why do you think you drank heavily during that one year?" I asked.

Giselle scowled. "Because I was a mess! At the beginning of that year, I found out that my dad was cheating on my mom. I saw him kissing some woman in a restaurant and I confronted him. He made me swear not to tell my mom, promising that he would tell her. But he never did, so for that whole year I had to keep his damn secret and I was miserable; it felt like I was betraying my mom."

"What a terrible position to put you in!" I empathized.

"I know—he was such a coward about it! He never did tell her—our neighbor found out and *she* told my mom. I was so relieved once my mom knew, even though she immediately filed for divorce. My heavy drinking stopped as soon as I didn't have to keep that secret. I didn't drink much at all in med school, or any other time. But I still feel shitty about that time—both the heavy drinking and the sleeping around that I did when I was drunk."

I smiled warmly at her and said, "Well let's ask your spirit for help in forgiving yourself for your actions during that rough year."

As soon as I closed my eyes and connected to Giselle's spirit, she floated toward me with warm, gentle energy. I repeated to Giselle what her spirit said: "Before you can get answers about your unwanted behavior, you must be willing to look at your behavior honestly and have compassion for yourself. Assume that any repeated behaviors have a reason behind them—a way that you were trying to take care of yourself. This approach can reveal the deeper levels of motivation behind your actions."

"Well, getting drunk and sleeping around was a lame-ass way to take care of myself!" Giselle replied.

I chuckled. "I think your spirit is suggesting a more compassionate approach than that."

She sighed. "Okay, okay. So let's assume that in some weird way I'm trying to take care of myself by getting drunk. What next?"

Giselle's spirit continued. "Can you feel that you were drinking to numb out the painful emotions that you were wrestling with?"

Giselle nodded, so I continued channeling. "You've assumed that the emotions centered on guilt, and you certainly felt guilty. But it seems that the primary feeling you wrestled with was that of feeling trapped. Trapped because there was no good answer; each choice seemed to lead to you causing pain to either your mother or your father. Does this resonate with you?"

Giselle thought about it and then said, "Yeah, that's really accurate! I was trapped with no good solution."

Her spirit continued. "And do you remember that someone was trying to convince you to be in a committed relationship at that time?"

Giselle winced visibly. "Yeah, Karen. She was sweet, but I was not ready to be in a relationship back then. So I'd spend time with her but then go out, get drunk, and sleep with someone else and feel like a cruel jerk the next day. Why Karen kept hanging around me I don't know, but I feel horrible for how many times I hurt her. Like, what is wrong with me?"

Giselle's spirit quickly responded. "You and Karen were drawn to each other because you were both wrestling with the idea that relationships were bound to fail and cause pain. After learning of your father's infidelity, you had little faith that relationships could last, and you were sabotaging any potential relationships. Karen's father had also been unfaithful in his marriage, and Karen was subconsciously trying to prove to herself that she could love someone so well that she wouldn't be cheated on. Because neither of you was conscious of the motivations for your actions, those concerns weren't addressed, and the 'distorted behaviors' continued. Neither one of you was taking good care of yourself."

"Wow! Really? That's fascinating to know about Karen. I hope that she's found someone who loves her well."

I smiled and said, "From this gentle, compassionate place that you're in right now, can you acknowledge that both you and Karen were trying to protect your own hearts? That neither one of you was seeking to be cruel or foolish?"

Giselle nodded. "Yeah, I can see that. It really helps to know what was motivating each of us to act the way that we did."

"Yes," I agreed. "On the journey of self-forgiveness, it's best to start with looking at your specific actions and admitting that you don't like how that version of you showed up. But instead of harshly judging yourself, get curious and ask, 'What pain was driving that behavior?' Getting to the bottom of the pain and distorted beliefs can take some time, but it helps us find a lasting feeling of self-forgiveness."

"Well, how do I do that exactly?" Giselle asked.

Giselle's spirit offered the next steps. "Forgiveness has some degree of understanding at its core. Some actions—like a mass shooting—are impossible to understand beyond the knowing that the person must have been deeply struggling with something much bigger than themselves in order to cause so much pain to others. But when the actions are your own, with compassionate inquiry you can reveal the many layers of pain and confusion that were underneath the regrettable actions you took."

Giselle brightened. "So when I understand some of the 'why' behind my actions, I can forgive myself more because I can sympathize with the part of me that was hurting and just trying to feel better?"

"Exactly!" I cheered.

Giselle's spirit offered more insights. "When humans feel regret and shame, they typically try to distance themselves from those memories without really examining them and finding understanding and self-forgiveness. Then those past actions remain an open wound emotionally, triggering what appear to be unreasonable reactions."

Giselle nodded vigorously. "Yup—sounds like me."

"It's helpful," Giselle's spirit continued, "to notice any disproportionate reactions and investigate more deeply. Imagine if you had said to your wife, 'Honey, I know that you worry about someone's drinking getting out of hand. The only time I overindulged in alcohol was when I was trying to hide from a very painful situation in my family. I understand why I drank heavily then, and I'm in no danger of repeating that coping mechanism now.'"

Giselle sighed. "I can picture Sophie tearing up and saying, 'Thanks for understanding and for the reassurance.'"

"Yes," I said. "You weren't able to offer her kind reassurance before because you were reacting to the internalized shame you felt, which made you defensive. Now that you've forgiven yourself for that difficult year and the behaviors you regret, you can remain calm when Sophie is feeling anxious on the topic of alcohol consumption."

"Definitely!" Giselle said enthusiastically. "I can't believe that it was this easy."

I smiled. "We humans think that once we've done something wrong, the path to redemption must be long and arduous. It just needs to be sincere and filled with compassion—for the people we've hurt *and* for ourselves."

I'm happy to report that Giselle's energy changed during our session as she forgave herself, and now whenever she talks about her college years there is no shame or regret in her voice or her energy. And her wife, Sophie, was so impressed by Giselle's metamorphosis on the topic of drinking that she booked a session for herself and worked on healing her childhood wounds that yielded her anxious relationship with alcohol. Both women can talk openly about their childhood wounds now, and they remind each other to tread compassionately when investigating the reasons behind their actions. And because they both meditate and have conversations with their spirits, they are adept at understanding the source of their occasional tensions and misunderstandings.

We all have actions that we regret taking and label as mistakes. I find that my clients typically believe that they make mistakes for one of two reasons:

- They're dumb/foolish. This may be how you explain why you bought the wrong type of paint for the deck or why you didn't check out the plumber thoroughly before you hired him.
- They lack willpower. This may be how you explain eating three cupcakes, not going to that gym you're paying for each month, or yelling at your kids again.

But my conversations with my spirit and the spirits of others have taught me that the *real reasons* that humans act in regrettable ways are:

1. Inexperience
2. Confusion or surprise
3. Suppressed or unhealed wounds

Let's examine each of these.

INEXPERIENCE

We don't know what we don't know. Most of us would never expect children to know everything. And when we are around them and they encounter a new skill or situation, we'd encourage them to be easy on themselves as they learn. But somehow, as adults we hold the unrealistic expectation that we should have everything figured out by now. Intellectually we know it's impossible, but emotionally we respond with shame and embarrassment when we make mistakes due to our lack of knowledge or understanding. So, to use the above examples, you may not have checked to see if the plumber was licensed because you haven't owned a home before, and your landlord had always handled the repairs. And you bought the wrong deck paint because you've never painted a deck before and didn't even know that there was a difference between stains, paints, and clear varnishes. This is totally normal when doing something for the first time. It's also normal to respond in unpredictable ways when we are confused or surprised.

CONFUSION OR SURPRISE

We can make "mistakes" when we're pressured to think fast or asked to make a decision on the fly. In these situations, we often freeze like a deer in headlights, stammering out a response that we later regret. This could be saying yes to volunteering for a school bake sale because the principal caught you at the supermarket and you were surprised to see her there. Or agreeing that your son could have a friend over to practice free throws when you were distracted, not understanding that he meant his entire basketball team! Misunderstandings happen. Confusion happens. We feel the pressure when someone wants an immediate answer, and in trying to meet their expectation, we act from confusion or people-pleasing instead of informed self-care. I've coached my clients to have several responses in their back pocket for surprise requests. My favorite is: "I'm not sure if that will work, so let me get back to you."

SUPPRESSED OR
UNHEALED WOUNDS

By suppressed wounds, I'm not only referring to big painful events that may have occurred. We each have millions of "tiny wounds," painful emotional papercuts that we didn't take the time to process when they occurred. Instead, we felt something unpleasant and quickly pushed that feeling down to get away from the discomfort. And because our culture doesn't encourage us to go back later and examine that discomfort to heal it, that negative emotion remains stored in our body. As Giselle's spirit said above, such unprocessed feelings remain as an unhealed emotional wound in us, triggering actions and outbursts that we can't easily explain. Then we experience two layers of discomfort—the underlying emotional wounding that is still lurking within us untreated and the emotional outburst that seemed disproportionate to the situation.

Many label such outbursts or regrettable actions as "being triggered." I see them as an attempt to avoid reexperiencing a disturbing emotion. In our attempts to escape a repeat of that terrible feeling, we can create new reasons for shame and regret, and then the original wound becomes deeper, so we're even more easily triggered the next time the emotion comes up.

How can we prevent these suppressed emotional wounds so that we're less likely to act in regrettable ways? The first step is to acknowledge when we feel something unpleasant. Often just pausing for a few seconds to silently label our experience can prevent us from shoving it down and pretending that nothing is wrong. I find that when I put just a few words to what I'm feeling, the acknowledged emotions are then either released or they reveal a deeper pain to be explored.

I've learned to give myself permission to say, "Hold on a minute, please—let me digest this for a minute. Okay, got it; that feels kind of _____(insert unpleasant feeling here)." Once I acknowledge what I'm feeling, most of the uncomfortable emotion seems to float out of my body. The important step is to have compassion for myself and my emotions without having to justify/rationalize why I felt that way. Doing this quick check-in with yourself is a great way to honor yourself and to prevent suppressed wounds that lead to regrettable actions.

I also recommend asking your spirit for help. Remember that you're looking for the deeper levels of emotional discomfort that were driving your (regrettable) actions. It may be that you were confused, inexperienced, or reacting from an old unhealed wound. Try asking your spirit these questions during your next meditation:

1. What is a past event that I need to forgive myself for?
2. What can I understand about the pain that I was feeling at that time?
3. Is there a topic that I'm too hard on myself about? Why is that?
4. How can I have more compassion for myself going forward?

Practicing self-forgiveness will yield such big rewards! You'll feel calmer and be less easily ruffled by others' actions. Approach your past regrets from curiosity and a desire to understand your motivations, not a harsh condemnation of yourself. Your relationship with yourself will flourish from this approach!

In your voyage toward a more accurate and loving view of yourself, notice how well you take care of your needs. Do you rush to take care of others before even noticing what your needs are at the moment? The next chapter reveals the price of being "too helpful."

CHAPTER 12

YOUR RELATIONSHIP WITH YOU

Helping Everyone but Yourself

My new client Jonathan confused me when he sent a text before his session asking if I needed him to bring me a coffee. Initially, I thought he sent me the message by mistake, but I soon realized that his kind offer was an indication of a troublesome pattern for him.

Jonathan's wife was already my client, and she'd urged her husband to have an emergency session to get help with his debilitating neck and shoulder pain. His doctor had diagnosed it as muscle spasms two months earlier and sent Jonathan home with muscle relaxers, but they weren't helping with the pain, just leaving him foggy-headed. Jonathan sat down very slowly in my treatment room, confirming that he was currently in a good deal of pain. I'd learned from his initial email that he worked in a high-pressure sales position, and my intuition was nudging me to focus on the demands of his job.

He gave a slight smile when I asked him about his work. "I've worked for this company for almost ten years, and we're like family there. My crew is great—we all work really hard, and we usually exceed our sales projections."

I nodded and then closed my eyes to connect to Jonathan's spirit, who said, "Ask him to describe his role in his family when he was around ten years old."

Jonathan looked momentarily surprised at the question but then said, "Well, my dad left us when I was about nine and a half, and my mom kind of fell apart. She'd always been insecure and anxious, but after my dad left, she got worse—lying on the sofa and crying all day, saying she didn't know what to do next, that sort of thing. So I stepped up and helped her—making sure my brother got up for school and that we both had our homework done and lunches packed—and I tried to reassure her when she got stressed. Which I guess was pretty often. As I got older, I helped her make decisions and pay the bills and stuff."

"How did your mom respond to your help?" I asked.

Jonathan smiled sheepishly. "She used to say that I was her lifeline." As Jonathan said those words his pain clearly spiked, and I watched him grimace and then try to resume a normal facial expression. I decided to postpone getting answers for him and instead focus on achieving some immediate pain relief, and I had him lie on my treatment table so I could put some healing energy into his neck area.

As I flowed high vibrational energy into his neck and shoulders, I watched Jonathan sigh and visibly relax as the muscle spasms quieted. With my hands hovering just above Jonathan's neck, his spirit sent me a visual of an ox pulling a plow in a field. What the heck? That made no sense to me, so I assumed it was a random thought and dismissed it from my mind, only to have it float gently back to me as messages from the spirit world often do. Huh.

Feeling a little silly, I asked, "This may sound random, but I keep seeing an image of an ox whenever my hands go near your neck. Does this mean anything to you—were you born in the year of the ox or something?"

Jonathan opened his eyes and looked at me like I was nuts. "Uh, no . . . that doesn't mean anything to me."

"Okay, sorry," I said self-consciously. "It's just that the yoke that the ox is wearing is exactly where your pain seems to be."

Suddenly Jonathan began chuckling. "I just remembered something! One day last year I said to my wife that I'm responsible for so many people at work that sometimes I feel like an ox pulling a huge cart, with all my people riding in it. That's so weird . . . do you think that's what you're talking about?"

Feeling braver, I said, "Yes, I do. And as you finished speaking just now, I heard your spirit say this sentence: 'It's okay, it's not a problem.' He actually said it twice."

Jonathan opened his eyes wide in surprise and then narrowed them suspiciously. "Hey, did my wife put you up to this? Did she tell you to bring that up?"

I held up my hands and backed away from Jonathan. "No! I promise! Why?"

Jonathan paused. "I'm famous for saying that at the office. Last year for Christmas my team actually got me a wall plaque that says, 'It's okay, it's not a problem.' That's my go-to response when someone comes in and tells me that they've messed up and need me to take over an account for them."

I smiled and gently said, "Well I think that it's *become* a problem. In the visual I received, the ox was really straining to do its job, and the yoke was right where your circle of pain is. And that statement that you're known for saying, reassuring someone that you'll do their work for them, paints a picture of you consistently taking on too much work, and I think that your body is showing you that."

Jonathan lay there quietly while I finished his energy treatment and then told me that he realized the pain had started the same day that he'd agreed to take over a big project that wasn't even part of his job description. He sat back down on the sofa in my treatment room, and we resumed our conversation with his spirit.

Jonathan's spirit helped him see that the frequent praise he received from his mother conditioned him to fixate on how much he could help others. As his focus centered on solving problems for his mother, he learned to ignore his own needs in order to keep his remaining parent functioning.

His spirit continued, "This problem-solving for others was a survival mechanism, not a joyful part of your childhood. But because it was consistently reinforced it became a habit and a source of pride for you. You tend to give yourself rationalizations like 'I'm a good team player' and 'I like helping people because that's who I am.'"

"But those things aren't just rationalizations—they're true!" Jonathan protested.

"They *can* be true—at times," his spirit responded. "But if they're your automatic response every time, then you aren't actually tracking your energy or how depleted you are—you're just acting reflexively."

"What do you mean by tracking my energy depletion?" Jonathan asked with raised eyebrows.

His spirit offered this analogy: "Imagine that throughout each day you absorb one hundred units of energy. You need sixty of those units in order to run your body and your mind. Each person who asks you for help is asking for five units of energy. And when others help you, they are sending you five units of energy. With the way things are going at work, do you think you end each day with the sixty units of energy you need?"

"Ha! Not even close!" Jonathan replied.

"Agreed," his spirit said. "You're not being encouraged to make every relationship transactional, but you *are* advised to track your energy output and prioritize your own needs. When you see yourself as the guy that's always helpful, it leads you to say yes to every request for help."

Jonathan was thoughtful for a moment. "I guess it's not the healthiest part of my identity to be 'the good guy that you can count on' if it's draining the life out of me!"

I smiled. "It's about focusing on living a more balanced life. You can still be kind and helpful but also be self-honoring and take care of yourself."

Jonathan grinned. "Well, given that my neck pain has gone from a level nine to a two, you and my spirit have made me a believer!"

In his next session, Jonathan said he'd gone back to work that day and handed the big project back to the proper team and that he'd been paying attention to when he said yes to other people's requests and why. He began connecting with his spirit regularly in meditation and was thrilled to receive constructive tips on how to maintain the new boundaries with his coworkers.

As I expected, he encountered some friction from some of the people who had benefited from his perpetual desire to be seen as helpful. But within two months his colleagues had adjusted, and the team's productivity remained high. And his neck and shoulder pain disappeared!

While you may not feel like an ox pulling a plow each day, you may benefit from noticing how much of your identity consists of being "the helper." Assisting people is admirable, but not when it's done to such a degree that you're denying your own self-care.

Many people who identify with being the helper do so for good reason. Perhaps, your childhood positioned you to pay more attention to everyone else's needs than your own. Let's look at the two most common ways that this dynamic can occur.

A STRUGGLING PARENT

If you were raised in a household where a parent was struggling in some way—with depression, anxiety, addiction, physical handicaps, or health issues—it's likely that you were asked to help take care of things at home. If the person struggling was the only parent in the home, then it probably felt even more crucial that you help that person function.

It's sad how often young children become "parentized," stepping in to serve as a surrogate spouse to one of their parents or filling in for a parent who struggles to cope with everyday life for various reasons. Such children are frequently praised for this behavior as the parent subconsciously grooms the child to continue the helpful behavior. These children learn that "helping" is their most valuable trait, and it gets incorporated into their sense of self ("People like having me around because I always help out").

I've had numerous clients who have taken on some version of the "assistant to the parent" role only to find that it has no expiration date. This leaves the grown child feeling perpetually responsible for that parent's emotional well-being. Too many mothers praise their daughter for being a good best friend, subconsciously hoping to lock her into that supportive role forever. While the parent knows that the adult child moving on is appropriate, feelings of abandonment and depression can result, leaving the adult child feeling torn and guilty about pursuing their own life.

If you played a critical helper role to a struggling parent in your family, you may have heard phrases like these:

- I don't know what I'd do without you.
- You're my best friend and confidant, and I know you'll always be here for me.
- You're always so helpful—that's what I love about you!
- This family couldn't survive without you.

While such statements may be intended as compliments, they also serve to ensure that the child continues the helpful behavior. In households where one or both parents feel that the child's help is critical, there's generally not much attention given to the needs of anyone not in crisis. If this describes your family of origin, you may have learned to ignore your own desires and needs. If you were conditioned to disconnect from what you need in favor of noticing what others need, it could be very healing for you to begin paying more attention to how often you're ignoring yourself in your efforts to help those around you. Now let's look at another common family dynamic that can cause people to fall into the helper role.

A SIBLING IN CRISIS

You may have grown up with a sibling who suffered from mental health issues, significant illnesses, or addiction. While it's certainly understandable that such children absorb a lot of parental focus and time, you may have felt ignored unless you were actively helping your parents care for your sibling. It's an unfortunate consequence of addiction, prolonged illnesses, and disabled children that the other children in the household can be asked to serve as caregivers and be shamed if they resist such duties.

I've also had many clients tell me they felt that their troubled sibling was "assigned" to them as their responsibility, requiring them to forgo friendships and activities in order to fulfill their caretaking duties. Just as with a struggling parent, children raised in these scenarios can have trouble tuning into their own needs once they're adults. If this describes your childhood in some way, you may have trouble seeing someone struggle and not jumping in to assist. And you may still feel responsible for your sibling, feeling guilty if you're thriving and they're not.

If you played a critical helper role to a sibling in crisis in your family, you may have heard phrases like:

- You're such a great brother/sister—your sibling would be lost without you.
- You're our little hero, always standing up for (sibling).
- I couldn't hold this family together without your help.
- I don't know what we'll do with (sibling) when you go off to college....

If you were once given the responsibility of taking care of a sibling, you may struggle with feelings of being irresponsible and feel guilty when you pursue something for your own pleasure. It's likely that you feel more comfortable in pursuits that involve taking care of someone else. This is because without realizing it, your parents may have trained you to feel guilty when you weren't actively caretaking.

Both of these family dynamics can produce adults who frequently give away more energy than is healthy for them, leaving them with insufficient energy for themselves. It's so common to hear people complaining about busy schedules that leave them drained that you may not realize your exhaustion is rooted in how much energy you expend helping others. Remember: if you have trouble saying no, your body may start saying it for you through pain, exhaustion, and a general lack of vitality.

Do you feel somewhat responsible for the happiness of your parents or other family members? If so, you may want to ask your spirit about this topic. Here are some questions that I recommend:

1. Was I made to feel responsible for someone else in my family—for their physical safety or emotional well-being?
2. Do I see myself as the most capable one in the family? If so, what responsibilities do I assign myself as a result?
3. How can I support my family members in a healthier way?
4. What are ways that I can achieve a healthier separation from unhealthy family responsibilities?

5. Are there others in my life that I have taken too much responsibility for?
6. Do I look for opportunities to be of service to others to boost my self-esteem?

The goal is to learn to notice your own needs as well as the needs of the people you care about. If spending time around a particular family member feels draining to you, you may want to consider the responsibility you feel for that individual. This may mean pushing through your fears of disappointing someone when you don't continually offer to help; trust that living a more balanced life is the pathway to better health for everyone in your family.

On your journey toward better health and better relationships, it's important to be a good friend to yourself. This includes noticing if you tend to overextend yourself and looking at the reasons why. I'm willing to bet that somewhere in your background you were praised for placing others' needs before your own, and this behavior pattern has led you to put yourself at the end of your long to-do list. Imagine your best friend stepping into your life for a week—would you worry about her being exhausted by it? If so, it's probably time to make some changes.

In the next chapter on your relationship with yourself, we examine the inner critic that never seems to run out of criticisms for you. Let's examine how that inner critic got to be so unrelenting and how you can turn down the volume on that unhelpful inner dialogue.

CHAPTER 13

YOUR RELATIONSHIP
WITH YOU

Softening Your Inner Critic

You know that voice in your head that never seems to run out of negative commentary about you and your choices? How did your inner warning system become such a Negative Nancy? That pattern—like some of the others we've discussed—began in your childhood.

If you've spent time with a child who was behaving obnoxiously, you probably doubled down on your commitment to raising your own kids to be polite and kind. Well-meaning people across the globe have held this intention, and most have utilized the tools of shame, punishment, and guilt to teach their kids to be responsible and well-mannered.

As a mother myself, I understand that well-utilized guilt can help children learn empathy. (As in, "Honey, imagine how sad Suzie feels when you keep all the toys and don't share them with her.") And appropriate punishments can help children understand that actions do have consequences. But I stand firmly against using the harmful tool of shame to manipulate children's behavior. Shame has a corrosive effect on a child's self-esteem, which generally results in self-loathing and a lack of confidence. Many of us were raised with methods like shame, guilt, and punishment as our parents and authority figures tried to motivate us to behave in certain ways, and we have the emotional scars to prove it.

THE CREATION OF OUR INNER CRITIC

In an effort to avoid criticism, punishment, and shame during your childhood years, you likely learned to self-monitor and adjust your actions. To guard against making mistakes or getting into trouble, most of us took our most critical parent's voice and played it repeatedly in our minds. We'd imagine what that critical parent might say and apply it to ourselves preemptively, believing that if we avoided that parent's censure, then we were probably on a safe track. Over time, the voice of your parent (or authority figure) blended with your own internal voice and created your inner critic. Essentially you began to police yourself with a steady loop of negative feedback.

Most of us don't speak very kindly to ourselves even when we're performing well, so when we think we're being lazy, messy, or foolish, well, the negativity gets turned up to full volume. The good news is that if you learn to listen carefully to your internal criticisms, you can start to distinguish between your own boundaries and the harsh feedback that you're repeating from your childhood.

YOUR INNER CRITIC
BECOMES A BULLY

One of the primary jobs of your brain is to keep you alive and safe; survival is the priority. It keeps track of things that cause you pain—emotionally as well as physically—and helps you remember not to repeat those actions. This is why we generally only have to touch a hot flame once to know that it's a bad idea. The causes leading up to physical pain are generally straightforward and easier to predict than the causes of emotional pain. So our mind tries to protect us from emotional pain by looking for causation connections that lead up to each painful emotion.

The problem with these cause-and-effect theories is that they can be woefully inaccurate. Your mind frantically grasps at all sorts of possibilities for the painful emotion you're feeling and concocts a theory. So that time you were laughed at for giving the wrong answer in your third grade math class? The laughter was actually because the teacher made a contorted face as she tried not to sneeze. But your mind concluded that if you give a wrong answer, you'll be laughed at, and for years you avoided speaking up in class. And so it goes with your mind amassing a huge pile of "things to avoid so you won't feel awful" that may or may not be accurate.

By the time you're in your forties and fifties, your list of unpleasant experiences is very long. You've also had many delightful experiences, but since you aren't trying to avoid repeating those, your mind doesn't keep track of them. Which is unfortunate because your list of "what can go wrong" isn't counterbalanced by a list of all the things that can work out beautifully. As a result, your mind becomes more alarmist and fretful every year. [Note: This is one reason why I recommend that my clients keep a "diary of successes." If you write down the wise decisions you make and the great help that shows up for you when you're struggling, your ego-mind will learn to hold a more balanced perspective.]

As your mind keeps adding to your list of "dumb things I've done and bad decisions I've made," you become increasingly distrustful of yourself. You start looking for evidence of how you're just bad at certain things so that you can avoid them (and the possible shame and embarrassment). You may decide that you're "bad at relationships" or "bad at communication," and then every relationship struggle fortifies your suspicions.

Years ago, my spirit told me, "You can find evidence of whatever theory you're looking to prove." Most of us don't realize that our minds are silently collecting evidence, building a case to prove that we are, say, "bad at technology" or "hopeless with directions." This stack of evidence then solidifies into a conclusion that becomes part of our identity. Do you find yourself uttering statements like "I suck at math," "I'm bad at remembering names," "I can't cook," "I pick the wrong people to date," etc.? Once these beliefs are part of how you define yourself, it's very difficult for you to notice any evidence to the contrary. So if you believe that you're bad at directions and you find your way home without your phone's map, you're likely to discount your success with statements like "I just got lucky."

Eventually that bully in your head can become downright abusive. Your inner critic may shorten his criticisms from "You should've remembered to call that person back" to "You idiot!" Now you've veered off the road of policing yourself and into the gutter of outright abuse. Most of us wouldn't let a stranger talk to us as viciously as we talk to ourselves. But the criticisms happen so quickly, and are so familiar, that they don't feel like the emotional slap across the face that they actually are.

When your inner voice deteriorates to a list of insults and unhealthy comparisons, it's definitely time to upgrade your inner critic. The first step is to realize that *harsh self-criticism does not protect you from future mistakes*. By harsh self-criticism, I mean negative comments that label you as unintelligent, inferior, shameful, or a failure. Here are some examples of statements that my clients have reported hearing from their inner critic:

- I'm such a loser.
- I should be more like _____ (someone else).
- I always waste money.
- I'm broken.
- I'll never be good at _____ (fill in the blank).
- I'm just too much of a mess.
- I'm unlovable; no wonder I'm alone.

Comments like these are indictments of who you are as a person, not helpful guidance about a specific action or decision. These internal character assassinations erode your self-confidence with no clear way to improve yourself. Commit to paying more attention to your inner critic. Does it feel like you're receiving loving guidelines or toxic condemnations?

Intuitively, we know that we respond better to encouraging phrases than critical statements, but we still find ourselves defaulting to the "bully" as a way to improve ourselves. Breaking this habit involves raising your awareness about your inner commentary. How many times a day do you judge yourself as scattered, lazy, dumb, etc.? Once you begin paying attention to the condemnations, it will instigate kinder guidance from your inner critic.

A helpful exercise for retraining your inner critic is to notice when you're speaking harshly to yourself and force yourself to pause and create a more compassionate, *useful* statement. In time, this breaks your inner critic's habit of name-calling and universal condemnation.

You can also ask your spirit to help you more objectively evaluate your inner guidance. In meditation, I recommend asking your spirit questions like these:

1. Are there damaging phrases that my inner critic uses frequently?
2. Are there conclusions and assessments that I make about myself that aren't accurate?
3. What activities do I avoid because my inner critic has made me too afraid of failure?
4. What phrases can I use to guide my behavior more effectively and lovingly?
5. Can you suggest a phrase that I can substitute in for my conclusion that I'm _____ (a negative statement you believe about yourself)?

Questions like these promote the development of your elevated intelligence as your conscious mind and your spirit work together to replace unhelpful condemnations with accurate, encouraging statements.

I'm always surprised to discover that some of my most successful clients wrestle with an inner voice that's very scathing. One example is my client Megan.

Megan started her online session with name-calling—of herself.

"I'm sorry I'm late, Christine. I'm such a jerk!"

My eyes opened wide as I reacted to that pronouncement.

"Megan, you're not a jerk for being five minutes late!" I said.

She waved her hand to dismiss my comment as either inaccurate or irrelevant and continued.

"I just hate when people in this industry act like their time is so much more important than everyone else's, you know? And here I am doing that very thing I hate!"

Megan is an executive at one of the major movie studios in Los Angeles. She's well-liked and very respected and has shepherded many successful movies into blockbuster hits. But none of her success has slowed down the rampant bullying that her own inner critic hurls at her on a regular basis.

Megan booked her session because she wanted help with her chronic headaches and low energy. Typically, I'd ask the client for details about her symptoms, but Megan's spirit nudged me to approach the topic from a different angle. So I asked, "Megan, can you tell me your top four things you like about yourself?"

Megan looked surprised and then flummoxed. "Shit, I don't know...I guess my hair's okay. And I do really try to listen to my staff. Why are you asking me this?"

I smiled. "Because your spirit says that if I'd asked you for your top four faults you could have rattled off many more than that, and quickly."

"Ha! That's true!" she said with a laugh.

"But the fact that you struggled to give me even two items that you think are admirable about yourself is worth noticing. Because I think that your inner 'scorekeeping' is grossly unbalanced."

Megan cocked her head. "My scorekeeping?"

"Yes. Your ego-mind seems to have a long list ready of all the things that are wrong with you, but it's not kept track of your admirable qualities—your assets. And so your view of yourself is very skewed."

Megan chewed on her bottom lip as she thought about that. "Yeah, you're probably right. But listen—I'm in a really tough industry, and I'm a woman! It took me years to get the good old boys to listen to me, and if I made a mistake, they were always ready to dismiss me again."

"I hear you, and I know that your industry is really challenging, especially for a woman. But you've been extremely successful for over a decade, and yet you're still riding yourself mercilessly."

"Hmmm," Megan murmured as she leaned back into her plush turquoise sofa. "I guess you're right. But in my head I just keep telling myself that if I take my foot off the gas, even for a moment, I'll fall behind somehow. And there are a thousand other people waiting to take my place."

"I believe that," I said sincerely. "The entertainment industry is known for being cutthroat. But I also believe that your inner critic uses that reason to justify constantly berating you, which isn't actually helping you. I refer to it as 'whipping the racehorse that's already running.'"

Megan made an exasperated noise. "Well, that sounds like me. And frankly, I'm exhausted! And I mean All. The. Time."

Megan's spirit asked, "When do you feel joy?"

"Well, I'm glad when one of our movies does well. Or when I hire someone who turns out to be really great at their job."

Her spirit shook her head in disagreement. "That's when you exhale. That's relief, which isn't the same as feeling joy, playfulness, or fun."

Megan chuckled with a grimace. "Well, she's got me there. I guess 'not feeling like a failure' is the closest I get to being happy most days. Geez! That sounds pathetic!"

"I'd rather you have empathy for yourself rather than judgment, but let's come back to that. Your spirit is asking you to connect with her now. I can feel that she wants to show you something—probably a significant memory."

We both closed our eyes and sat quietly while Megan gathered her energy and raised it above her head. I watched as her spirit sent information to Megan (it appears to me like a ray of light entering the person's head) and Megan's eyes flew open as she received the message.

"Oh! My spirit just showed me a scene from my childhood! My mom would walk through the living room when my brother and I were playing with our toys and say, 'It must be nice to have nothing to do all day except sit around and play!' Then I'd feel guilty and clean my room or something that looked like I was working as hard as she was."

I smiled and said, "Your spirit is nodding her head, letting me know that you received and understood her message accurately. That memory reveals some of the origins of your intense work ethic, and it's sad that your mother felt that play had no value, even for children."

Megan sighed. "Yeah, both my parents were hard workers, and my mom never seemed satisfied with anybody's efforts. Like we could always be doing more."

I nodded as I was listening to Megan and then channeled her spirit's response. "Your mother's disapproval of any activity that wasn't considered 'work' taught you to fear being seen as a slouch."

"That's so true! My mom used to use that word—I haven't heard it in years."

"Maybe not, but you've been running away from the label for a long time," her spirit said gently. Megan's defeated exhale confirmed her spirit's remark.

In a quiet, small voice Megan asked, "Is this why I'm exhausted all the time?"

"Yes," her spirit confirmed. "You've trained yourself to ignore your body and mind when it feels tired and needs to rest or play in order to recharge. Your fears about being seen as lazy lead you to overcompensate and never feel comfortable relaxing. When your body gave you feedback that it was tired mentally and physically, your inner critic belittled that feedback in order to pressure you to keep working. When you don't listen to your body's feedback, it begins speaking in bigger symptoms."

"That would be the headaches, right?" Megan asked.

"Absolutely," I confirmed. "When we get chronic headaches, they're frequently stemming from feeling a lack of power in some area of our life. In this case, you were tired but your inner critic wouldn't let you take enough of a break to really recuperate. Then your work becomes a sort of prison, and you lose your enthusiasm for getting out of bed each day."

"Yes! Oh my God, that's exactly how I've been feeling! And then beating myself about it. I'll be in the shower saying, 'You fool! Don't you know how many people would absolutely kill to have your job? And you don't even appreciate it!' "

I smiled with a pained look on my face. "I'm guessing that such comments from your inner critic didn't make you go to work happily, but they did shame you into showing up every day."

"You got that right," Megan said, nodding. "No wonder I feel exhausted all the time—every day is just another day on the hamster wheel that I never let myself off of."

"That's a powerful realization," I said. "Too often we move the finish line or bar up so high that we'll never get over it and see ourselves as winning or even being done. And when the goals are impossibly out of reach, internally we give up mentally and emotionally. But since we can't hide under the covers all day, we use fear and shame to push ourselves to get back on the hamster wheel again."

"Man, that really describes my last three months!" Megan said. "How do I change this? Take a two-month vacation on a tropical island?"

I grinned. "That sounds lovely, but you can get rejuvenated without the lengthy time away. The first step is to question your inner critic's assessments. For instance, today is Friday. If you don't take any work home this weekend and you commit to only doing things that would nurture you, how does that feel?"

Megan grimaced. "My first thought? It feels bad. Like, uncomfortable. I know that some of my people will be working this weekend, so I'll feel guilty if I'm at home just lying by the pool."

I tried a different approach. "Why don't you see if your spirit can give you some coaching on this topic?"

It took Megan several tries to reconnect with her spirit and be open enough to hear the advice being offered. When she did hear her spirit's remark, Megan barked out a short laugh. I raised my eyebrows with curiosity.

Megan grinned. "My spirit asked me, 'Is your goal to out-work every single person at your studio?'"

"Interesting question," I responded. "What's your answer?"

"Well, no . . ." she said sheepishly.

"Then the fact that others are working should not be the sole determinant of your work schedule. That compulsion to work is stemming from your history of trying to avoid your mother's shaming comments when she was working and you weren't."

"Ugh! That lands—my mom's voice is definitely in my head," Megan said with resignation. Then she continued channeling her spirit's counsel.

"My spirit says that the goal is for me to be tuned in to both my own needs and the requirements of my job. She reminded me that I have a talent for recognizing great storytelling and for creatively solving problems that come up in production. But my creativity and enthusiasm require rest and rejuvenation to flow well."

I nodded my agreement. "Yes! So with this understanding, please see your time off work as an investment in yourself. You are being wise to rest, not lazy."

"Wow, that's a different way to look at things!" Megan beamed.

I nodded. "Once we question our inner critic's accusations and horrible verdicts, we can take a more compassionate—and accurate—approach to guiding ourselves."

Megan grinned. "My energy already feels better! Like I'm giving myself permission to honor how I feel rather than just do everything so I don't feel guilty or like I'm a screw-up."

Smiling at Megan, I agreed. "Yes, it's so important to notice when all of our motivation stems from trying to avoid shame and inner criticism."

"Now I wonder what other bullshit I've been using on myself to whip the racehorse that's already running!"

I paused, then offered, "Why don't you promise yourself that you'll try to notice when you self-criticize and search for a better way to motivate or correct yourself?"

Megan agreed, and when we had our next session a month later, she showed up looking refreshed and her energy field was once again bright and vibrant. She reported that she'd begun noticing when her inner critic became the "nasty cop," and she would utilize her spirit's suggestions to rewrite her inner critic's dialogue as if it belonged to a character in a movie. Her enthusiasm for her work had returned, and her headaches had disappeared.

We all benefit from paying attention to our inner critic and softening the phrases that we use to motivate and "correct" ourselves. If you struggle with speaking kindly to yourself, think about what you'd tell a good friend or younger sibling who came to you with a similar problem. Remember that harsh judgments don't prevent you from making any mistakes in the future; they simply lower your self-confidence. Offering ourselves the kindness and love that we needed when we were young often gives us the permission we need to explore our own happiness and future possibilities.

For the past three chapters, the focus has been on your

relationship with yourself—how you see yourself, forgive yourself, and talk to yourself. Our next topic is a big one—our romantic relationships. Because romantic love can involve the most meaningful energy exchanges that we do each day, imbalances here can feel devastating. The next three chapters will examine the most common issues I see in romantic relationships.

CHAPTER 14

ROMANTIC RELATIONSHIP CHALLENGES

Transactional Love

Do you ever find yourself keeping score to make sure that your partner isn't getting more than you are from the relationship? How often have you said, "He owes me for this!" or "Now I've earned that weekend away" or "Uh-oh, I'm in trouble—that's going to cost me"? These can be indications that you and your beloved are in a relationship that has become transactional.

In an overly transactional relationship, you each keep tabs on what you give and receive, and the union can begin to feel more like a business deal than a romantic connection. You may believe that the focus of the relationship is on "fairness" or "equality," but it's usually more about avoiding feelings of scarcity or not getting what you feel you're owed. If you feel that you've put in more than you've gotten back in the relationship, your response might be righteous indignation.

It's important to distinguish between scorekeeping in relationships and a healthy practice of observing your own energy levels. Many of us developed the habit of "over-giving" in all of our relationships. This tendency to give without noticing when we're depleted can lead us to exhaustion, frequent illnesses, and even depression. If you've noticed this imbalance in any of your relationships, I encourage you to pay attention to how much energy you typically invest and see if it feels like the other person invests similar amounts of energy. But in the overly transactional relationships I'm describing here, the issue is not that you consistently deplete yourself. The problem is that the focus for each person is on the benefits and gains that feel "owed" to them in the relationship.

In a relationship that's become overly transactional, there may be a list (spoken or unspoken) of expected duties for each person, with the implication that if you don't perform all of your tasks, then you're breaking an agreement. Resentments arise easily as the scorekeeping is usually not very accurate; each person tends to discount what their partner does and inflate what they've contributed. This pattern leads to both people feeling unappreciated for the efforts they've made and complaining about the unfairness of the situation.

In a romantic relationship that relies heavily on a transactional model, both people remain very focused on what they stand to gain from being in the partnership, such as material wealth, status, affection, connection, or sex. Each person is keeping tabs on how well they're achieving all of the goals they've set for the relationship, and they view the union as an investment of their time and effort. Meaning they expect a return. The inherent competitiveness ("If only one of us can come out ahead, then I hope it's me") tends to block intimacy, as there is naturally a hesitancy to be vulnerable with a potential competitor because that vulnerability could be exploited later as a weakness.

Relationships that begin as romantic unions but deteriorate into transactional arrangements tend to use positive and negative systems of reinforcement. These penalties and rewards can look like earning a night out with friends, being in the "doghouse" and having to do extra chores, and being "owed" flowers, sex, or other gifts. Children raised in such households where transactional behavior was the norm generally adopt this same approach toward relationships, evaluating potential friendships based on how much the other person can help them advance in popularity, academics, career, etc. Such children frequently don't generally value loyalty, love, or teamwork, as they haven't witnessed the benefits of it within their family.

The focus on what you're "earning" from the relationship tends to block feeling empathy for your partner, so each person is likely to feel like they're not truly seen and heard. The lack of empathy and vulnerability offered by each partner can lead to each person feeling justified in developing strong emotional bonds with others, adding to the lack of connectedness. Eventually there is little emotional safety in the relationship, which doesn't lead to great outcomes.

In a romantic relationship that is *not* overly transactional, each person wants to step forward and give to their partner because the happiness of your loved one is contagious. When you invest in things that make your partner joyful and fulfilled, you get the rewarding experience of giving without keeping track of what you receive back. The relationship is treated more like a joint bank account with the awareness that both people benefit from the accruing happiness that is created and nurtured. There's an optimistic willingness to put in effort—toward chores and even awkward conversations—because of the core belief that the result will be a flourishing relationship that nurtures everyone. As each person holds the intent to be a steady, reliable partner, there is a gratitude-rich awareness of how your life is enhanced by the relationship.

Despite starting off as a beautiful romantic relationship, many partnerships suffer from this lack of attention and eventually deteriorate into little more than conversations about schedules, kids, and frustrations with work. These partnerships can devolve into relationships that are overly transactional without us ever intending that result.

How do you know if your romantic relationship has become too transaction-based? Consider these questions:

- How often do you find yourself feeling cheated or taken advantage of by your partner?
- How often do you and your partner talk about what's owed or what's fair?
- Do you and your partner rely on rewards and punishments to coerce desired behavior from each other?
- Do you feel competitive toward your partner?
- Does your relationship feel like a job or a contract?

This isn't a quiz in a magazine, so there's no perfect score. These questions can help you reflect on the state of your partnership and decide how you'd like to move forward. If you'd like to make your relationship less transactional and more romantic, here are some wonderful suggestions that my clients' spirits have offered in sessions:

1. Prepare to talk to your partner by getting yourself in a soft space emotionally. This may mean watching videos of babies or puppies or listening to your

favorite music—it doesn't have to be a practice based on romance. Then gently let your partner know that you've decided to love them better. You're going to put forth an effort to flow love over them without a tabulation of whether or not it's appropriate, earned, etc. You've simply decided to turn up the dial on the love that is flowing between you. Be careful not to focus on how you hope your partner responds. This is meant to be a declaration and then a set of actions taken so that you can experience the joy of being in a different kind of relationship.

2. Trade "chore lists" for two weeks. Each day mention to your partner something that you hadn't realized/appreciated about the chores that they do. (For instance: "I never thought about how on Mondays you have to walk down our very steep driveway to put the trash cans out and bring them back in, even when it's pouring rain!") These comments of appreciation can begin replacing the scorekeeping with genuine appreciation.

3. Ask your partner to share a big dream or goal with you so that you can brainstorm together about how to bring that goal to fruition. Adopt the goal as your own, focusing on the roles that your partner feels comfortable with you taking on. (Be sure to "stay in your lane" so that the accomplishment still feels like it belongs to your partner.)

4. Ask your partner if they're willing to have a "Relationship Appreciation Month." Each day you can sit together and list several reasons why you're blessed to be in this relationship. There are no wrong answers; the goal is to pivot the focus of your daily interactions.

When you sit in meditation, you can ask your spirit for feedback on your current romantic relationship, as well as the relationship(s) that your parents modeled for you. Here are some questions you may want to ask your spirit:

1. When I was growing up, did my parents relate to each other in more of a transactional way or more of a romantic way?
2. Did my parents leave me with the impression that investing in a romantic relationship was a good idea?
3. Do I focus too heavily on what I'm receiving from my current romantic partner?
4. What are some specific ways that I can shift away from a transactional relationship?
5. What are some projects that my partner and I could work on together so that we can remember the pleasures of teamwork?

You may have once had a beautiful romantic relationship. But the mundane has a way of killing that romance, especially with our busy lives and daily to-do lists. One day, you may look up and find that your relationship has transformed into a very different partnership than the one you originally created. That's what happened to my clients Lance and Heather.

Lance and Heather were both single parents, and they met while dropping their young daughters off at gymnastics camp. They dated for a year and have been happily married now for over a decade. Lance is a CFO for a shipping company, and Heather provides consulting services for people seeking care for elderly parents. They arrived at my door looking stiff and irritated, and they sat on opposite ends of my sofa, leaning away from each other.

I smiled and asked what they wanted to focus on. They both said "better communication" simultaneously. I've learned that when couples ask for a session to work on communication, they usually mean that they have each stopped listening to the other but are frustrated about not being heard themselves.

So my next question was: "Can each of you give me a one-sentence summary of what you feel the biggest problem is between you?"

Heather spoke first. "I feel like no matter how much I do it's never enough."

Lance said, "No, I think the problem is that we can't talk to each other anymore. If I say anything that isn't a compliment, you get defensive."

Since their statements and body language indicated that they were in a fairly locked-down position, I asked if I could pose the same question to their spirits. They both nodded.

When I connected to their spirits, Heather's came forward first and spoke. "I believe that Heather is venturing away from the unspoken agreement that they had when they got married and blended families."

I opened my eyes, and both of them looked perplexed, so I continued channeling to get more details.

Heather's spirit said, "When they originally moved in together, Lance was traveling a lot for work, and Heather worked a job that was flexible in how many hours she spent in the office versus at home. Heather arranged her schedule so that she went into the office early and was then available to pick up all the kids after school. Now that the last two children are in high school and driving, Heather has not been home every afternoon."

This time when I opened my eyes, both of them were nodding. Heather turned to Lance and asked, "Do you think that I should be home every afternoon even if the kids are out with friends or doing after-school activities?"

"No! I'm not saying that you should always be home even when the kids don't need help. I'm just frustrated when . . . things fall through the cracks."

"Like what things?" Heather said icily.

Lance hesitated. "It's annoying when I get home and we have no food in the fridge and nothing going for dinner. Then I end up going back out to get groceries instead of just stopping on the way home, which would've been simpler."

Heather bristled. "So it's only my responsibility to plan all the meals and go grocery shopping?"

"No, but . . . it's how we always did it before," Lance said sheepishly.

At this point, Lance's spirit jumped in. "I agree that an unspoken agreement had existed between them. Because it was never discussed, as circumstances changed, a new agreement wasn't discussed either. And now there are resentments."

Heather nodded emphatically. "Yeah, because apparently all the household duties were assigned to me. And so now that I'm not doing all of them, Lance is resenting me. Is this because you make more money than I do, so you feel that I should do all the housework to make things even?"

"That's not true—any of it!" Lance replied. "We've always divided the household chores together and worked great as a team. You're right—picking up the kids and figuring out dinner always fell on you because you were home in the afternoons and I couldn't be. But I NEVER thought that you OWED me those household chores because my salary is higher!"

"Really?" Heather said quietly. "I guess I just always assumed you did. Or I felt guilty about the different salaries and thought I should do more to make up the difference."

Lance reached over and grabbed Heather's hand. "Oh, honey! I'm so sorry that you've been carrying that angst around for all these years!"

Heather smiled lovingly at her husband and then looked over at me. "I think when the kids didn't need me after school, I started spending more time at the office, and I got a promotion last month because of the improvements I've made there. Like a dummy I thought that Lance resented my promotion because it meant that I might not be home doing my 'wifely duties.'"

Heather's spirit chimed in. "When Heather believed that Lance resented her promotion, Heather began acting in a passive-aggressive way. She sort of 'went on strike'—for a job that she was never officially given."

Then Lance's spirit spoke. "Lance could feel the resentment coming from Heather but wasn't sure why Heather seemed so hostile about the topic of cooking and grocery shopping."

Lance exhaled and sank back into the sofa. "Wow, it's so good to realize how we got here! For the last few months I haven't known what to do!"

Heather looked guilty. "I'm sorry! I'm hearing what our spirits are saying, and I realize how much my reactions were based on inaccurate assumptions that I was making."

Lance grinned. "Believe me, I was making a few assumptions of my own. I was worried that you wanted me to stop traveling for work so that I could be home cooking and running the household in the evenings. Like now it was my turn to do that role. And I didn't know how to respond to that idea—that I'd made up!"

Heather rubbed Lance's arm. "Honey, I'm fine to do the cooking—I enjoy it, actually. But I think that since half the time the kids aren't even home for dinner now, we need to have a family meeting each week and figure out everyone's schedule."

Lance jumped in. "Sure! And then you and I can make a grocery list, and I'm happy to pick stuff up on the way home when I'm in town."

Heather smiled. "And I'm happy to do the cooking."

Lance grinned. "Or if the kids aren't going to be home till later let's start going out to dinner more. You've taken on a heavier load at work, and I think we both could use some time to just sit and catch up together."

Heather's spirit offered sage advice: "The way to prevent the relationship from feeling overly transactional is to have a conversation about what you each expect from the other person. It's actually a pretty short list for each of you. In general, you both enjoy pitching in and taking care of each other and the children."

Lance grinned. "Well, I'm happy to go first. Honey, my expectations for you are that you communicate with me about how you think we should run the household. You're more organized than me, so I love it when you throw out ideas of how we should set things up. I'm happy to get food, make food, and pick up kids from events. I just need to have conversations about it because I usually don't think about meals until I walk in the door hungry at the end of the day."

Heather looked lovingly at him. "My expectations for you are that you talk to me too. Like telling me when you're feeling overwhelmed—by work or the kids or anything. There aren't specific jobs that I think belong exclusively to you—except taking out the trash 'cause you know the raccoon that lives out there terrifies me. But when you're stressed and don't communicate why, the kids and I tend to avoid you 'cause it can feel like you're looking for a reason to get angry."

Lance grimaced. "That's fair—I do tend to do that. Okay, I'll let you know when I'm having a draining day at work. And I'll try not to come home looking for something to be resentful about."

Both of them acknowledged how their hesitancy to ask for what they wanted in the relationship had led to taking on roles "by default." And as circumstances changed, there wasn't an easy way to bring up the shifts needed in their roles and responsibilities at home. By remembering that their first priority was the happiness of themselves and the person they loved, they could easily converse about the best ways to divvy up the household chores.

When most of us hear the term "transactional relationship," we may imagine the stereotypical older rich man dating a beautiful young woman. The gains for each seem clear, as do the expectations. But in reality, most relationships are not this black and white, and over time even a healthy relationship can see the romance dwindle and the scorekeeping increase. My spirit's advice is to pay attention to how it feels to be in the relationship.

Do you like how you show up for your partner? Do you enjoy this version of yourself?

The next chapter also describes a relationship dynamic that can occur over time because most of us aren't watching for the warning signs. If you've ever looked at your partner and thought, "Am I the romantic partner or the parent figure in this relationship right now?," then this next chapter is for you.

CHAPTER 15

ROMANTIC RELATIONSHIP CHALLENGES

The Unintended Manager

Have you ever said, "I'm really hoping to date someone who's my manager at work"? Me neither. This unequal kind of power dynamic can lead to feelings of inequality. But one of the most common challenges I see in long-term relationships is a dynamic in which one person unintentionally becomes the manager, leaving their partner feeling undervalued and rather powerless.

Here's an example.

As my clients sat down on the fawn-colored suede sofa in my treatment room, I noticed that Martina's energy felt taut and righteous and Liam's energy looked sad and deflated. I'd had private sessions with each of them and knew that they were empowered, successful, and joyful people. But their relationship dynamic together looked pretty miserable at the moment. When I asked them each for a sentence about what they'd like to focus on in the session, Liam spoke first.

"I'd like to stop feeling like the kid that's always being scolded!"

Martina immediately sat up ramrod straight and retorted,

"Well, I'd like to stop feeling like I'm the only one who cares about this family!"

I looked at Martina. "What's the topic that you're the only one caring about?"

Martina sighed. "Well, I want to say 'everything,' but I know that when I use words like 'always' and 'never' I'm just being dramatic."

I smiled gently. "I'm not going to label you as dramatic. But I do like to avoid those kinds of absolute words because they can make everyone in the dynamic feel stuck, like things are locked down and unchangeable."

Martina nodded. "Okay, fine. So I'll just say that it feels like I'm the only one that worries if things are being taken care of—with the kids, with our meals, with our health, and grocery shopping."

"I care about that stuff, but not to the same degree that you do," Liam countered. Then he turned to me and said, "My wife got an MBA, but you'd think she got a medical degree the way she supervises my food intake and my vitamin regime."

Martina first looked hurt, then angry as she said sharply, "Well, let's get to the real reason why I booked us this appointment! I found Liam in the garage sneaking a can of soda and eating a bag of BBQ potato chips!"

Liam scooted forward on the sofa as he said, "Well, maybe I wouldn't have to hide in the garage to eat snacks if you didn't run our house like a dictator running a mandatory health clinic!"

I saw Martina's face scowl as she took a big breath to retort, so I held up my hand to referee in what was obviously an ongoing conflict between them. "Martina, may I ask your spirit and Liam's spirit to give us input?"

She sank heavily back into the sofa, her long dark hair falling forward as she exhaled. "Sure, go ahead."

Martina's spirit came forward and spoke first: "Martina's mother had a heart attack six years ago and it scared her. Since then, she's been on a quest to achieve the best health that she can for herself and her family."

I opened my eyes to see Martina nodding in agreement. "Yeah, that's true. My mom's heart attack was a wake-up call for sure. All of the women in my family are overweight; we jokingly say that our Latin bloodline dominates everything, and that's why we all look exactly like my mom. But after her heart attack, I started wondering what else I was inheriting from her. So I threw away all the junk food in the house and focused on really healthy foods. I jumped into researching the best vitamins, and I have all of us taking supplements so that we're fully armed against germs and any health problems."

Martina's spirit continued. "Those steps are all positive, but there's so much fear motivating your actions that it makes you rigid in your approach. You're not able to hear Liam when he says that he wants to eat some foods that make you uncomfortable."

"But if he buys junk food, then that's all the kids will want to eat!" Martina wailed. "Once that crap is back in the house, I'll lose this battle for sure!"

Martina's spirit commented, "Notice your wording. You've referred to arming yourself and your family and losing the battle. Such violent word choices can help you see that you feel threatened—by a possible heart attack or other health issues that could take you from your family."

Martina began to cry silently as she nodded. "God, I AM scared. We almost lost my mom—when she was in the hospital we didn't know if she was going to live. What if...what if I die, and my kids have to grow up without a mother?"

Liam reached over and squeezed his wife's hand. "Honey, you may look like your mother, but you've been working out for years and eating healthy. You've lost lots of weight, and your doctor said that you passed your physical exam with flying colors!"

At this point, Liam's spirit joined the conversation: "Liam had always enjoyed the partnership he had with Martina because they listened to each other and made decisions together. But when Martina's fear intensified, she grabbed the reins of control and decided—subconsciously—that the situation was too life-threatening for any debate or discussion. Because she'd done the research and had the most information, she appointed herself the manager of everyone's health care, including the foods that each person ate."

Martina put her head in her hands. "Oh...that IS what happened! Liam, I'm sorry, but I guess when my fear combined with my controlling tendencies, a dictator emerged!"

Liam chuckled. "Honey, I love your 'take-charge' attitude most of the time. But if I tried to talk to you about the foods that the kids and I missed having, you'd accuse me of not supporting your health or not caring about the kids. There was no opening for us to actually have a discussion, so I just stopped trying."

Liam's spirit continued. "When one partner begins to manage the other's behavior, a type of parental dynamic occurs. This parent-child dynamic usually leads to resentment on both sides, as well as a dampening of sexual attraction for each other. In an attempt to regain a feeling of adult empowerment, the partner in the child role can act out, much like a rebellious teenager."

"Like sneaking food and sodas in the garage," Liam said with an embarrassed look on his face. He ran his hands through his short red hair and asked, "Okay, so how do we break this parent-child dynamic?"

Martina's spirit offered, "The first recommended step is for Martina to acknowledge that there is no imminent threat—to her or her family members."

"Done!" Martina said decisively.

Her spirit continued, "The next recommended step is to have Liam become more of an equal partner on the topics of food, supplements, and health care. If he feels that he needs to be more knowledgeable on these topics, he should do his own research rather than read the material that his wife has collected. Then he can have a conversation with Martina about how they want to move forward in their household in a way that focuses on healthy living without decisions being made primarily out of fear."

Liam thought for a moment. "Ya know, since the kids were born I've let Martina become the expert on so many things. She likes reading more than I do, so I just got lazy and let her handle the research on everything. I think I'm also to blame for being in the 'child' role."

Martina touched her husband's cheek lovingly. "Thank you for saying that, mi amor. I know that I sometimes manage you and the kids like I manage the huge distribution center at work, and that's not a good approach for any of us."

Martina's spirit spoke up. "While you both do household chores, Martina holds the responsibility for all the scheduling and assigning of duties. When one person has to assume this type of 'managerial' energy, it can become a heavy burden energetically and can lead to feelings of resentment."

Liam's spirit chimed in. "The person who becomes the de facto manager and delegates responsibilities to their spouse can often feel superior to the other partner. Once there are feelings of superiority, it can lead to a dismissive attitude. The challenge is to delegate without diminishing the other person."

Martina cringed. "I know that I'm guilty of bossing Liam around like I do the kids, directing everyone to put their clothes away and stuff. I just get in that mode of getting things done quickly, and I don't pay attention to how I'm coming across."

Martina's spirit added, "Remember that equal division of labor doesn't mean that there's equal division of responsibility. And the responsibility for the scheduling and managing of the family can be as draining as the labor involved in running a household. The current resentments between you stem primarily from Martina's frustrations about feeling solely responsible for so many decisions regarding the running of your household."

Liam blushed. "Her spirit is right. I have let her take over the running of things. I think I justified it by telling myself that she has stronger opinions about the laundry and the brands we buy, but really, I was ducking out of the responsibilities. Damn! I'm sorry, honey. I've been resenting you for a situation that I encouraged!"

Liam and Martina received more insight from their spirits about how their relationship had veered off course and how to steer things back to a connection that felt mutually respectful, and we were all delighted when their resentments vanished.

This dynamic of the unintended manager can show up in relationships whenever one person is deemed the expert in a particular topic such as finances, childcare, or scheduling. Couples can agree to an equitable separation of duties based on experience and preferences ("I like cooking, and he's happy to take care of the yard"). But what begins as a healthy division of chores can become a manager/employee dynamic when the "expert" dismisses the partner's questions or attempts to be involved.

Frequently, the partner who spends the most time with the children becomes the expert in all things kid related, and the person who handles the paying of bills and managing the money can become the authority on all money matters. The "expert" may feel overworked and underappreciated for their contributions while not realizing that they are blocking their partner from participating.

The partner who's become an expert in a crucial area like money, child-rearing, or health care may then start assuming that they're also more knowledgeable about other topics and begin criticizing their partner's efforts in a multitude of topics. The frequently criticized partner may develop a type of "learned incompetence" wherein it feels safer to retreat into a passive approach and wait to be told what to do in order to avoid criticism.

It's natural for the partner on the employee side of the dynamic to resent the lack of power and respect that accompanies that position. The desire to feel more empowered can lead to attempts at reestablishing their sense of autonomy. This can look like sneaking a cigarette, drink, or "forbidden foods"; going out with friends and avoiding texts from home; or developing other secretive behaviors in an attempt to feel independent.

How do you know if your romantic relationship has devolved into some version of a manager/employee dynamic? Consider these questions:

- How often do you feel like you're being "directed" by your partner, like he/she is your manager?
- How often do you give directions, and when you do, are you speaking as if you're talking with an equal partner?
- Do you resent your partner's lack of help and/or appreciation of what you do for your household?
- Do you feel "shut out" of certain topics, uncomfortable bringing them up for discussion for fear of the censure or dismissive responses you'll receive?

If you find yourself cringing at some of your answers to the above questions, then let's get your spirit's help in addressing this joy-sucking dynamic in your romantic relationship. Here are questions that you may want to ask your spirit:

1. What are the topics and activities within our relationship that I have appointed myself the expert on?
2. What are the topics that I have deferred to my partner on, assuming that they know more than I do and I should "butt out"?
3. How can we achieve more appreciation for the work that we each do to contribute to the overall success of our relationship?
4. What are the areas of excellence in my partner that I'm overlooking?
5. Which areas of my own competence am I not being recognized for?
6. How can we achieve more balance in our view of each other's skills?

Once your spirit helps you gain more clarity on this topic, you can approach your partner and say that you want to do a better job of appreciating what they contribute to the relationship. Suggest making a list of the areas of excellence and knowledge that you each have, including areas that you both are skillful in. Ask your partner if he/she feels diminished or dismissed by you trying to participate in an area that you are the expert in.

Using the list that you've both created as a starting point, you can decide how the household duties can be distributed in a way that makes each of you feel appreciated. Just having this type of conversation can go a long way toward redistributing power that has slid into your lap or your partner's lap over time. Once your awareness has been heightened about your partner's contributions and areas of expertise, you can each make more of an effort to complement the work that you each do to contribute to the health and prosperity of your household.

If you were eating a sandwich and a stranger grabbed it right out of your hand and took a bite, I hope that you'd stand up for yourself and set a boundary about what was appropriate at that moment. But it's often a different story with our romantic relationships when our partner snatches away our power and we never say a word. The next chapter is about how your partner might be "grabbing your emotional sandwich" and what you can do about it.

CHAPTER 16

ROMANTIC RELATIONSHIP CHALLENGES

Tiptoeing Around an Emotional Tyrant

How often do you find yourself walking on eggshells around your romantic partner? We all have topics that are tender for us, and we all hope for a partner who treads delicately when discussing our personal sore spots. But this chapter is about romantic partners who have a long list of subjects that can all lead to BIG reactions. Or perhaps there's no set list of subjects to avoid; instead, the reactions seem to occur at random. Such BIG reactions might look like one of these behaviors:

- Explosive yelling
- Hysterical crying
- Throwing things
- Storming off and staying gone for a while
- Silent treatment
- Shaming, critical lectures

With this particular type of partner, the list of topics that are emotional minefields may seem to expand each year so that more and more topics become "off-limits." Eventually you may realize that you're spending a lot of time anxiously trying to anticipate and manage your partner's reactions. When you start to second-guess yourself regularly, you might be living with an emotional tyrant and giving too much of your energy away.

Think of your partner's BIG reactions as a form of "power grabbing," an attempt to coerce you into conforming to their preferences. The bigger their emotional upset, the more likely you are to avoid repeating the "offense." The person who has the strong reaction is seeking to be in control, believing that if they get their way, they'll feel safer and happier. In your desire to keep the peace and avoid the big upset, you may frequently give in and comply with their desires. But after many of these BIG reactions, your partner's behavior begins to assert a type of emotional dominance, oppressively controlling the way that you both feel.

The result is that the household revolves around the person who is the least emotionally healthy. Allowances are continually made for the emotional tyrant's behavior because the first time the upset around a particular topic occurred, your partner gave a justification that felt reasonable to you. Your agreement to accept/tolerate such reactions has given your partner carte blanche to ignore any requests to modify their behavior.

The emotional tyrant in your life is undoubtedly aware of the typical norms of polite behavior, but they have given themselves special permission to step over those boundaries. They believe that they are special or unique and therefore an exemption should be made for their bad behavior. These individuals may believe that they're very important, very delicate, or just very particular. The result is that this person dominates the dynamic in the household. Here are some justifications that clients' spouses have used to rationalize their BIG reactions:

- "I have very high standards."
- "I have significant health issues."
- "I have unhealed trauma."
- "I have a very important job."
- "I'm more intelligent than most people."
- "I'm supersensitive." (This is a frequent description of someone who's just easily offended.)
- "I can't help it if my emotions are all over the place; I just feel deeply." (Therefore, you should indulge my emotional instability.)
- "I can't help it if you (or others) are too sensitive." (Typically said to give oneself permission to be rude and insensitive.)

You may have tried to set boundaries around your partner's outbursts, but if the behavior continues, then it's safe to say that your boundaries were not respected. Living in such a relationship can be exhausting and disheartening, and over time the continual violation of your requested boundaries can lower your self-esteem. So if these descriptions resonate with you, let's talk about how to transform the feeling of living with an emotional dictator.

Before we go further, I want to stress that if you feel in physical danger, please do not attempt to transform your romantic relationship! Any lack of physical safety should be taken very seriously, and if your partner has harmed you or threatened to harm you, then please consider leaving the relationship. Enlist the aid of friends, family, and agencies that can help you exit a relationship that feels unsafe. Even if you love your partner, sometimes the best way for everyone to be safe is for you to put some physical distance between the two of you.

Assuming that the boundary violations between you and your partner do not have you fearing for your safety, I recommend that you write down the behavior that you find unacceptable. Be specific, as it's difficult to transform something as vague as "he's always upset" or "she's just too high maintenance."

Once you've listed the BIG reactions that you no longer want to live with, write down the worst-case scenario for each one. Beyond the yelling, crying, or lecturing, what could happen after that? Are you afraid that your partner will leave you? Are you afraid that they'll stop loving you? Criticize you for hours? Not speak to you for days? It's important to acknowledge the underlying fear that inhibits you from taking an effective stand against your partner's behavior.

Once you have some ideas of your worst-case scenario, you can begin to make peace with it. I'm not suggesting that this unwanted outcome will happen; I'm asserting that your fear of it has kept you locked in a subservient position in your relationship. Until you make peace with this dreaded result, you will be hesitant to firmly insist on permanent behavior changes. Making peace with the result you fear the most will help you reclaim your power in your relationship.

For example, if your partner gets angry and gives you the silent treatment when you make plans with friends, imagine the worst-case scenario. Is it that he never talks to you again? Or that he leaves the relationship? Or that he makes you feel lonely and rejected for days?

Let's assume that your worst-case scenario is that he will

pack up and leave you. You might think, "Well, seeing my friends isn't worth potentially losing my relationship, so I'll cancel on my friends and stay home." But instead of weighing visiting your friends against potentially losing your relationship, I encourage you to think of it as keeping your relationship but only if you're willing to abandon parts of yourself. This has you living as a very limited version of yourself, with much of your power residing in the back pocket of your partner. In such a case, is he loving you, or is he loving his projected ideas of a good partner (that he's bullied you into being)?

I want you to recognize the power play happening when your partner deploys the silent treatment. It's very disempowering when only your partner can end your discomfort and they actively choose not to. Your partner is counting on your discomfort being greater than his inconvenience of not speaking. Previously, in an effort to feel like you had some power in the dynamic, you may have changed your actions to appease him so that he didn't get angry and shut down. But each time, you've given up more than just spending time with your friends; you've reinforced his opinion that his ideas about your choices are more valid than your own judgment. Are you willing to live according to his script of "the ideal partner"? I encourage you *not* to continually "audition" for a role that you don't really want.

It's staggering how easily we can find ourselves feeling like a trained dolphin, doing backflips for a small morsel of praise. When you can make peace with your partner leaving—your worst-case scenario—you will reclaim some of your power and begin to have more trust in your decision-making.

Once you've decided that you're willing to risk losing the relationship rather than losing yourself, you're ready to set and enforce healthy boundaries. In a calm moment, explain to your partner that you've decided that the behavior of the silent treatment (or other unacceptable behaviors) no longer works for you as part of a healthy relationship. You can then ask him what other responses he can use to express his frustration, responses that can lead to a respectful conversation. The two of you can come up with a list of acceptable responses that each of you can offer when you're upset, disappointed, or angry.

The next step is to let him know how you'll respond if he reverts back to the silent treatment when he's unhappy with you. Because you're now clear that his behavior blocks you both from having a healthy, respect-filled relationship, your energetic boundary will feel more solid. Your response to any further incidents of silent punishment could be going to stay with a friend or taking a brief, impromptu vacation. The key is to emphasize that you won't be anxiously avoiding his reaction/punishment anymore. If you're clear in your own mind that you will no longer live in a relationship that feels emotionally prickly and fragile, then your energy will convey to him that you're serious and that this boundary is a requirement to staying in a relationship with you. It's important to commit to yourself that you'll hold firm on the "promises" that you make now regarding your responses to his silent treatment.

When tackling this issue, your spirit's help will be instrumental. Here are questions that you can ask your spirit:

1. Do I give too much power away to my partner in order to keep the peace or garner approval?
2. Am I trying to anticipate and manage my partner's reactions too often?

3. What fears block me from advocating for more considerate behavior from my partner?

4. Do I believe that I must share my partner's upsets in order to show solidarity?

5. What behaviors do I tolerate that have a corrosive effect on our relationship?

Your conversations with your spirit can focus on identifying what you're actually afraid of, making peace with your fears in order to take your power back and then having a conversation to spell out your requirements for the relationship to go forward.

Once you have some acknowledgment and consent from your partner, then the next time a BIG reaction occurs, you can refer back to your agreement in that conversation and walk out of the room. Your participation in the BIG reaction is a necessary component of it continuing, and my clients have been surprised by how quickly things resolve once they get clarity about the fears that keep them hustling for their partner's approval and acceptance.

Here's a case in which a client got clear and confident about what she wanted and was delighted when it led to a speedy result.

Because Maggie had worked as a photographer for *National Geographic* and had traveled all over the world, I was used to her showing up for our online sessions dressed in a variety of attire. But I was still a little surprised when I logged on to our session and saw her in her pajamas. She looked sad and exhausted, and her energy looked fragmented like a car windshield that had been fractured into a million tiny pieces. Something intense had happened, and I was eager to hear about it.

Maggie took a deep breath and exhaled slowly. "Sorry for my disheveled appearance. I thought you might as well see me as I really am today."

I smiled and offered, "No worries—your pj's are fine. Why don't you tell me what's happened to have your energy looking so fractured?"

Maggie paused to collect her thoughts. "It's Don. We've been married for eleven years, and each year it's gotten a little worse. And I keep saying that I'm at my limit, but apparently he's not hearing me 'cause his behavior continues."

"What behavior?" I asked.

"His temper tantrums—at least that's what I call them, because they remind me of our kids' tantrums when they were toddlers. Except this is a grown-ass man doing it!"

"Can you describe these temper tantrums?" I asked.

Maggie frowned and said, "It's really embarrassing. But here's his most recent one. Last night I was on the phone with my sister while I was making dinner. We were laughing as she told me about her husband's attempts to fix their washing machine. Don walked in and overheard part of the conversation and mistakenly thought that we were somehow laughing at him.

"He began storming around, slamming cabinet doors, and yelling at the kids to clean up their school stuff. Finally, my twelve-year-old daughter came up to me and whispered, 'Mom, I think you should get off the phone 'cause Daddy's really mad.' So I hung up, and then it took me twenty minutes to convince Don that we weren't even talking about him! We were laughing *with* Laura's husband, not at him."

I could see how upset Maggie was getting as she was reliving the incident. I asked her, "How did Don react once he realized that he'd misunderstood your conversation with your sister?"

"Well, he didn't apologize if that's what you're thinking! He never does—he just gets defensive and brings up every mistake I ever made in the past. Seriously, his tirades can go on for hours."

"How did this incident come to a conclusion?" I gently probed.

"With me in tears, which is frequently how they end. It's like he has to break me down and then he stops and eventually comes back to soothe me. It's so messed up!"

"That sounds awful!" I said tenderly. "How often do these outbursts happen?"

Maggie brushed her wavy brown hair back off her shoulders and straightened her chunky black glasses. "It used to happen once or twice a year. But over the past few years it's happening more often, like every few weeks. He got a big promotion at work, and the stress has left him with a shorter fuse. I try to be understanding about his stress levels, but this is ridiculous. I was up half the night either fuming or crying; I'm really at a loss for what to do next."

I closed my eyes and connected to Maggie's spirit, who suggested that I ask Maggie to describe her parents' marriage.

Maggie looked puzzled. "My parents never acted like this toward each other, so why is that relevant?"

I responded, "I've learned that when someone's spirit makes a suggestion like this it's usually leading us toward something helpful."

Maggie took a deep breath. "Okay, well my parents probably erred in the other direction—just holding everything in and not communicating with each other when things bothered them. The most damaging part about my childhood wasn't my parents fighting—it was having to move all the damn time. Dad wasn't good with money and..."

At this point Maggie's spirit interrupted her to say, "It's not that he made poor investments. He actually had a gambling problem."

Maggie grimaced and said, "Yeah, that's accurate. I guess neither of them ever labeled it that bluntly. Mom would tell us kids that dad had trouble saving money or that the economy was bad. And then we'd move again! My sister and I hated it—we went to nine different schools before graduating high school."

I repeated the question that I heard from Maggie's spirit: "How did your mother handle the financial difficulties and resulting chaos?"

Maggie thought for a moment. "She never really said anything negative about Dad. She just told us to be 'team players' because we were a family, so we had to stick by one another."

I smiled at Maggie and said, "Well, your spirit is telling me that your mother stayed in the relationship because she was afraid of trying to support herself and two children. And that she learned early in the relationship that if she complained to your father about his gambling, he would retaliate with criticisms of her or avoid her for long periods of time."

Maggie's eyes opened wide. "You know, I do remember my mom shushing us when we would complain about not having money. She would say, 'Don't hurt your dad's feelings.' And if Dad did happen to overhear us, he'd look hurt and leave the house. I'd completely forgotten about that! I guess we learned to stop complaining in front of him."

Maggie's spirit offered this: "I directed your attention to your childhood because during that time you were conditioned to accept the justifications offered by a loved one as a way of demonstrating that you are loyal and loving. But love does not mean that you must accept all the rationalizations your partner offers for unwanted behavior."

I watched Maggie's face and knew that she was making important connections between her childhood and the current situation with her husband.

She looked at me and said, "I get it! I watched how Mom focused on just keeping the peace, and I started doing that without even realizing it. I was so focused on stability because I didn't want my kids to have to move all the time like I did. And Don earns good money and is cautious with it. Once I found a man who provided the financial stability that I was hell-bent on giving myself and my kids, I didn't want to question much else in the relationship."

"Yes," Maggie's spirit said, "and your fear of losing the relationship has had you handing over too much of your power to Don. He can intuitively sense your fear of losing the relationship, and it gives him a stronger position of power."

Maggie frowned. "Basically, it allows him to become a bully, and I just keep tolerating it. Okay, how do I fix this mess?"

"The first step," her spirit explained, "is to reassure yourself that you can survive and be happy even if your worst fears are realized. If your marriage ends, this does NOT mean that you'll be subjecting your kids to a childhood filled with financial instability and multiple moves. You earn a good salary yourself, and you are very responsible with money. And you've been married for long enough that you would be dividing your assets, so you would be able to secure nice living arrangements for yourself and your children."

Maggie realized that she had been looking at her situation in an overly simplistic way—either staying married and having a great lifestyle or divorcing and reliving the chaos of her childhood. This "all or nothing" outlook kept her from insisting on respectful treatment from her husband when he was upset. Then Maggie's spirit gave her a startling homework assignment.

"It is suggested that you speak with a divorce attorney. Not because your spirit is predicting that you are likely to get divorced, but because you must make peace with this dreaded outcome. Get a rough estimate of the assets you'd have if you left the marriage and go look at housing options."

Maggie's eyes opened wide. "My spirit seriously wants me to talk to an attorney and then go look at apartments and rental houses?"

I smiled gently. "Yes. Not because she's recommending divorce, but so that you feel less afraid of this worst-case scenario."

The session ended and Maggie left not knowing if she'd follow through with her spirit's suggestions. But four weeks later she returned for another session, and she was positively glowing. She excitedly shared her progress.

"I can't believe how well my spirit's advice worked! My spirit nudged me twice in my morning conversations with her, reminding me to see the attorney, and it turns out that if I left my marriage, I'd have enough money to buy a pretty nice place to live. And I can live off my salary—I've done it before. So yesterday I went to look at possible places to rent or buy, and I found several cute options! And get this! I came home from house hunting, and Don walks up to me and says, 'I know that

I've been a jerk to live with lately, so I've made an appointment with a therapist.' Can you believe it? I almost fell over!"

Maggie's spirit was quick to chime in. "Don's willingness to change his behavior came from the shifts that occurred in your energy. As you took your power back, you didn't have to tell him that you had changed your boundaries—he could feel that they'd changed."

"Well, this is freaking awesome!" Maggie said, pumping her fist in the air.

"I don't mean to rain on this parade, but I think there's still more work to be done here," I said cautiously.

Maggie's spirit nodded her head in agreement and added, "Now it would be helpful to communicate to your partner the specifics of your new boundaries. You have made peace with the idea of ending the relationship if necessary, but it's clear that you still have love for each other and would prefer to heal the relationship if possible."

"Definitely!" Maggie enthused. "I know that I was a mess last time I saw you, but Don really is a great dad and husband most of the time."

"Agreed," Maggie's spirit said. "But because Don's mother tolerated Don's father yelling whenever he was upset, what was modeled for Don was a lack of anger management and an abusive type of domineering male energy."

"Yeah, I can see that," Maggie said, nodding.

Her spirit continued. "It's recommended that you sit with Don and tell him that you appreciate him deciding to work on his anger responses because you've decided that you aren't willing to live in a relationship that contains such disrespectful behavior. Then you can decide together on some responses that you can both offer when you're upset."

Maggie smiled. "I think he'll be very open to this conversation now. And if he isn't, then I feel comfortable holding my ground and insisting that the tantruming behavior stops."

Maggie's spirit gave her suggestions on phrases that she and Don could use to signal to each other that a conversation or reaction was feeling disrespectful. Some of these included:

- I can see that you're upset, but I'm not willing to discuss this with you while you're yelling at me or insulting me.
- I'm going to ask you to leave the room until you feel calm enough to talk about this. Otherwise, the kids and I will leave—we can go out to eat and give you some space to process your feelings.
- I hear what you're saying, but your reaction feels very intense, so I wonder if there are other things bothering you as well. Can you reflect on your stress load and then we can talk more about this later?

Two weeks later Maggie returned for a session. Her energy felt calm and steady, and her radiant smile let me know that she was doing well.

"I'm loving this new chapter in my marriage!" she announced. "We still have work to do, but I'm determined to keep moving forward. We've had a few bumps where he started to get mad about something, but I was really clear in my reactions. I was abrupt and just left the room. And both times he came and found me and apologized! A real apology too, not a fake apology that is the lead-in for his excuses or blame."

Maggie's spirit congratulated her on having the emotional bravery to confront her worst relationship fears as a way to reclaim her power. Today, Maggie and Don have a healthy, tender relationship, and they're modeling for their children how to express negative emotions in respectful ways. They both hold the intention to incorporate their spirit's guidance into their relationship and live in a marriage that reflects their elevated intelligence.

If while reading this chapter you recognized *yourself* as a potential emotional dictator, please consider this an invitation to compassionately explore the idea. Examine the reasons that you use to give yourself permission to act out. Then with your spirit's help, you can determine if your emotional outbursts are oppressively shaping your romantic relationship. We all get occasionally reactive, but when one person's emotional state frequently reigns over the entire household, it will undoubtedly have a corrosive effect on the relationship. Your spirit can gently help you notice how often your mood sets the emotional tone in your household and how often your partner walks on eggshells around you. This topic can feel scary to tackle, but it's an opportunity to let your spirit guide you into having a relationship that's emotionally safe for both you and your partner.

The next two chapters will help you obtain a new perspective on the people you grew up with. Let's examine your family through a new lens.

CHAPTER 17

YOUR FAMILY

Questioning Childhood Labels

"You're too sensitive!" "Why are you so dramatic?" "God, you're demanding!" "You really are mouthy." These are some of the labels that may have been assigned to you as a child when you were vulnerable and oh-so impressionable. They cast a harsh, negative light on positive attributes like energetic sensitivity, emotional intelligence, curiosity, and decisiveness. And these monikers are often given to us by the people who are supposed to love us the most. Do any of them sound familiar? Were you ever labeled as being "too much" or "too little" in some way?

You aren't alone. It would be wonderful if we lived in a world where parents would always acknowledge and nurture their children's unique gifts, expressions, and feelings. But (insert dramatic music) that world doesn't exist. At least not yet. None of us were raised this way. Not because our parents didn't love us but because they had their own insecurities and unhealed wounds to contend with. When faced with not having all the answers, parents often label their children as the problem rather than acknowledging their own limitations. Unfortunately for all of us, those labels are things we can carry with us as part of our identities unless we pause and investigate their accuracy.

If you're reading this book, it's very likely that you're a highly sensitive person, which means you were also an energetically sensitive child. You may have felt emotions (and energy) more acutely than your parents and siblings seemed to, and your reactions may have seemed "too intense" compared to theirs. I've had hundreds of clients tell me that their parents said they were "too sensitive," "ridiculous," "overly dramatic," and "high maintenance." These labels can be a way for parents to subconsciously give themselves an easy out. Once a child has been classified as being unreasonable, her requests can be ignored without the parent feeling guilty.

Children who ask questions about the reasons or fairness behind family rules and/or religious beliefs are branded as "defiant," "disruptive," or "disrespectful." Once characterized this way, the child is often shamed into compliance. Most parents don't intentionally set out to use ridicule and shame as a weapon against their children, but it can be tempting to abruptly belittle the child to avoid awkward questions. And when a tired mom doesn't feel like she has enough energy to explain her reasoning or make adjustments to help an anxious child feel more comfortable, she may just insist that the child "toughen up" and accept the situation.

Children are very sensitive to energy but frequently don't have the vocabulary to describe what they're experiencing and may ask the adults for help in understanding what they're feeling. Such children can be thought of as "the canary in the coal mine," registering something that feels uncomfortable and then attempting to alert others. But this "truth telling" may be unwelcome as children ask for answers to things like icy tension between relatives, Uncle Pete's "weird comments" when he drinks, and the anxiety and depression occurring in certain family members. Parents may assume that the child is too young to understand what's going on and needs to be protected, and they therefore believe it's appropriate to give evasive answers or deny the child's experience altogether. This can be a devastating experience for emotionally sensitive children who then learn to distrust their own feelings.

As adults these sensitive children can feel anxiety about speaking up at work or in personal relationships, as the history of being shamed for telling the truth creates a mental and emotional block to being honest in relationships.

Let's review some of the labels I see given to people that fall under the umbrella of being "too much" and share how they may be playing out in your life.

TOO SENSITIVE

If you were labeled as too sensitive or overly dramatic as a child, you may be subconsciously trying to disprove this family label by working to be some version of "tough and resilient." This may look like signing up for rigorous sports or endurance events, volunteering for the extra assignments at work and pushing yourself to go without sleep, or being numb to what you feel and pretending you're happy all the time ("Nothing gets to me anymore"). Such behaviors can create a barrier to vulnerability and intimacy, so you may feel that no one really knows you, and your partner may complain about feeling shut out.

The pendulum can also swing the other way, and you may have believed your label of overly sensitive, viewing yourself as fragile and in need of people and situations that offer safety and protection. You may seek to date rugged, tough partners or find partners who are confident and take charge so you can avoid making decisions. If you've learned to see yourself as delicate, you may also find yourself perpetually seeking help—seeing therapists, doctors, and holistic practitioners in an attempt to "fix all your weaknesses." You may worry that because you're so delicate and fragile, you are "too much to deal with" and hesitate to express your needs for fear of being abandoned.

TOO DIFFICULT

If you were labeled as defiant or disrespectful, you may have accepted your characterization and chosen to be the "rebel," adopting an attitude of aloofness and flippancy. You may take pride in dressing "differently" or wearing your hair in a style and color meant to startle others. In childhood the label of difficult and disruptive can feel very disempowering, so frequently these children grow up with the desire to take power from others, either through intimidation or making others feel uncomfortable in the moment. You may consider yourself a "skeptic" and be prone to scoffing at new ideas and taking pride in not just "blindly following the pack." You may treat yourself as an outlier and avoid joining groups and making friends because you assume that you're difficult to be around.

If instead you've worked hard to disprove your label of unruly and difficult, you may have become highly focused on following the rules and appearing cooperative. You may have felt drawn to a career in law enforcement, accounting, or other fields where there is an exact set of rules to be followed. You may now prefer to spend time with other rule followers, those who also feel the most comfortable when no one challenges the status quo. You may find yourself judging others for not following the rules and find yourself reporting them to authorities, like the overzealous neighbor who reports people to the homeowners association, the school board, etc.

Underneath all of these "too much" labels are people who were made to feel that they were often more trouble than they were worth. The result is nearly always an adult who fears being seen as a burden. Is this a fear that you currently carry?

Whatever behavior patterns you may have developed in reaction to being labeled as "too much," you'll benefit from giving yourself permission to question your family's categorization of you. My spirit suggested years ago that we each view our old labels like shoes that *may* have fit us at one time but that we've long since outgrown. And some of the labels never actually fit us at all. It's empowering to question their accuracy and look at the influence that they still exert over us.

For an example of how childhood labels can influence how someone perceives herself, here's Miku's story.

My first session with Miku had me feeling like I was handling a delicate glass sculpture; one wrong move and everything could shatter. When Miku signed on to her Zoom session, I was struck by her beautiful glossy dark hair and flawless skin. But while her physical beauty was striking, her energy looked weak and thin and felt fragile. I was immediately curious about the reasons for the lack of vitality in her energy field.

After we exchanged hellos, I asked Miku what she wanted the focus of her session to be and she replied, "My health." I knew from reading her client intake sheet that she was thirty-nine and had been suffering from autoimmune issues for many years, but I wanted to know her specific symptoms. When I asked, Miku's answer was vague.

She lowered her lovely brown eyes and said, "I know that I should feel fine." Hmmm, not very helpful. I decided to try a different approach.

"Can you tell me the three symptoms that you currently struggle with the most?"

She sat up straighter, took a breath, and replied, "Very low energy, frequent skin rashes and digestive issues." Okay, now we were getting somewhere. I started to ask her when her symptoms began, but her spirit interrupted me and pointed me in a different direction.

"Miku, this seems like an odd place to start, but your spirit wants me to ask you about the labels your family had for you when you were in middle school."

Miku looked embarrassed for a moment and then looked back at the camera on her laptop. She explained that she grew up in Canada. Her parents were the first generation of her family to emigrate from Japan to the US, and they maintained much of the traditional Japanese culture in their home. One of those traditions was that the children were to refrain from questioning or complaining—about anything.

Miku went on to explain, "During my first year of middle school, my parents started calling me 'the disrespectful one' because I would come home from school and ask why we did things differently than other families. My father would yell and banish me from the dinner table. My mother would shake her head disapprovingly and say, 'Disrespectful girls never have friends.' So after a while I just stopped asking them questions."

Miku's spirit then asked, "When did the stomachaches begin?"

Miku thought for a moment and then said, "I guess the following year, in seventh grade."

I smiled and gently said, "Your spirit is telling me that by then you had begun doubting yourself and believing that you usually came across as difficult and irritating. You stored the stress and negative energy from that painful belief in your stomach area, which adversely affected your digestion."

Miku nodded. "That makes sense."

Her spirit continued, pushing me to ask Miku about the labels she acquired in high school.

Miku thought for a moment and then answered, "Well, after middle school I became pretty shy. I stopped talking in class and asking the teachers questions and just focused on getting good grades. I didn't really talk to the other kids much, so they started calling me the Ice Princess. One girl, Danielle, used to say, 'She's so pretty that she thinks she's too good for us!' But it wasn't that at all! I just didn't know what to say to them, so I kept quiet."

"That sounds painful," I said. Miku was on a roll and kept talking.

"And then my uncle moved in with us when his wife left him. And he used to look at me funny. When I told my mom that I didn't feel comfortable around him when he'd been drinking, she told me to stop being so dramatic. She accused me of trying to focus all the attention on myself!"

I grimaced in sympathy. "That sounds awful. I can understand why you responded by avoiding talking about what was true for you."

Miku nodded solemnly. "I guess I avoided telling anyone what I was experiencing because anything I said could be turned into evidence of how I was too high maintenance or difficult to please."

"Your spirit is telling me that without realizing it, you also chose a husband who repeated the labels that your family gave you."

Miku looked deflated. "Yeah, I guess I did. When I met Robert during college, he was so nice and seemed to really listen to me. But over the years he has lost patience with my constant physical symptoms, and now if I tell him that I can't go to a business function because I don't feel well, he rolls his eyes and says, "I know, my corporate environment is always too much for you to handle."

I tried not to register any reaction to that comment as I asked, "Do you have kids? How do they respond to your symptoms?"

"They've learned from their dad, I guess. If I tell my son or daughter that I am too tired to stay up till midnight to pick them up from a party, they sigh and tell me that my not feeling well shouldn't limit their social lives. Which is true, I guess..."

At this point Miku's spirit jumped in. "Because Miku still believes her family's characterization of her, she hesitates to ask for what she needs for fear of being labeled a burden. And when she does make a request, her apologetic tone leaves the door open for pushback from her family, who dismiss her preferences and label them as excessive weakness."

Miku was nodding as I continued translating what her spirit was sharing with me. "Her perceived fragility causes her to feel guilty about not measuring up and disappointing her family's expectations of her. But she is not fragile; she is sensitive—there is a big difference!"

Miku looked surprised. "What does that mean—'I'm sensitive'?"

"It means that you feel energy and emotions deeply, usually before the others in your family feel them. In childhood you were reporting on things that your parents either couldn't perceive or chose to ignore, so they attributed your claims as overly dramatic and annoying. And since your parents had previously shamed you for asking questions, you believed their assessments of you and doubted your own intuition—about your uncle, your sense of belonging at school, and even your own physical symptoms. But you were right! Your intuition was giving you very precise and valuable information."

I stopped because I heard Miku quietly crying. I gave her a moment to digest the information, and then she nodded and said, "Please go on."

Her spirit continued. "When you're trained to abandon what is true for you, you're also conditioned to relinquish your power to others. The people around you who appear confident in their perception of the world become dominant over you, and you agree to do things their way because of your self-doubt."

I paused as I reflected on that nugget of truth. It explained why so many sensitive people are hesitant to talk about the impressions they get when they walk into a room or observe a conversation; they doubt their own impressions because they have so little experience being validated.

Miku's spirit continued. "When you met Robert, you were attracted to how confidently he stated what was true for him and what he needed. You subconsciously hoped that he would advocate for you the same way, so you handed your power to him and let him make most of the decisions in your relationship. But when your sensitivity to energy meant that he couldn't accurately anticipate and advocate for your needs, you were left living by his perception of reality and his opinions about what you should need."

Miku took a deep breath and exhaled. "Wow, my spirit's right. I do try to adapt to whatever Robert thinks I should be feeling and needing. I've come to trust his opinions more than my own! Ugh!"

"There's more," I said. "Your spirit is telling me that your autoimmune issues are a physical manifestation of how you deny what is true for you, assuming that your husband's perception of reality is more accurate than yours. And now that your kids are teenagers, you frequently value their interpretation of what's 'appropriate' for you too. By doing so, you're rejecting yourself—your intuition and your own inner wisdom—and so your body is rejecting itself to demonstrate this for you."

Miku smiled. "That's actually kind of brilliant, how my body and my spirit are working together to get my attention. Now how do we fix it?"

"By acknowledging what is true for you. Begin with journaling. Writing down what you feel and perceive is important because journaling provides a format where your truth won't be denied or debated by your family members. This is where you begin to honor yourself by believing what you feel. And it's recommended that you not share your observations with others until you have clarity and confidence in your opinions. Otherwise, your family may try to talk you out of your position if it's inconvenient for them or if they can't relate to what you're describing."

Over the next six months, Miku worked diligently to reclaim her power by honoring what was true for her. She eventually stopped apologizing to her family for her specific needs and preferences, and they soon learned to accept what she asked for herself. Her relationship with her husband proved to be the most challenging, as he was used to his wife accepting his version of reality without question. But each time Miku had to advocate for her own experience and what she needed, she became more confident in reacquiring her voice.

And as she reclaimed her voice, she began to open up to the natural abilities that come with being energetically sensitive: increased intuition, enhanced creativity, and accuracy in reading people quickly. The more she trusted herself, the more her symptoms dissipated until her only remaining symptom was a slight skin irritation when she let someone else's opinion of her requests "get under her skin." When the itching occurred, Miku learned to sit quietly and reflect on how she was denying her reality in order to make someone else feel comfortable.

Today, Miku is considered "cured" of her autoimmune issues by her doctors. I'm pleased by this, but I'm even more thrilled at the empowered version of Miku that shows up for our occasional sessions—confident, glowing, and with a strong energy field that looks healthy and radiant. She proudly works on developing her elevated intelligence, knowing that it is a gift that comes easily to her now that she's owned the benefits of connecting with her spirit regularly.

Each of us played different roles in our family, and we were frequently given nicknames or labels that went unquestioned. When you're ready to ask your spirit about this topic, here are some questions that I recommend:

1. Which words that my family used to describe me do I still hold on to?
2. Which of these labels do I still use to define myself?
3. Am I seeking to disprove these labels or live into them?
4. Which of my behaviors are primarily a reaction to past labeling rather than an accurate expression of who I am now?
5. How can I acknowledge and honor the needs I had as a child that led to these labels?
6. How can I now relate to my family without making them wrong or living with a label that feels dishonoring?

As you interact with friends and family, notice when you label yourself as some version of a burden and question the way you describe yourself. Is it really an accurate depiction of who you are now? Who would you be if you dropped that label and accepted your desires, questions, and experiences as valid and important?

The next chapter is a big one, and I encourage you to keep an open mind. Have you ever wondered if it's possible to have healthy boundaries with your family? Your elevated intelligence can help you create boundaries that honor who you are today.

CHAPTER 18

YOUR FAMILY

Creating Healthy Boundaries as Adults

As adults, it can be really hard to manage the thoughts, feelings, and reactions that we developed during childhood. It's so easy for us to stay in patterns that aren't serving us, but that's why creating healthy boundaries is crucial as we get older. The goal of establishing healthy boundaries with family members can feel like navigating a treacherous maze. But your spirit can help you heal past hurts as well as create respectful boundaries that resonate with your inner peace and growth.

I love when clients tell me that they can now inwardly thank their parents for the gifts they received from them *and* make healthy boundaries around their current toxic behavior. If you can accept that your mom is narcissistic, then you can give up trying to change her and instead focus on how you want to live as an adult who has a narcissistic mother. Whether you choose to drastically limit your interactions with such a parent or set firm, mutually respectful boundaries, it's important to decide what's healthiest for the current version of you rather than accepting old dynamics.

But setting new boundaries with family members— especially when your parents did not allow you to have healthy boundaries as a child—can feel like climbing Mount Everest alone. Here's some good news: your spirit can help you select the best teachers, therapists, and healers to help you recover from your childhood wounds and your current familial issues, and your elevated intelligence can guide you as you set healthier boundaries.

Setting boundaries can be tricky in any relationship, but with family members who have known you for decades and have participated in creating the unhealthy family dynamics, there is typically a resistance to any change. Subconsciously, many family members count on the relationship dynamics remaining static and unchanging because the lack of change helps them feel a sense of predictability and stability.

I find that my clients frequently need to set new boundaries with their parents or siblings when their family members' behaviors fall into one of these three categories: 1) frequent criticizing, 2) frequent dumping/complaining, or 3) frequent requests for help. Let's look at each of these in more detail.

FREQUENT CRITICIZING

If you were raised with a parent or sibling who felt entitled to repeatedly criticize your decisions and actions, this can be a tough pattern to break once you're an adult. Your tendency may be to react defensively like you did when you were a criticized child—a reaction that can reinforce the dynamic instead of changing it. Here's how being defensive reinforces that behavior: as soon as you begin to defend your choices, you've inadvertently stepped back into the energetic exchange you had as a child.

It's critical that you pay attention to which version of yourself shows up in dialogues with your family members. If you're triggered by their comments, your inner child may reflexively step forward to protest or defend yourself in a familiar way. Taking a moment to consciously switch gears into your adult self (one that has resources and independence) will allow you to break your habit of perpetuating an old dynamic that does not serve you.

Imagine you were raised in a family that adored ballroom dancing, particularly the waltz. Every conversation in your household was conducted to the rhythm of waltzing music, the only accepted mode of communication. As an adult, you've developed a passion for the tango, a very different dance style. However, your family dismisses the tango and refuses to acknowledge your talent for it. When you visit your parents, the familiar sound of waltz music triggers an automatic response, and you find yourself waltzing without even realizing it—it feels reflexive. Similarly, when you find yourself defending your decisions, you're instantly drawn back into the old dynamic of being the young child defending her actions.

Instead of doing the old family waltz when your family member criticizes you, I recommend saying some version of this statement: "Thanks, but I'm not taking feedback on that topic right now. I'll let you know if I feel open to discussing it in the future." While the mere thought of offering such a response may make you nervous, it is a statement made by an adult, not a child hoping to convince her parent or sibling that her actions are appropriate. The energy behind such a comment is meant to convey that you're comfortable with your actions, and so you have no need to defend their appropriateness. If your family member continues to offer their opinion/critique, you can respond with "I don't feel that you are hearing me, so I'm going to end this conversation if you insist on staying on this topic. What is your choice?"

As nerve-racking as it may feel to keep repeating these statements, they'll help establish a healthier boundary with a critical family member. Some clients have shared that when they set this boundary, that family member distanced themselves, no longer interested in a relationship where they weren't permitted to openly criticize. But in each case, the client found that the loss of the seemingly close connection was well worth the increase in self-confidence and peace from the cessation of the constant criticism. Often the sibling or parent who justifies their critiques as "I'm just caring about you" will be initially offended when their "advice" is no longer allowed, but most will eventually accept the new dynamic based on mutual respect between two adults.

FREQUENT DUMPING

The second type of behavior that calls for a boundary is when a family member frequently seeks support, typically solicited through complaining or tales of sadness and woe. Many children grew up in families where their role was to be a sympathetic ear, listening to complaints as a way of showing love and support. If this resonates with you, it can be challenging to no longer entertain the constant stream of negativity whenever you visit or answer their phone call.

Shifting away from your childhood role and allowing your adult self to emerge requires you to question the assumption that listening to continual complaining or stories of helplessness truly signifies healthy love and support. By challenging this belief, you begin to break free from the pattern of being parentified or treated as a constant source of support to your parent or sibling. While supporting those we love can certainly involve some time spent listening to them describe their difficulties, ideally the conversation is a healthy balance of empathetic listening and assisting your family member in problem-solving.

Too many children were assigned the role of listening to complaints without being allowed to offer a solution or describe their own difficulties, and this one-sided dynamic has you playing a supporting role at your own expense both emotionally and energetically. You can imagine that being the recipient of the negative energy that accompanies complaining is like holding a cauldron in front of you while your family member constantly pours boiling acid into it. No one benefits from this activity, and you are weighed down (and possibly scarred) by this dumping behavior along with your feelings of being trapped in that role. Even if your relative believes that they feel better afterward, indulging in frequent complaining reinforces the concept that one is a victim of their circumstances, which is an unhealthy perspective. So in changing this pattern you are not abandoning this family member, but shifting your connection into one that is healthier for both of you.

If you find yourself cringing when the phone rings and you see that your family member is calling to vent to you once again, it's probably time for a healthier boundary. The first step is to redefine what healthy, loving support looks like between you and this family member. Then you can communicate your new goals for the relationship—the roles you want to play for this person and the types of balanced conversations that you're seeking (rather than a one-way stream of negative reporting).

You can communicate your boundaries with statements like "I've been noticing how oftentimes our conversations end up feeling very heavy and negative to me, and I want to shift that feeling. I think that we've gotten into a pattern of complaining to each other (this comment is you being generous if the other person is the only one who complains, and your role is to listen). So from now on, let's allow each other five minutes to 'dump,' and then we either problem-solve the situation or move on."

The recipient of your new boundary may not be delighted with these new guidelines, as it requires them to recognize the desires of the balanced, adult version of you. But the next time this family member begins to rant about how terrible things are for them, you can wait a few minutes and then remind them of the new "policy" that you agreed to. Often, the other person only agreed to the new boundary begrudgingly when the idea was initially introduced, but your job is to reinforce this new policy that you both committed to.

If your family member is not able or willing to be self-reflective regarding their behavior, there is a slightly different version of this dynamic shift that I've successfully helped clients utilize. Your conversation will appear to be a request that you're making of this person and will go something like this: "I'm trying something new. I want to be less negative, so I'm asking the people closest to me to let me know when I'm just ranting and complaining, okay? I'm trying to notice when I'm just whining and being in victim mode instead of taking charge in my life. And I'll do the same for you—I'll point out when you're complaining and we need to problem solve or change the topic, okay?" Just like the more honest approach, the recipient is unlikely to be excited about this plan, but it's tough for them to assert that they should be allowed to complain unceasingly, so this plan typically works if you stick to it.

Similar to the first instance of boundary-setting above, I've had clients report that the family member contacts them less often, as their primary goal was simply to offload their negative thoughts. Again, I advocate for holding firm with the new boundary, even if you are accused of "no longer caring" about that family member. You may have to repeatedly explain that while you still love this person, you believe that listening to regular complaining did not benefit either of you. And in the end, you may have to accept this person's label of you as "unsupportive" if the only way they believe that you can show your support is to listen to them indefinitely.

FREQUENT REQUESTS FOR HELP

The third type of family dynamic that necessitates a new boundary is when you've been conditioned to constantly rescue a parent or sibling. If I hear a client say, "I'm the only friend my mom has" or "I'm the only person that my sister will trust to help her," my antennae go up as I'm alerted to the possibility that my client has been convinced that only they can help a family member, and thus they have been made overly responsible for that person's physical, financial, and emotional well-being.

In this chapter I'm not referring to the care of an elderly parent or a health-challenged sibling. I'm describing the situation where you've been awarded the dubious title of "the favorite person" to talk to when they're lonely, need transportation to social events and doctor's appointments, or want advice on cleaning up frequent crises of their own making.

Once you identify that you feel the weight of someone's physical or emotional care on your shoulders, question the idea that no one else can help this family member. I find that most clients were not allowed to challenge such an assumption when they were first "assigned" the responsibility because it was presented as an honor, as if only they had the skills and love necessary to properly care for that person. See this for the manipulation it is and challenge the notion that accepting help from others will devastate this family member. When I've asked my clients what would happen if they were in a car accident that left them in a coma for the next four months, they begin to broaden their thinking around the duties they've been assigned. They realize that if they suddenly disappeared, their family member would find other solutions, and this is an important realization.

The next step is to begin getting yourself and this family member better resourced. While you may be your mother's first choice for a ride to every doctor's appointment, you're not the only option. Investigate ride-sharing, senior vans, and other options for people who need transportation to appointments. I've learned that if I have a dilemma, chances are good that others have experienced this and come up with an affordable business that provides solutions. It is money well spent if it liberates you from a role that you resent because it feels permanent.

My clients often realize that a family member reaches out incessantly because they're lonely, and a concerted effort to find your loved one more community can yield big dividends. There are generally low-cost options available for socializing, and if you can urge your family member to allow others into their life, you will feel much of the weight for their emotional well-being slide off your shoulders. It is not your job to ensure that your loved ones are never lonely; their social life must also be their responsibility.

Once you have alternatives to being the only person who provides all the care or rescuing for your family member, then you're ready to have an honest conversation in which the adult version of you relays that you need more assistance in the role of helping this person. Sometimes it's helpful to list a reason for your decreasing availability that is something your family member respects, like work or parenting. If your dad values your job and how responsible you are in that role, then you can state that you've been given additional responsibilities at work, and so you'll need to adjust how often you can help him. It's surprising how quickly such family members typically adapt once they're given no choice. The delightful result is that both you and the family member begin to think broader when it comes to getting that person's needs met, which is empowering for both of you.

I understand that frequently finances do not allow you to bring in extra help for errands and the caretaking of an elderly parent. In such cases, I recommend warning your family member that you may not be able to answer the phone immediately and to work out a system where you're texted a code that means your help is needed urgently. Unless you receive that code, I recommend waiting a while before responding to texts and phone calls. Most of my clients have used this technique to wean dependent siblings, teens, and anxious parents from the scenarios of multiple "urgent" phone calls and texts each day. Being less available, combined with complimenting the family member's problem-solving skills when they did not require your help, typically results in a gradual elimination of your role as the "only acceptable helper."

If any of these weighty roles sound familiar to you, here are some questions that you can ask your spirit while in meditation:

1. Which roles have I been given by my family that don't serve me?

2. How can I find other resources for this family member?

3. What are some phrases that I can use to help this family member see how unbalanced our relationship is?

4. What healthy boundaries are missing between me and my family?

5. How did I end up in this role (the role you play in your family)?

6. How can I help this family member see themselves—and me—more accurately?

Here's Pamela's story of successfully convincing her mother to eliminate her daily ninety-minute phone calls.

Pamela had come to see me for sessions six years earlier when her chronic migraines stopped responding to conventional medications. In our work together, I channeled Pamela's spirit as she advised Pamela on how to heal her migraines by addressing childhood wounds that prompted her to give her power away to men that she dated. Later, Pamela enrolled in my program and learned to communicate with her spirit on her own, so now I only see her when she has trouble understanding her spirit's message or needs help in implementing her spirit's suggestions.

When I logged in to our online session, Pamela looked anxious. She smiled a tight smile and then blurted out, "God, I hope that you can hear my spirit! She seems to have gone missing!"

I raised my eyebrows in response, but since I could already feel the energy of Pamela's spirit I wasn't concerned. I grinned and said, "I'm sure that she'll show up—tell me what's been happening."

Pamela raised her finger for me to wait a moment and then hit "record" on her phone. (I encourage my clients to record their sessions so that they don't have to take notes and can relisten to their spirit's advice multiple times, especially if the messages are unexpected.) Then she updated me on her current situation.

"My dad passed away a few years ago, and as the oldest, I've become Mom's 'go-to' person. As in, I'm the one she tries to talk to at least five times a day. And since I'm in meetings at the hospital all day, I get a slew of messages on my cell phone about everything that's gone wrong or inconvenienced her that day. I don't even listen to her messages anymore because she's going to cover the same complaints when I call her on my way home from work. My commute home is spent listening to a ninety-minute tirade about what's wrong with the neighbor's dogs, the teenagers who live down the block and play their music too loudly, etc. It's a crummy way to end my day, let me tell you."

I nodded sympathetically. "It sounds like an exhausting daily habit you two have developed."

Pamela pointed at me and exclaimed, "Ha! You're right—I participated in creating the pattern, and my spirit worked on me for months trying to get me to break the draining end to my day. But my mom's been so lonely since my dad died, and I'm all she has. My brother, Paul, lives far away, and he only calls once in a while, but my mom says that he just tries to solve her problems, and I am nice and just let her talk. So I've been letting this go on for months, and by the time I get home I'm so drained that I usually eat something quick and fall asleep in front of the TV. When I meditated and asked my spirit why my energy was so low, she kept telling me that I was allowing my mom's bad habit to drain me."

"That sounds accurate," I said, nodding. "What did your spirit recommend?"

"My spirit said that I should tell my mom that I only wanted to have mutual conversations where we each shared about our day. But here's the thing—if I shared about my day, then I'd have to hear my mom's comments on all my decisions! No thanks! She's quite negative, and I didn't want to share things and then have to convince her that I had it handled. So I just let her keep doing all the talking."

I was watching Pamela's energy as she spoke, and I knew that she was downplaying how draining her conversations with her mother left her. So I wasn't surprised at the next piece of her story.

"Then I started getting symptoms—my migraines came back. They'd been gone for years! But I knew that the headaches meant I was at my breaking point. So I sat down and asked my spirit for help. And she gave me a visual that really got through to me. She showed me my mom sitting in a little rowboat that had a big leak in it. But instead of fixing the leak, she was bailing out water and tossing it into my rowboat! That's when I really understood that it wasn't helping my mom for me to listen to her complain every day, and she was drowning me!"

"That's great!" I enthused. "I like your spirit's visual—very effective."

"Agreed," Pamela said with a smile. "So then I asked my spirit for help in weaning my mom off our daily complaint calls. She gave me some great ideas for wording, and I got brave and had the conversation with my mom. I told her that I loved her and wanted her to be happy, but that these calls were not helping either of us and I wanted to try to have conversations about what went right for us each day, not the bad stuff."

"That sounds productive. How did she receive it?" I asked.

"It went over like a lead balloon. Mom got weepy and said that no one understood her since Dad died. But honestly, Dad used to complain about her all the time! That's part of why he played golf every day—to get away from her constant gossiping and bitching about everyone. So I didn't back down. And my mom hasn't spoken to me in three weeks! And now my spirit isn't speaking to me either, so I want your reassurance that I haven't botched this."

I smiled at Pamela. "Your spirit is right here waiting to speak with you, so let me assure you that you haven't botched anything. I think that you're feeling so emotionally conflicted about this topic that you're having trouble raising your energy up high enough to hear your spirit."

"Oh, that makes sense. I've been racked with guilt for the past three weeks, and when I couldn't hear my spirit, I really went into a downward spiral of self-doubt. So what does my spirit recommend?"

"Well, first let me reassure you that your spirit was never unresponsive; you just couldn't hear her because of your fears and guilt. In the future, try meditating and asking your spirit questions about something that's less emotionally charged for you—that can help you reestablish your connection."

"Got it—good tip!" Pamela said gratefully.

I reconnected to Pamela's spirit and then said, "Okay, here's your spirit's advice: go by your mom's house. Tell her face-to-face that you really wanted to change the type of conversations you guys had, but not end them. Then if she's not open to talking with you, hug her and leave. It's important for your mom to agree to this new style of communicating with you."

Pamela grimaced. "What if she won't open the door?"

"Then you say what you came to say through the closed door, and you leave. It's important that you show up as the adult who is intent on a healthy relationship and not as the child who is afraid of being rejected by her mother."

"Oh, crap! I am reacting out of a fear of rejection, aren't I?"

I let Pamela breathe for a moment and feel through her fears and discomfort. Then her shoulders dropped as she relaxed into her discomfort and said, "I can do this. I can wait for Mom to agree to my terms of a healthier relationship."

A week later Pamela emailed me to say that when she went by her mom's house, her mother greeted her a bit stiffly but invited her in. She tried to act nonchalant as she told Pamela that she'd resumed going to the country club for Monday afternoon bridge games and that she was pleasantly surprised that so many of their friends were still there playing bridge. Pamela could feel her mother's embarrassment at their conversation weeks earlier, so she didn't mention it. But the next day when Pamela called her mother as she drove home from work, her mother asked her about her day and only briefly complained about the neighbors. Pamela was thrilled with the shift in her relationship with her mother, and she also reported that her spirit was "back on the job" conversing with Pamela in her morning meditations. And, not surprisingly, her migraine headaches ceased.

The relationships we have with our family members frequently serve as the model for our friendships. So the next three chapters deal with the challenges I commonly see in my clients' unhealthy friendships.

CHAPTER 19

TOXIC FRIENDSHIP PATTERNS

The Friend in Crisis

Your phone rings. You look down at the caller ID, and when you see Molly's name you cringe, dismiss the call, and immediately put your phone on silent mode. Yep—we're talking about *that* friend. The one you love and the one you also feel compelled to periodically avoid.

Your spirit hopes that you have friendships that enhance your life and form a solid part of your support system. A healthy friendship offers mutual support for both people and an energy exchange that's generally very positive. Ideally our friends are there for us on our most distressing days and our most celebratory ones. A good friend will embolden you to advocate for yourself when you're feeling uncertain, and she knows when to show up and drag you out for ice cream because it's time to get out of the house and breathe some fresh air. Your friends likely know how you like to celebrate your birthdays and what to say when you're feeling discouraged and need a pep talk. A wise friend can help you see other perspectives in a situation you're wrestling with and alert you when you're being too hard on yourself.

But most of us have had at least one friendship that drains us more often than it delights us. There are three categories I think of when I hear stories about challenging friendships: the friend in crisis, the critical friend, and the competitive friend. Each of these types of relationships deplete our energy, and they indicate that certain dynamics are in play. It's important for you to learn about each type so that you can revise these draining patterns in your friendships.

THE FRIEND IN CRISIS

This is typically a friend who lives below your standard of living in some way. She may be single and you're happily coupled, or she may be struggling financially more than you are. But in some way you're frequently worried about her, and you feel that she's going to need help. And you believe—either consciously or subconsciously—that you're probably the best person to help her. This belief holds both of you in the dynamic of rescuer and person-in-crisis.

This situation can also arise when the friend in crisis believes that being in need is the most reliable way to get people to support her and send her energy. These friends may have been raised in a household where the children were given attention only when they were sick or in a dire situation that required adult help. If this is the case, your friend is likely focusing on one crisis after another because it's her insurance policy against feeling forgotten and abandoned.

If you find yourself repeatedly playing the rescuer, it's worth reflecting on your own childhood to see if this role was modeled for you. Was one of your parents a rescuer? Or were *you* the rescuer in your family, responsible for keeping a sibling out of trouble or keeping mom or dad sober or out of depression? Such "assignments" can predispose you to continually volunteering to play this role for others once you're an adult, unwittingly assuming that it's your responsibility.

As the rescuer for your friend, you're expending a lot more energy than you're receiving each time you assist her. This is the energy drain in your friendship that is readily apparent. What may not be as apparent is the belief that you're both operating from while you're entangled in this type of dynamic. On some level, you and your friend both believe that she is less capable than you are, and therefore it's appropriate that you lend her some of your skills and resources on a continuing basis. By validating her belief that she's not as capable as you are, you're guaranteeing that she'll feel desperate for your help whenever her next predicament arises.

You may also be operating from the belief that her spirit, or God/the Universe (whatever higher powers you believe in), has not taken proper care of her, and thus her life is "unfair." Once we've decided that someone has gotten a bad deal in their life, we'll usually feel inclined to help correct that oversight in some way. I understand that there are life circumstances in which people are going through real crises or are in need because they've been marginalized or oppressed. That's not what I'm talking about here. I'm referencing the friend who repeatedly believes she's in an unfair/undeserved crisis and is calling you for help, sympathy, or financial rescue.

It's healthy and appropriate to empathize with a friend who's normally very capable but is currently going through a difficult time due to illness, injury, divorce, or other occasional circumstances. This is different from deciding that because God hasn't provided for this person adequately, you will make up the difference. Be on the lookout for the rationalizations that you and your friend use to justify your repeated rescue missions.

If you've identified your friendship as existing in this toxic pattern, what questions can you ask your spirit to garner the most helpful advice?

Here are some questions to pose to your spirit before meditating:

1. Am I perpetuating the rescuer paradigm with this friend? How am I doing that?
2. Do I have a history of rescuing people that you can help me see?
3. How can I help this friend see her own strengths and skills for solving this problem?
4. Am I trusting myself to solve her problems more than I'm trusting her, her spirit, or God/the Universe?
5. How can I encourage this friendship to move away from crisis management and into a healthier exchange?
6. What are helpful comments and questions I can ask her to encourage the development of her self-reliance?

Here's Sherry's story to help demonstrate this type of friendship:

When the typically vivacious, confident CEO of a large company won't make eye contact with me, I know that something's up. Sherry was sitting in my treatment room wringing her hands and looking at the floor, the walls, anywhere but at me. I started wondering if she was going to confess something like having an affair. Instead, she took a deep breath and said, "I'm feeling terrible about avoiding my friend Amelia, but I just can't bail her out of one more catastrophe!"

It was so unusual for me to witness Sherry looking flustered that it took me a moment to absorb what she'd said. This woman was a successful business owner with four hundred employees, and she was typically assertive and confident in her handling of urgent matters. But as she sat before me twisting the zipper pull on the side of her expensive leather handbag, I recognized the body language of someone who felt trapped in an unhealthy friendship.

Seeking a neutral question to start out with, I asked, "How did you guys meet and how long have you known Amelia?"

Sherry brushed her dark, curly hair back behind her shoulder and took a deep breath. "We met in high school. Amelia was the brainiac—class valedictorian and proud nerd. When she moved into our neighborhood, we became friends, and she got me through Spanish classes with the dreadful Mrs. Harrington. Then I went off to college, and she got married and stayed in that stupid tiny town in New Jersey. Five years ago, her husband left her with three kids, and I feel like I've been taking care of her ever since!"

Sherry slumped back on the sofa, looking relieved to have dumped out her current struggle. I've learned that frequently the fastest solutions come from me asking just enough questions to know the topic that's troubling the client, and then to connect to her spirit and begin translating the guidance. In this case, Sherry's spirit had an accurate assessment to offer.

I took a deep breath and said, "Here's your spirit's take on this friendship. She says that you and Amelia haven't had much in common since she had children and you were in graduate school, but you've stayed loosely connected because you appreciated all her help in high school and you had fond memories of your time together."

"What's wrong with that?" Sherry asked.

"Absolutely nothing," I reassured her. "Your spirit is just sharing her perspective."

Sherry relaxed her shoulders and nodded for me to continue.

"Your spirit also says that when Amelia's husband left her, you were shaken not just because the guy abandoned his wife and kids, but because you felt that in some way God had abandoned them too. Does that resonate with you?"

Sherry considered the question for a moment. "Well, I definitely haven't thought of it that way before...but yeah, I guess I did feel like Amelia deserved better than to be left by Doug the dirtbag."

I smiled at her nickname for Amelia's ex-husband. "Your spirit goes on to say that because you're doing very well, and Amelia's been struggling since her husband left, you've unknowingly felt responsible for making sure that she lands on her feet."

"Except she never does!" Sherry complained in exasperation. "I swear, that woman is always in crisis. She ignored late payment notices and so she lost her health insurance, then her kids kept getting sick, and so now she's in even more debt. It's never-ending! I feel like I help her put out one fire and another one starts before I can take a breath."

"I get it," I said empathetically. "That sounds exhausting."

"It really is," Sherry said sadly as she leaned forward and put her head in her hands. "So here I am, a grown-ass woman avoiding her calls like I'm a kid avoiding curfew."

I chuckled and then channeled her spirit again. "I'm hearing that this isn't the tragedy you think it is. Your spirit says that part of why Amelia married Doug was because she doubted her ability to go out in the world and make good decisions. And marrying Doug shielded her from doing that because he liked to make all the decisions in their marriage. So when he left she was scared, and she has floundered a bit, but her spirit is confident that she can rise to the occasion if given the chance."

Sherry looked confused. "What do you mean 'if given the chance'?"

"Your spirit says that Amelia's mother and you both worry that she won't make good decisions, and so you both jump in to intervene before she can make too big of a mistake."

"Well, yeah!" Sherry said defensively. "Did you miss the part where I told you that she let her health insurance lapse? With three kids! Who does that?"

I held up my hand to pause Sherry's righteous rant. "I know that it was a big mistake with real consequences, but Amelia needs to experience those consequences in order to hit her own low point. Amelia's spirit is actually excited for Amelia to have a resurrection story where she overcomes her self-doubt and feelings of victimhood and experiences all the strengths that she possesses."

Sherry took a deep breath and exhaled slowly. "Well, this is a different spin on things! But how do I pull back from rescuing her without her feeling like I've abandoned her too?"

Sherry's spirit was ready with an answer. "First, be clear in your own mind that you're not abandoning her. You're supporting her from a place of greater understanding, which is more helpful to her in the long run. Next, be alright with her struggling. Not because you don't care, but because you want to support her as she relies on her own problem-solving skills instead of yours."

Sherry took a deep breath and nodded. "Okay, not easy, but I can do that. What else?"

"Try to remember that your pain threshold is different from everyone else's breaking point. So what might motivate you to jump into action—say, getting the first late payment notice from an insurance company—might not be scary enough to motivate other people. Because your discomfort threshold is generally lower than Amelia's, you jump in to rescue before she reaches a level of discomfort that causes her to shift her behaviors."

Sherry sat back on the sofa with a relieved smile on her face. "Wow, I never thought of it that way! My spirit's right—I never would've tolerated half the stuff that she did with her ex-husband; he really abandoned her in a million little ways before he actually walked out the door."

"Yes," I agreed, "and your spirit says that she's near her discomfort limit, which is why she's reaching out to you more often."

"Makes sense," Sherry said thoughtfully. "But what do I say when she calls me with this week's latest calamity?"

"Your spirit suggests that you validate her feelings of stress and then ask her how *she* wants to solve her dilemma. If she says that she doesn't know how, resist the urge to give suggestions or jump into action. Instead, tell her that you have confidence in her problem-solving skills because she's always been very smart. People tend to rise up to meet our positive expectations of them if we hold space for them to do so."

"I'll do it!" Sherry said excitedly and then laughed. "I feel like I just lost 150 pounds! I guess that was the extra person I had on my shoulders when I walked in here!"

I'd love to report that Amelia responded beautifully to Sherry's withdrawal of frequent support and instantly found her own wings. But Amelia spent about four months being frustrated that she'd "been abandoned yet again." After four months, Amelia hit a new low—she was denied an appointment for her son with a doctor specializing in asthma because she didn't have health insurance. Not being able to give her son good medical care galvanized Amelia into action. She took a corporate job that had great benefits to secure insurance coverage for her family. Then she enrolled in nursing school in the evenings, and now she has a great career that she loves. Nine months after Sherry shifted away from her rescuing behaviors, Amelia reached out to her and they spent an evening reconnecting and establishing the grounds for a new, healthy friendship.

Once you recognize this pattern in one of your friendships, you can begin to explore ways to change your behavior to support your friend without rescuing her. It's helpful to notice how uncomfortable you get when that friend is in distress and to observe your belief that she may not be able to take care of herself. It's natural to want to help her, but remember that allowing her personal growth is often the most beneficial thing you can do for her.

Let's move on to a different friend who may be depleting your energy—the one who's eager to offer you her opinion in ways that feel unhelpful at best and just plain cruel at worst: the critical friend.

CHAPTER 20

TOXIC FRIENDSHIP PATTERNS

The Critical Friend

If you've just finished painting your bedroom wall a new, bold color, who's the first friend you want to share it with? Who's the *last* friend you want to show it to? This chapter is about that friend—the one who's likely to pop your balloon of excitement and then look at you innocently while you deflate. Let's call this friend Shirley.

Sometimes we want a brutally honest opinion from a trusted friend. I want to know if my new haircut looks bad or if I was overly harsh when I told my neighbor I wouldn't dog-sit for a month. But we've all had that friend who seems to enjoy being more brutal than honest.

Healthy friendships can include healthy criticism. When your friend offers constructive criticism, it's because she wants to help you achieve your desired results. Her comments will include specific, actionable suggestions on how you can more effectively reach your goals. This can look like your friend suggesting a more effective way to set a boundary with your neighbor or strongly encouraging you to pause and reflect before calling your brother to finish a heated conversation. Notice that when you receive constructive criticism, you may feel slightly self-conscious, but you should not feel diminished.

The focus of unhealthy or destructive criticism is not to help you achieve your desires; the real underlying goal here is to lower your morale and confidence. Such criticism can be vague and lacking in actionable suggestions for improvement, or it may be specific but offers no hope for improvement. An example can be when your friend Shirley tells you that your mother-in-law will probably never like you because you're just not ambitious enough. Or that it's not your fault your project wasn't well received because your position in the company isn't valued. Destructive criticisms can be tricky to spot because they can include some bits of supportive language. Like the friend who, after hearing what you wrote in an email, says, "That's pretty good so far, but is that all there is?"

The result of such destructive criticism is that your friend Shirley takes significantly more than half of the energy that's created during your conversation as you cringe, feel self-conscious, and back away from the energy created by the conversation. You may even relinquish additional energy as you ask her for more "advice," not realizing she's offering criticism that's presented as if it's advice. In such exchanges, Shirley feels more empowered because she's pointing out your flaws, and your shame keeps you listening, hoping for a way to improve yourself. But Shirley has no real interest in you becoming a better, stronger version of yourself; her toxic comments are meant to convince you that she's more knowledgeable than you are and should therefore be the leader in your relationship.

Why is Shirley like this? Typically, such behaviors begin in the family that raised her. In many families, whoever is "the most knowledgeable" has the most power. So conversations frequently look like a grab for credit or authority as each person tries to establish that they are the most deserving of power and respect. By telling someone how they're "doing it wrong," Shirley asserts herself as the most knowledgeable and therefore the one whose approval is sought. Shirley was most likely raised with one or both parents engaging in this behavior, criticizing the children in an effort to control their actions.

If you convince a child that you know the best way to do everything and then you shame them for not doing things "correctly," they're likely to defer to your preferences and seek your advice and approval. This makes for very cooperative children, but they tend to lack self-esteem and confidence in their decision-making abilities.

Many children were raised with some version of this paradigm wherein one person in the family is the "wise one" or "expert" in nearly everything and is allowed to openly criticize everyone else. In such families, constant criticisms are tolerated because the "expert" feels justified in being annoyed by how little others know and judges the "inferior" way they do things. Generally, the children in these families do not attempt to replace the person in power, and the "expert" parent remains the one who everyone tries to please throughout their life.

Such children, as adults, try to insulate themselves from ever feeling like a bothersome, incompetent person by striving to be the expert as often as possible. These adults may choose career paths in which they're seen as an expert or seek to be the most knowledgeable person in their peer group at work. They frequently choose friends who are receptive to being criticized.

They feel more secure when their friends and coworkers recognize them as the "expert," but the dark side of the position of the expert is that it's often accompanied by the freedom to offer harsh criticism at will. Because this is subconscious, your friend may have little awareness of how critical she can be.

Addressing this imbalance in a friendship will require you to communicate to your friend that she seems to feel comfortable offering criticism. It's likely that your friend will have difficulty seeing herself as critical and claim that she was only trying to "help." Don't be daunted by defensive responses like: "Oh, well fine, I thought you wanted my help." Or "I just assumed that you'd want to know (how it could be done better, what others thought of you, etc.)." Try to avoid debating whether the comments were criticisms or helpful tips, and instead focus on how they made you feel. It's beneficial to ask the friend for constructive steps that she thinks could be taken if she's adamant about wanting to help. And know that because this is a comforting pattern for many people, your friend may choose to end the friendship if you're no longer open to hearing her critical feedback. Sometimes we're not aware of the implicit contracts underlying our friendships until we attempt to change the dynamic and encounter staunch resistance.

Before addressing your critical friend, I recommend sitting in meditation and asking your spirit some of these questions:

1. Which of my parents was the most critical of me?
2. How are those criticisms still influencing my behavior?
3. Do I have friends who I'm overly critical of? How am I rationalizing my criticisms?

4. Which friends are critical of me that I'm tolerating because I assume they're trying to help me?

5. How can I bring this pattern to their attention in a respectful way?

Obtaining the answers to these questions will help you engage with your elevated intelligence when you're interacting with friends who reign over you in a toxic way.

I noticed that a new client named Olivia had rescheduled her session four times, so when the day arrived and she logged on to our Zoom call, I was curious about the nature of her schedule. Olivia, it turns out, had booked under a pseudonym because she's a Grammy award–winning singer who's used to concealing her true identity. Olivia told me her sister had recommended that she contact me to help her clear up a persistent throat irritation before she went on tour the next month, and she apologized for the rescheduling.

With thick mahogany-colored hair and large blue eyes, Olivia was as beautiful and charming "in person" as she appeared in her TV interviews. She seemed rather quiet and reserved—not what I'd expected given that her pop hits were frequently about strong, bold women. She mentioned that her manager was the reason for her repeated rescheduling.

"My time is not my own, generally," she said with a shy smile. "Most of the time I'm going where I'm told to go by Sharon. But that's the nature of this business, I guess."

Olivia's spirit vehemently shook her head no, so I paused the conversation and asked, "Can you tell me more about Sharon?" (Olivia's spirit confirmed that my question was important by showing me a giant image of a target with an arrow landing in the bull's-eye.)

Olivia looked momentarily confused but quickly recovered. "Uh, sure. Let me think. Sharon's been with me since the beginning. We were high school friends and then she got a job working as an assistant for the president of my record label. She's the one who got me my first meeting with Barry, my producer, and the rest is history. I hired Sharon right then as my manager, and she's been with me ever since."

I smiled and asked, "How would you describe Sharon's personality?"

Olivia immediately responded, "Oh, that's easy—take charge!" She chuckled as she continued. "When we're on tour, everyone calls her Sharon to her face, but behind her back they call her the Little Emperor, after Napoleon. She's on top of every detail and seems to know how everything needs to be done. She's brilliant and pretty amazing."

I was watching Olivia's energy as she described Sharon's personality, and I noticed how her energy receded as if she was hesitant when interacting with Sharon's energy. The energy in Olivia's throat also began pulsing, which drew my attention.

I asked, "What's the interaction like between you and Sharon? More specifically, who has more power in that relationship—you or Sharon?"

Immediately Olivia bristled and sat up straighter. "Well, I do—she works for me!"

I smiled reassuringly but pressed on. "Of course, but who typically gets their way if the two of you have different opinions on something?"

Olivia hesitated and then said, "Well, I guess it depends on the situation." But her energy had already clued me in on the answer as it dimmed and seemed weaker.

I decided to offer a hypothetical to help her see the pattern. "What about if you want to take a lunch or dinner break and she wants to delay that break?"

Olivia looked thoughtful. "That actually happened two days ago, and Sharon insisted that we practice for another hour before breaking because she thought she'd heard me hesitate on one line of a song."

"But you felt like you were prepared, and you were ready for a break?" I asked.

She looked down before answering. "Yeah, I knew that we were all set. And Enrique, my bass player, looked beat and I knew that everyone else was tired and hungry."

"And what happened?" I asked.

"We listened to Sharon and kept playing and stayed for the extra hour. Which was fine—she was probably right that it was better to stay and practice some more."

"But you felt prepared, and you wanted to stop and take care of your band members?" I asked.

Olivia smiled self-consciously. "Yeah. I mean, they've all been working really hard lately, and we're ready for this tour. But Sharon likes to practice until *she* feels that we're all prepared."

I didn't want to sound too critical of Sharon, so I said, "That sounds difficult—to be in a position where you want to take care of yourself and the people in your band but also follow the advice of someone you respect."

Olivia nodded glumly and then looked up quickly. "Wait!

Are you saying that Sharon is the reason my throat has been so irritated?"

I channeled Olivia's spirit: "Sharon isn't causing your throat irritation directly, but she is causing you to doubt your intuition and your own experience. Because she took the lead in the beginning of your career, guiding you and teaching you the business, she's assumed that she'll always be the expert and that everyone should defer to her. And now that you know as much as she does, this hierarchy no longer feels comfortable for you."

Olivia twisted a tendril of her shiny hair around her pointer finger as she digested that. "I think you're right—I mean, I think that my spirit's right—about that. But I don't want to fire Sharon!"

Her spirit continued. "It's not recommended that you fire Sharon. It's far more valuable to remodel the relationship to accurately reflect both her skill set and yours."

Olivia scrunched up her nose in confusion. "What does that mean? And what does it look like?"

"It means recognizing that you frequently defer to Sharon even when you feel that her decision isn't in your best interest because you try to avoid her criticism."

"Ugh! That's true! Crap—it's like I'm living with my dad all over again!"

"Please tell me a little bit about that," I invited.

Olivia made a face like she'd tasted something sour. "My dad thinks that he knows better than everyone else—about everything. I grew up with him saying things to us kids like 'Why the hell did you do that?' 'That was dumb; now I'll have to redo it'—you know, shit like that. I hated feeling like whatever I did was never good enough, so I left home as soon as I could."

I smiled. "Life has a way of repeating those painful patterns once we're grown so that we can work through them as empowered adults."

Olivia laughed bitterly. "Well, apparently I'm not doing a very good job at that!"

"Don't be too hard on yourself. We often don't even realize that we've replaced a critical parent with a critical friend because the behavior is so familiar that it goes unnoticed. Especially when the friend starts off the relationship being legitimately more skillful in an important area."

Olivia had picked up a pen and was tapping it nervously on her desk. "Okay, let's play this forward to tomorrow when I disagree with something that Sharon has a strong opinion about. Which frankly is just about everything. Let's say I tell her that I want to do it differently..."

"What do you think will happen?" I asked.

Olivia looked worried. "I remember a few times when I pushed for what I wanted or stood up to her criticism of me or the people that work for us. She either stormed off in a huff or looked hurt and said, 'I thought you trusted me to do what's right for your career.'"

Without waiting to hear from Olivia's spirit, I shared. "I've learned through years of channeling clients' spirits on this topic that the first step is to decide that you can live without that friendship if necessary. Can you and your career survive without Sharon's guidance?"

Olivia sat up straighter and smiled. "Absolutely," she said confidently. "I don't want to lose her as a friend, but my career would be fine. There are other managers out there."

"Good!" I beamed. "As soon as you realized that you began

reclaiming some of your energy from Sharon, and the dynamic between the two of you shifted. I can already see it registering in the energy in your throat—can you feel that difference?"

"Oh, wow! I actually *can* feel that!" Olivia exclaimed. "It's like my throat cleared and relaxed instead of feeling tight and itchy."

I continued. "Great, so now it's a matter of turning up the dial of awareness whenever you're interacting with Sharon. Try to notice when you defer to her way of doing something in order to avoid receiving criticism or guilt. Be willing to advocate for yourself and your employees. Sometimes it means honoring your own wisdom instead of choosing what will keep the peace in that moment."

Olivia looked concerned. "But it's not always going to feel like a battlefield, is it? 'Cause that sounds too stressful."

I shook my head no. "I encourage you to decide right here and now that you won't allow your work environment to feel like a constant battleground. Making that decision pulls even more of your energy back from Sharon. Once you're clear on that intention, you'll have an easier time making boundaries with Sharon. And typically in such cases the so-called expert backs down and adapts to the new, more equal relationship."

Olivia raised her eyebrows. "Okay, what happens in the not-so-typical cases?"

I gave a small smile. "The friend can't accept anything other than being the leader in all matters, and she leaves the relationship. It doesn't happen often, but occasionally it feels too uncomfortable to not always be seen as the expert."

Olivia pondered what I'd said. "Well, my spirit was smart to give me a symptom in my throat, 'cause that definitely has me motivated to resolve this!"

Olivia's spirit chimed in. "The throat symptoms were used to help you notice an unhealthy dynamic that was depleting your energy in a myriad of ways and leading the other band members to doubt your leadership. It's time for you to recognize your own expertise and to honor your ability to make good decisions."

Over the next few months, Olivia had four more sessions and received her spirit's guidance on handling specific discussions with Sharon. During the first month Sharon considered finding another job, and during the third month Olivia considered firing her! But after a few months of power struggles and awkward conversations, they settled into a healthier dynamic where each of them respected the other's wisdom. Olivia points out when Sharon is being critical so that she can pressure others into doing things her way, and Sharon does her best to accept the feedback and become more flexible. Their friendship remains, they're still working together, and "Olivia" is performing in London as I write this chapter.

If you have a friendship that includes unhealthy criticism, your first task is to notice the hurtful feedback and the effect that it has on you. Do you point out when your friend's comments feel painful, or do you assume that she's right and resolve to try harder? I encourage you to have conversations with your spirit and obtain guidance on how to gently but firmly set new boundaries with your critical friend so that you can feel emotionally safe within your friendship.

In the next chapter, let's look at a different friend—the competitive friend. The one that tosses out statements that make you feel like you're running dead last in a race you don't even remember entering.

CHAPTER 21

TOXIC FRIENDSHIP PATTERNS

The Competitive Friend

As Levi walked into my treatment room, I noticed that his normal confident stride was missing; this Levi looked tired and defeated. His sandy hair was tousled like he'd been running his hands through it, and his brown eyes looked pleadingly at me as he said, "I really need my spirit's advice today."

I smiled and replied, "Sure, let's jump right in."

Levi sighed as he slumped down into the chair across from mine. "This is probably a small matter compared to the big injuries and illnesses that other people come in here and ask you about..."

I interrupted him to say, "Levi, if it has you feeling this deflated, it's absolutely worth asking your spirit about. Don't rank your stressors on an imaginary scale with other people's issues."

He sat up straighter. "Okay, so here's the thing. It's my best friend, Tony. We've been friends since college—we were both poor kids from out of state, attending on scholarships. He was the best man at my wedding, and I love the guy, but..."

I waited for him to finish his sentence.

"...but he drives my frickin' crazy! Everything's a competition with him. Which is cool if we're playing basketball at the gym, but Jesus, he never lets up! Our jobs aren't at all similar, but Tony finds a way to compare them anyway; and of course, he's always doing better than me. I feel like I can't even have a normal conversation with him—he's always asking me questions just so he can top my answer. I mean, I could tell him that I got in trouble at work, and he'd tell me about some time when his boss had a meltdown and threw a printer at him. Anything to top whatever I'm saying—good or bad."

When Levi finished, I asked, "And do you find yourself getting caught up in the competition?"

"Yes!" Levi exclaimed angrily. "It's so stupid! And when I hang up the phone, I'm mad at myself for getting drawn into some imaginary contest. I used to love hanging out with him, and now half the time I feel like I want to punch him in the face."

Levi sat back looking spent and a bit guilty. "I'm hoping that my spirit has some wise words to offer me."

Let me pause here and offer some insight into the friends that are competitive. What drives this behavior, and how can you transform it? Highly competitive people frequently believe that if they're not "the best" or "the most," then they're essentially invisible or unimportant. This belief can stem from a family culture or experiences in school.

A childhood that can produce hypercompetitiveness in adulthood may look like a parent who favors whichever child is the most impressive that day. It's not uncommon for parents to set their children up to compete for their attention and approval. This may take the form of comments like:

- Why can't you be more responsible like your brother?
- Your sister gets As in English—why can't you?
- Score a goal in today's game so I'll be proud—don't embarrass me.
- See how thoughtful your brother was? He took the trash out for me.

Once children are encouraged to compete for love, it becomes deeply ingrained in them to perform for acceptance and inclusion. Hearing your parents comment that your brother is Dad's favorite and you are Mom's favorite can cause division and competition between siblings as everyone tries to maintain their favored status.

School can also be a place where children learn to be competitive for popularity. Sports are only one way that kids compete to see who's "best." Gossip is also a hot commodity— information is power, and people will compete to gather information so that others will come to them to hear the latest. Even being worried about performance—on an exam or in an oral presentation, for example—has become a topic of competition for some teen girls, and parents have reported to me that their daughters seem to compete for who is most in need of comfort, and the swarm of girls will swoop from one girl in need to the next like a murmuration of soothing starlings. It's understandable for people to seek ways to solicit attention and reassurance during times of insecurity and self-discovery.

No matter how your friend developed their competitive behaviors, they currently believe—on some level—that unless they are the "most" or "best" at something, they aren't worth noticing. This is a painful position to be in and can be painful for those around this person too. Transforming this behavior involves noticing your role in the dynamic and then gently bringing your friend's attention to the competitiveness.

It's natural for us to notice our friends' goals and accomplishments and to compare ourselves. But when these comparisons trigger our own insecurities and we feel anxious whenever we aren't "winning" or being viewed as the best, this tendency becomes corrosive to the friendship. We can even slip into not wanting our friends to do well because their achievements raise the bar for us, putting pressure on us to keep up with their success and the material possessions they acquire.

If you have a friendship that includes an unhealthy amount of competition, you may find yourself simultaneously wanting to spend time together and dreading it. What begins as playful sparring can quickly turn into intense pressure to outdo the other person. In the midst of all that competition, it's easy to overlook the damage that is done to both people's self-esteem and the casualties the friendship suffers in the process. Luckily for us, our spirits are quick to notice these sorts of patterns. Levi's spirit had some valuable information for him on this topic, so let's return to his session.

I channeled Levi's spirit, who said, "Let's talk about the inflammation in your body that's been creating joint pain for you over the past six months."

Levi looked surprised. "Does that mean my spirit has nothing to tell me about Tony?"

I smiled. "Not necessarily. It means that this is where your spirit wants to start. I suspect that it's related to your friendship issues, so let's just go with it for now."

Levi nodded his head in agreement, so I closed my eyes and resumed listening to his spirit.

"When you think an inflamed thought, you produce corresponding inflammation in your body. This is true for all humans."

Levi interrupted me. "Wait—what counts as an inflamed thought?"

I translated his spirit's answer. "An inflamed thought is one that has strong negative emotions behind it such as anger, exasperation, indignation, or outrage. It may help to imagine writing down your thoughts; if you'd put an exclamation point at the end of the sentence, then you can assume that such thoughts create inflammation in the body."

Levi threw his hands in the air. "Well hell, I'm a dead man because I have about a million inflamed thoughts a day!"

I smiled in reassurance and kept relaying what his spirit was saying. "You do indeed produce many inflammatory thoughts each day. But you also produce many positive and reassuring thoughts, which send signals to the body to produce soothing chemicals, which reduce inflammation and calm the central nervous system."

Levi considered this and then asked, "How do I know which kind of thoughts I'm producing more of? Is this like a big math problem that I need to be calculating in my head every day?"

His spirit patiently answered, "The inflammation levels in your body will tell you which thoughts are in the majority. Currently, your relationships with Tony and your boss are prompting your thoughts to center on the feelings of exasperation, indignation, and powerlessness. Such feelings and thoughts greatly increase the inflammation in your body, which is felt most acutely for you in your knees and shoulders."

Levi's eyes opened wide. "Yes, my knees and shoulders have been killing me! I just assumed I was getting too old to be playing basketball with the twenty-year-olds at the gym. But I'm surprised that my spirit mentioned my boss, Jim. How is that relationship leading to inflammatory thoughts?"

His spirit paused for a moment and then continued. "While you're aware of Tony's competitive nature, you don't seem to be aware of how you entertain competitive thoughts with your boss. You question his approach to work projects and meeting sales quotas. Your thoughts tend to focus on ideas like: 'I would do a better job of handling these leads. I should be doing his job—he's not any more skilled than I am; he just has better connections.'"

I opened my eyes and saw Levi looking sheepish. "Damn! That's so true! So does that mean I'M the nightmare? Is Tony competitive with me because I'm the jerk who makes everything into a contest?"

"No," his spirit reassured him. "That's not what's being reported. But your scrutiny shouldn't be limited to only noticing other people's competitive nature. Comparing yourself to others is common, but when your observations focus on how you'd do things differently and be better, it creates a competitive vibration in your energy field. This energy is likely to attract other competitive people and will influence the thoughts and feelings of the people you interact with."

Levi rubbed his hands through his hair, making it stick straight up. "Well, this is humbling!" He laughed. "It's sounding like I'm more of the problem than Tony is! Okay, what does my spirit suggest? How do I fix this?"

"It's not that you are *more* of the problem. It's that you've become so comfortable with competitive thinking that you're not noticing yourself doing it until you're upset or insulted by it. The first step is acknowledging that you want a different dynamic in your relationships. This will raise your awareness when you're engaging with others. Then, notice your thoughts and be more deliberate with them. Focus on how you can be supportive instead of better-than. Your success has never been limited by someone else's achievements. Try not to view life as one finite pile of success or money in which others' achievements deplete the amount of success that's available for you."

Levi sighed. "I think I do approach success that way—like it's a giant pie, and if someone gets a slice, then there's less available for me. That sounds pretty self-absorbed!"

I quickly spoke up to stop his berating thoughts. "Your spirit says that this competitive way of assessing yourself began in childhood and was fueled in college. Does that resonate for you?"

Levi thought about the question and then said, "Yeah, it does. My dad loved sports, and the better I did in basketball the happier he was with me. I mean, he always said that he was proud of me no matter what, but man, he beamed and strutted around like a peacock when I scored a lot of baskets in each game. Then in college I got accepted into a tough program in the business school where we were all competing for a small number of internships. I worked my ass off and got one, but that time period definitely reinforced the idea that other people's winning came at my expense."

I empathized with Levi. From the time we enter grade school, we are frequently pitted against our classmates to coax us into pushing ourselves to perform better. And our methods of marketing products are typically based on ideas of scarcity like: "Limited quantities—buy quick to get yours!"; "Limited time only"; and "Look younger than your friends; leave them all wondering how you did it." All of this can amount to a culture that sets us up to pay very little attention to our overly competitive thinking and leads us to compare ourselves to others and feel lacking in some way.

His spirit offered, "Notice when your thoughts about someone else—Jim or Tony—include judgments. Judgments about how you would perform better, be more patient, sensitive, driven, successful, etc. Then pause and ask yourself to come up with a thought that is supportive or complimentary to that person. It will shift your energy and shift the dynamic of the conversation."

Levi squinted at me. "Will that really work?"

"Let's try it now," I suggested. "Go back to the last conversation you had with Tony. What were you discussing?"

Levi closed his eyes. "Okay. We were talking about my in-laws coming to stay and how my mother-in-law drives me crazy. So of course, he launched into a story about how his MIL drinks too much wine and gets sloppy drunk every night."

I grimaced. "Yikes. Okay, let's imagine that after Tony said that you said something complimentary to him. Play it forward in your mind; how do you think it would go?"

Levi chuckled. "Well, this is embarrassing. I actually don't know how it would go because I'm always so focused on holding my half of the conversation that I don't think I've ever acknowledged him like that before. It's like I'm afraid if I give him a little bit of credit that he will puff up like a giant puffer fish and dominate the whole exchange."

"Well, just try imagining saying something positive and encouraging to him. Make one statement out loud."

Levi took a deep breath. "Tony, man, I'm sorry that your mother-in-law gets boozy when she visits. I'm sure you handle it gracefully though."

I sat and waited for Levi to open his eyes. When he did, he looked surprised.

"Wow. That was really... unexpected. As I said something nice and supportive, MY energy changed. I didn't feel competitive! That's what you and my spirit are trying to show me, isn't it?"

I smiled and nodded. "The energy of competition takes two people to maintain. The first step in transformation is to notice the pattern, and then look for how you get caught up in it. I agree with your spirit: if you can train yourself to shift gears and offer supportive comments instead of trying to engage in one-upmanship, you'll change the dynamic."

Two months later when Levi had another session, he breezed into my treatment room looking confident and relaxed. He reported that his knee and shoulder pain had almost completely vanished and said he was pleased with the progress he'd made since our last session.

"It's crazy!" he said beaming. "I had no idea how often I was inviting the competitive conversations with Tony; I rose to take the bait every time he made a comment about his work or other successes. And one time when he topped me on a story I shared, I actually said, 'Sure, Tony, but I don't want to compete with you, so if you want to talk about your work some more, then we can.'"

"How did he respond?" I asked.

Levi chuckled. "He stammered and said, 'Dude, I'm not competing with you.' But after that he was more aware during our conversations too. It's so much better now, and I actually enjoy playing basketball with him again! He's been less competitive there too."

"That's great!" I replied. "And what about with your boss, Jim?"

Levi grinned sheepishly. "I admit that it took me a bit longer to get those competitive thoughts under control. I had to acknowledge that there was a lot of jealousy underneath my competitive judgments. I was trying to make myself feel better about not getting his job, and the truth is that he is really qualified and good at the job, even if he has a different approach than I do. So I've calmed my ass down about that situation too, and I have the reduced inflammation to show for it!"

"I'm impressed!" I said. "And pleased for you too because you feel happier and more content, which is the ultimate win, right?"

"Absolutely!" Levi agreed.

If you're aware of a competitive pattern between you and a friend of yours, here are some questions that I recommend asking your spirit in meditation:

1. How do I fuel the competitive dynamic in my friendships?
2. When did my competitive patterns get reinforced in childhood?
3. How can I break the competitive exchanges that I tend to have with my friend?

4. What insecurities do I have that lure me into getting triggered to have competitive exchanges with others?
5. How can I define success for myself rather than comparing myself to my friend's ideas of success?

We all desire success and recognition, but it's vital to define success based on your own goals and trust that your friends have their own visions of success. How do you define success for yourself? It's worth taking some time to write down your thoughts on what comprises a successful life for you—personally and professionally. This can help us to stay centered in our own path instead of abandoning it to pursue what we think will impress our friends.

There are many possible dynamics in friendships that can be challenging, but hopefully the examples given in these Toxic Friendships chapters can help you begin to understand and transform some of the dynamics that feel upsetting or draining to you. The suggested questions for you to ask your spirit can also serve as a stepping-off point, as they can be adapted to ask about other frustrating situations within your friendships. May we learn to build healthy friendships with energy exchanges that form a solid foundation underneath each of us!

The next three chapters deal with the subjects we sometimes love to hate—money, annoying coworkers, and career goals. Let's talk about work!

CHAPTER 22

WORK ISSUES

Your Relationship with Money

What's the craziest thing your parents ever told you about money? My friend's mother told her, "You're too pretty to work." Yikes! For every zany money statement that you remember, there are likely three others that you've forgotten about. But guess what? You haven't *really* forgotten them. They're lurking in your subconscious mind, shaping how much money you allow yourself to earn, spend, and save. If you're unhappy about how much money you currently have, this chapter is a valuable resource for uncovering the hidden blocks between you and financial abundance.

Your parents aren't the only ones who deposited limiting beliefs into your subconscious; we receive input from every family member, teacher, and even from our culture. Maybe your grandma has been commenting about how women have to work harder than men ever since you were a toddler, so you don't even question the statement anymore; it just lives in the background of your mind. And last Tuesday when you were at work and thought that a man was working harder than you that day, you started worrying about being fired. Then you beat yourself up for having anxiety "for no reason." This is an example of how our subconscious uses familial or societal beliefs, perceived "rules," and policies to influence us.

So how do you start uncovering the limiting beliefs that affect the jobs you get, the money you have, and your sense of worthiness on the topic of abundance? You take a quiz.

My spirit gave me this quiz years ago to help me flush up beliefs that I held on the subjects of money and work. Here's the catch: For this to help you, you can't give the response you think sounds good. I want you to give the answer that you're afraid might be true. The goal is to have our subconscious fears speak up and reveal themselves. Speed is your friend during this quiz.

I recommend answering every question in less than thirty seconds. Jot down the phrase that answers the question and move on to the next one. Don't stop and groan about any one answer you find yourself giving—finish quickly so that you don't give your conscious mind time to start analyzing your answers. I recommend writing your answers on a separate piece of paper so that you can repeat this quiz in the future to see how your answers change. Ready? Rapidly answer these questions:

1. When I was growing up, my mom's strongest fear about money was _____.

2. The main reason that I don't have more money is _____.

3. I think my dad's biggest belief about money is _____.

4. In order to get more money, I will have to _____ _____.

5. If I was very wealthy, one problem I'd have would be _____.

6. It's not good to be seen as impressive or successful by lots of people because then this happens: _____ _____ .

7. One choice I made in the past that affects my abundance now is _____ _____ .

8. People who are wealthy are judged as being _____ _____ .

9. I don't have enough _____ to be really successful.

10. If I tried something big and failed, _____ would never let me forget it.

That's a lot of "unveiling" to do, and if you're feeling disheartened, please take a deep breath—I've got you. Now that you're aware of these limiting beliefs, you can start to reprogram them, and you'll see big changes in your life as a result. We reprogram these oppressive beliefs by:

1. Discovering them
2. Finding evidence that they're not always true
3. Choosing a new belief/rule/policy that we can believe

Let's start with looking at the fears and beliefs that you listed as belonging to your parents. Does your financial situation reflect that you may believe what your parents believe? You don't have to prove your parents wrong, but can you find some evidence that contradicts their beliefs? Try to identify several people who are similar to you and who are not appearing to validate your parents' beliefs. Once you find several exceptions to the rule, see if you can shift the rule from being *always* true to something that is *occasionally* true. Then you can decide to make yourself an exception to their rules as well.

What do you believe you will have to do to make more money? Is your response to question four universally true? Or is it something that you're afraid might be true for you? Again, look for evidence that supports the theory that your belief is a maybe, not an absolute rule. Then decide on a new answer that honors who you are and what you're capable of now that you have your spirit's guidance. For example, if you answered that in order to make more money you'll have to work harder, you can now use this substitute: "In order to make more money, I will need to use my intuition to guide me toward increased income."

Questions five through eight reveal hidden fears you may hold about the dangers in being "too big" or too successful. Sometimes just noticing/writing down an irrational fear that we hold helps us release it. Other times we will have to actively unwind that belief and its stranglehold on our desire to shine. And of course, question ten deals with the fear of failure that we can all experience to some degree.

In the next few days, you may notice yourself remembering old sayings and money stories from your childhood. The comments from your past that bubble to the surface can be great material to take into your next conversation with your spirit, who is happy to help you dissolve any limiting beliefs you uncover.

Here are some questions that you can ask your spirit:

1. Where did this limiting belief (_____) originate?

2. What evidence is my ego-mind holding on to that "proves" this belief?

3. Where have I seen or experienced evidence that contradicts this limiting belief?

4. How can I move forward feeling less restricted by this limiting belief?

5. What is the biggest limiting belief that I'm ready to release?

6. How do I see myself as unworthy of abundance?

Here's a story of my client Ethan who broke free from a limiting belief that had put a ceiling on his income for decades.

While I was living in Southern California, a new client showed up at my door looking like he wasn't sure he wanted to be there. Ethan had booked a session after one of his friends at work raved about the great advice he'd received from his spirit during one of my group classes. His smile looked nervous and his energy looked tentative, but that's not unusual for a client's first session.

When he'd booked his session, Ethan had listed "stomach issues" and "stress" as his primary concerns, so I began there.

"Please tell me about the biggest areas of stress in your life right now," I asked.

Ethan began shaking his leg and fidgeting with the lid to his water bottle. "My work is super stressful, which is probably why my stomach is always a mess. I live on antacid tablets."

I cringed inwardly at the thought of him frequently downing antacids, and I asked, "What do you do for work, and what makes it so stressful?"

Ethan thought for a moment. "I work for a big talent

agency—we represent a lot of A-list celebrities, so it seems like everyone wants to work there. I want to say that it's stressful because it's such a competitive environment—and it is—but really I think my stress boils down to frustration that I'm not making more money. There are agents who started at the same time that I did, and they're easily making $200k more than me. And representing actors who do bigger projects. I just... I really can't figure out why I'm so stuck at this level. I've been making the same salary every year for the past five years—it's ridiculous."

I smiled. "Well, that might explain your digestive issues. Frequently, when we spend a lot of time beating ourselves up, that negative energy gathers in the stomach area, compromising digestion and leading to problems."

Ethan sighed. "Yeah, I beat myself up constantly. I'm always looking for reasons why I'm not signing more talent, and I'm sure that the problem is me. But I work really hard for my clients, and I get them great movie deals and endorsement contracts! I just don't get it..."

I connected to Ethan's spirit, knowing that would be the fastest way to figure out why Ethan's career was not matching his expectations. Ethan's spirit requested that I ask him about his father.

Ethan looked puzzled and said, "My dad's not even in the entertainment industry! He's in politics—a career I'd never go into."

I raised my eyebrows to ask Ethan why, and he continued. "My dad is very successful, but he's... well, he's not a very good man. He uses his power to take advantage of people. I grew up swearing that I'd never be like him 'cause he only cares about himself."

Ethan's spirit showed me a bull's-eye, so I knew we were on target. I returned to channeling and repeated what I heard: "Your spirit says that as you watched your father's behavior, you connected his success with money and power and selfishness. Now, in order to avoid being cold and selfish like your father, you block yourself from becoming successful and powerful."

Ethan looked like he was going to fall off the sofa. "I...I... I want to say that's wrong, but I can feel it take my breath away, so I know it's true! So does this mean that I'll never let myself be successful?"

I shook my head. "No, it means that we have to unravel this inaccurate limiting belief. Right now, your subconscious mind is using this policy as a guardrail, protecting you from being like your father. Can you think of someone who is successful and powerful but is kind and generous?"

"Sure—the guy I coach kids basketball with down at the YMCA. Phillipe is one of those guys who made a ton of money from a tech start-up, and he's very generous with both his time and money. Oh! And there's a guy at my office who's known for having really high integrity—the top talent all want to sign with him because he's so authentic and he's protective of his clients."

"Great!" I responded. "Growing up, your father's selfishness was hard on your family. Your spirit says that it was painful for you to watch how cruel he could be to your mother."

"He was such an arrogant prick to her sometimes," Ethan agreed.

"Well, your ego-mind was determined not to treat others the way that your father treated his family, so your child's mind made up a rule based on the causative factors that you could understand at the time. And that rule was something like: to avoid being an arrogant, selfish person, don't get too successful and powerful."

Ethan nodded. "Makes sense. So how do we unravel that dumb guideline and replace it with a more accurate one?"

"The more examples that you can think of that 'disprove' your ego-mind's rule, the more you weaken your belief in it. The problem with our inaccurate, limiting beliefs is that when we're not aware of them, our ego-mind is in the background collecting 'proof' or evidence of how those beliefs are accurate. But the ego-mind doesn't even notice the facts that disprove its theory."

Ethan frowned. "It sounds like my ego-mind is, like, the worst scientist ever! Only noticing the evidence that backs up its lame theory."

I chuckled along with Ethan. "Yeah, it's true. Your mind wants to help you avoid being someone you don't like, but it's not doing it in the best way. So the first step in eliminating your limiting belief is to notice it, which your spirit helped us do quickly. Then you find evidence that the policy isn't the best way to get you what you want because others have found a way to be both successful *and* a good, kind man. Then you reassure yourself that you can pursue your goals of success without being like your dad."

"How do we do that?" Ethan asked.

"Well, I know that you want to be more successful, but your spirit is telling me that you're fairly successful now. Have you behaved in any ways similar to your father so far?"

Ethan shook his head no. "I really don't think so. Can you double-check me and ask my spirit?"

I repeated the answer from Ethan's spirit. "You are very kind to people, but sometimes you can be so kind and accommodating that you don't negotiate firmly enough for your clients."

Ethan shrugged. "So there's nice, and then there's me being a doormat."

I held up my hand. "It's not that bad, I promise. Your spirit just says that sometimes when you're working so hard to avoid being thought of as mean or selfish, you can 'overcorrect' and be too accommodating. Trust me, this is a minor flaw! But your spirit shares this to reassure you that you are far from being selfish and thoughtless."

Ethan's spirit helped him shift his focus away from getting everyone to like him and instead to trust his own business instincts so that he deferred to others less. His spirit also helped him unearth another similar belief, which was that as long as he made less than a certain dollar amount each year, he would never be like his father. Ethan quickly agreed that it was not the high salary that made his father behave hurtfully, and as he released this belief, I saw the energy around him change dramatically. Suddenly it looked like the Aurora Borealis above his head. When I asked my spirit what was happening in Ethan's energy field, she told me that he had just opened the floodgates for himself regarding abundance and success.

I was eager to hear about Ethan's progress in his next session, and when I opened my door and saw his big Cheshire cat grin, I was delighted. He was animated and started talking even before he sat down.

"You're not going to believe it!" he almost yelled. "Well, you're you, so maybe you will believe it. I left here seven weeks ago, and since then I've signed four major actors and already closed movie deals for two of them! I've completely broken through my self-imposed income ceiling."

My grin matched Ethan's. "And you're still not like your father!"

Ethan nodded. "Yeah, I get it now, and as soon as I notice myself being hesitant to advocate for myself or my clients, I remember what my spirit said and I trust my knowledge of the industry."

By the end of that year, Ethan was representing six more lead actors on hit TV shows, and his income reflected his success. That is the power of discovering your limiting beliefs around money and success and working to release them. This isn't a promise that you'll become a millionaire overnight. But trusting in the process and sticking with it helps you break through your blocks and change your narrative so that you're more open to receiving abundance.

Trust me, the quiz in the beginning of this chapter can change your relationship with money, work, and abundance. And once you're on the lookout for those hidden limiting beliefs, you're going to start hearing them come out of your mouth, and you'll smile knowing that once you've discovered them, you're on your way to releasing their hold on you.

What about the issues you have at work that aren't related to your own limiting beliefs? For instance, that annoying guy who works in your department and constantly takes credit for your work? Or the woman who helps herself to your lunch from the breakroom fridge? The next chapter can help you move through those "people issues" at work.

CHAPTER 23

WORK ISSUES

People Issues

It's not surprising that the most common topics clients ask for help with in sessions are health, relationships, money, and work; these areas of our lives are huge determinants of our happiness and fulfillment. I want to set you up for success in every area of your life, so let's talk about getting your spirit's advice on the people who can make your work life difficult.

Numerous studies have shown that *who you work with* is a bigger influence on your job happiness than the *kind* of work that you do. In other words, "work issues" are almost always "people issues."

In your current workplace, do you feel appreciated? Do you feel respected and listened to? Do you enjoy most of the people that you work with? If the answer to some of these questions is "no," then it's time to ask your spirit for some help.

Workplace advice from the spirit world inevitably focuses on setting effective boundaries by using clear communication. Most people with lots of work stress need help in articulating their desired boundaries and then enforcing them. And one of the big factors in confidently laying out your boundaries is having clarity about what you need in order to excel at work and how to ask for it. Your spirit can provide great coaching in this area.

Most of us decide that we need better boundaries once we've been upset by someone else's behavior. Your boss or coworker may have been dismissive or disrespectful, or they may have ignored your requests. When you're agitated or your feelings are hurt, it can be difficult not to lash out or complain to others about the person who's mistreated you. But my clients' spirits typically advise that the first step is to address the "offender" directly so they have a chance to clear up any miscommunication on their part.

Try to share your point of view while staying neutral and not assigning motive to the other person's actions. For example, don't shoot off an angry email that says, "You left me off the invite to that big planning meeting purposefully to keep me from doing my presentation!" Once you've pushed someone into defending themselves, it can be challenging to return the dynamic to a professional one and clarify any misunderstandings.

In your communication, list the behavior that you've observed and share the resulting experience you had. For example: "I'm curious why I was not invited to the planning meeting; I was disappointed not to be able to share my report with the group. Can we discuss what happened?" Keep this section brief; many people are tempted to go into elaborate detail about how offended or distressed they are, which tends to come across as ranting or harsh criticism.

Once you've shared the behavior that negatively affected you and had a conversation for further clarity, you can state your boundary. For example: "I'd like to be included in all future planning meetings so that I can be more effective and more collaborative in my work." It's important that your boundary not come across sounding like a "wish" but rather a declaration of what you believe that you need to be effective at work. Then you can ask for their feedback by asking questions like "Is there anything that might prevent or get in the way of that happening in the future?" or "Are there additional details that need to be discussed in order to come to an agreement?"

Once you reach an agreement, there is one more important step. If possible, you'll want to include "witnesses" to your boundary setting. Including a witness could look like cc'ing your boss's boss or someone else in your company on an email detailing what you discussed and agreed upon. This witness helps you enforce the boundary later if the agreement isn't respected. The additional person should be someone who has influence over the person you're negotiating with and who's invested in your work performance. This may be a manager you report to, or if the communication is with your manager, then you may want to include your manager's boss on the email. I advise "going above your boss's head" when you need others in power to be on notice regarding your boss's behavior. To be clear, this is not about getting your boss in trouble. You are simply advocating for what you need to excel at work and doing it with the most neutral language you can find.

Frequently in sessions, my client's spirit will dictate some language suggestions to help the communication seem non-threatening but clear. Here are some examples:

- I know that our goals for this project are _____.
  I want to do my part in helping us meet those, and to do so I need _____. (Used by a client whose

boss kept taking credit for her work. By copying the management level above her boss, she was quickly given a raise in recognition of her work product.)

- In the interest of making sure that I'm executing this correctly, I'd love your input on my calculations. (Used by a client whose boss was ignoring her work, leaving her unsure if she was doing well. After this email her boss paid attention to and commented on her work product. Her boss's boss also gave her glowing feedback, realizing that she handled the situation smoothly.)

- My understanding is that my job description includes me being responsible for this deliverable: _____.
  I am happy to include that duty in my work output, but I'll need these resources to do that. (Used by a client whose boss kept ignoring her requests for additional team members because he wanted the praise from the CFO for keeping his budget low.)

- I want to ensure that I'm focusing on the highest-priority work first. So I'm requesting a list each week of our team's priorities for that week, understanding that the priorities can change in emergency situations. (Used by a client whose boss constantly changed his mind about what he wanted the team to work on. With the peer pressure of others witnessing him, her boss became more consistent.)

As you can see in these examples, the focus and tone of the communication is on being a successful employee, not criticizing someone else's behavior. By having witnesses to your communication and your requested boundary, you increase the chances of a reasonable, helpful response. You also put that person on notice that you're willing to notify others if your career is significantly impeded by their actions. During meditation your spirit may suggest a variation on the examples above, but this gives you an idea of the recommended approach.

Once your boundary has been set (hopefully somewhat publicly), then you must be ready to enforce it if necessary. Many clients assume that enforcement looks like getting angry at someone and yelling or threatening a consequence. But I find that determined questioning can be even more effective than ranting or raving. Again, it's important that your energy remains relatively calm but very firm. It's this unwavering quality that will make your boss or coworker uncomfortable since you're coming across as calm but unwilling to let go of the issue until you receive a satisfactory answer.

It might be helpful to hear a few more examples from my clients' work situations:

Julianna had emailed her boss and asked him to give her assignments in a written email because he had a habit of changing his mind regularly, making it impossible for her to successfully complete her assignments. He wrote back and said, "Yeah, sure" and then changed the subject. Then he gave her another assignment orally while they were walking down the hall. Julianna sent him an email that afternoon repeating the assignment he'd spoken to her and restating her need for written priorities. She began the email with the statement: "I appreciate you agreeing to give me my assignments in writing so that I'm clear on what's expected from me. What I heard you asking me for as we walked today was this: _____. Did I hear you correctly and is this the new highest priority?" Julianna copied her boss's manager on the email so that she'd have a witness. Her boss wasn't happy, but Julianna looked innocently at her boss and said, "Well, you know that it's very important to me to do well here at the company. I'm just trying to make sure that I stay on target." Both her boss and her boss's manager have now been paying more attention to Julianna's work, and her assignments are now sent to her in writing.

Trevor had repeatedly asked his coworker Duncan not to present their team's work without the rest of the team present, but Duncan couldn't resist bragging about the work project at a gathering of the managers. Trevor asked a colleague to stand with him as he pulled Duncan aside during a break and said, "Duncan, I remember us talking about you not presenting teamwork unless all of us were in the room. Can you help me understand what was so urgent that you felt compelled to break that policy?" Duncan waved his hand and attempted to make a joke about how it was no big deal and that Trevor and the other team members shouldn't be so sensitive. Trevor replied, "They're not being too sensitive. They're protecting their work product so that you don't keep taking credit for work that isn't yours. If it happens again, I will have to bring this to our boss's attention." Duncan never did it again.

Amy had spoken to each of the upper management team members, asking for an additional member for her team. Each of them individually agreed, but collectively they never voted to increase her budget so that she could hire someone. When Amy again asked each of them, they put her off by saying that a budget increase needed to be voted on by the entire group of partners. Since Amy wasn't invited to those meetings, she was feeling blocked and frustrated. Two days before the next partner's meeting, Amy sent an email to all of them collectively that said, "I wanted to take a moment to thank each of you for agreeing that my department needs an additional staff member. I know that you have many items to address in your meeting, so I wanted to ask that you please remember to vote on the budget increase needed for me to make the hire that you've all agreed I should make." She was given her increased budget within the week.

Here are questions that you can use as a starting point when talking to your spirit about your work:

1. What are the primary reasons that I'm not enjoying my work?
2. How can I more effectively communicate with _____ _____?
3. How do the actions of _____ interfere with my success at work?
4. What obstacles currently exist at my work that I can remedy?
5. Are there ways that I can be a more effective communicator in my job?
6. What boundaries are recommended for me in my current job?

Marlene's story can provide another example of the effectiveness of clear communication and boundaries.

Marlene arrived at her online session looking professional but frazzled. She was wearing an ivory silk blouse and striking jewelry, but she also had two pairs of reading glasses perched within her shiny auburn hair and a cell phone in each hand. She looked more ready to spring into action than to sit calmly and talk with her spirit.

"I don't even know where to start," Marlene began. "I just know that something's got to change, or I'm going to work myself into an early grave."

I sent Marlene calming energy as I asked her where she worked and what her job title was.

"Well, my job title *should be* 'Doer of everything that my boss doesn't feel like doing'! But my actual title is assistant supervisor of shipping, and the company is one that no one's ever heard of but we supply 30 percent of the boxed cereals in the grocery stores."

"Please tell me the aspects of your job that you think cause you the most stress, and then I'll ask your spirit how she would answer that same question for you."

Marlene pulled one of the pairs of reading glasses off her head, glanced at them and frowned, and tossed them aside. She sighed and said, "My boss recruited me two years ago. We'd both worked for a big consulting firm, and when he got his job he convinced me to leave the firm and work for him. I've been very loyal to Bruce ever since, and he takes advantage of it. He doesn't even read most of his emails now—he just forwards them straight to me! So I'm doing my job and at least half of his job. And there's no one that I can complain to about it; his manager is in another state, and I have no real access to him. So I'm perpetually overworked and underappreciated."

I nodded, then connected to Marlene's spirit, who said, "Bruce recruited Marlene because he knew she was a hard worker and could figure out new systems quickly. He trusted Marlene to figure out the procedures and computer programs used in the new company; he trusted her so much that he didn't even learn some of them himself. And now he's used to passing along that work to Marlene and is oblivious to how he's overloading her with work."

Marlene fumed. "Argh! How can he be oblivious to how much I'm working? I'm literally ALWAYS here! As he leaves the office every day, he walks right past my desk and sees me still working."

Marlene's spirit responded, "Sometimes people choose to be blind to things that would make them uncomfortable. Bruce doesn't want to see himself as someone who exploits the people who work for him, so he does not pay attention to your long work hours."

Marlene slumped in her chair. "Yeah, that sounds about right. He's choosing to be ignorant about how his laziness affects me because then he might feel bad. So do I need to quit?"

I smiled. "Actually, your spirit recommends that you stay in your role but that we work to change your daily experience to one that feels satisfying to you."

Marlene perked up momentarily. "Well, I'm all for that! But I admit that I don't know if we can really change this situation."

Marlene's spirit was a lot more optimistic than she was and had great advice. "Your spirit is saying that we need to get more people witnessing how hard you're working. The suggestion is to start off with an email to Bruce's boss, Mark. In this email you can state that you're concerned that you may not be doing everything correctly and that you don't want to create issues down the road for Mark or others. Then ask if you can copy him on some of the issues that you're handling so that he can confirm that your work is on target. Once you have Mark's permission, then you can let your boss, Bruce, know about your email to Mark and that you will also copy him on these 'check-in emails.'"

Marlene's eyes opened wide. "Whoa! That sounds risky. Won't Bruce be upset?"

I repeated Marlene's spirit's response: "He certainly won't like it, but it is not an offense that he can terminate you over. And you'll stick to your assertion that since you're relatively new, you want your work to be reviewed. This is your excuse to get other sets of eyes on your work output. Your goal is to stop focusing so much on keeping Bruce comfortable and instead be strategic."

As she tapped her pen nervously on her desk, Marlene said, "Okay, I can see that it's time to do things differently. Saying that I can't get anyone higher up to notice my workload is just me feeling stuck. And my spirit's right—one of the upsides of me doing so much of Bruce's work is that he is pretty dependent on me, so he's unlikely to fire me for writing one email that goes over his head."

Over the following months Marlene studied with me and began hearing her spirit's advice without my aid. Her spirit coached her on how to continue drawing attention to her work products. She also coached Marlene on making boundaries around her time. In one group meditation session, Marlene's spirit dictated specific wording for an email to Bruce that said, "Our company promotes the importance of having a healthy work/life balance. To invest in my mental health, I'm embracing this idea and will be shutting down my computer after 7:00 p.m. each day. If there's an urgent matter I can be reached via text, but I trust you to only text me if absolutely necessary." Marlene was nervous but trusted her spirit's advice and her own elevated intelligence about her value to Bruce, and she sent the message. The email yielded a sarcastic comment initially but then a 70 percent reduction in after-hours requests. Marlene learned to get comfortable with the initial discomfort of pushing back on Bruce's demands.

Marlene appeared for her fourth private session looking delighted but quickly blurted out, "I'm scared shitless! Wait till I tell you what happened!"

The emails to Bruce's boss, Mark, had the desired effect of alerting the managers above her to how little work Bruce was actually doing. Bruce was fired and Marlene was offered his job.

She looked alarmed. "I've gone from delighted at this promotion to terrified that I'm going to fail. I know how to do half of the things that Bruce was supposed to be doing. But the other half is new to me, and I'm feeling in over my head."

I smiled and passed along the message from Marlene's spirit. "Your spirit says that you need to hire someone like you to be your assistant. But you'll differ from Bruce in that you won't overwork that person."

Marlene confirmed that her old position had not yet been filled, so she was actually performing two full-time jobs. Her spirit advised, "This is a chance for you to practice getting clear about what you need and then asking for it."

Marlene chewed the end of her pen as she thought. "I need someone who learns fast and likes to work collaboratively. Actually, I think that I could really excel at my job if I had two people under me because now that I'm here I can see how inefficiently this department has been run."

I grinned at her. "Your spirit is nodding her head enthusiastically and is ready to coach you through reorganizing your department. Let's start with getting clear about the way you think it should be structured, and then your spirit will help you articulate your vision."

Over the next few months, Marlene laid out a detailed plan of how she thought her department could be running more efficiently, and her plan included two assistants reporting to her. Marlene was given the budget and the go-ahead, and she reorganized her department, listening carefully to the people who reported to her. In her morning meditations, Marlene's spirit coached her on listening attentively to her staff so she could provide them with the tools they needed to perform well. As a result, Marlene's department doubled its productivity within eighteen months, and she was offered yet another promotion. Marlene refers to her spirit as her "favorite career coach," and we still work together occasionally so that her spirit can elaborate on messages that Marlene may have misunderstood or not been present enough to hear. Marlene has learned that with her spirit's help, she can shine at work and still have a balanced life.

It's true—your spirit can be an excellent "career coach," helping you navigate tricky dynamics at work and identify areas that will bring you more fulfillment. Your spirit has additional "work goals," and understanding them can bring peace to your career journey, even during frustrating moments. In the next chapter, we'll explore your spirit's key career objectives.

CHAPTER 24

WORK ISSUES: WORKING WITH YOUR SPIRIT'S "CAREER GOALS"

YOUR EGO-MIND'S CONCEPT OF SUCCESS

How do you define career success for yourself? Do you have an idea of where your definitions came from? As discussed in Chapter 22, our beliefs about money and success are typically shaped by the perspectives of our family, friends, and the culture we live in. You might not realize it, but your spirit probably doesn't share your same views about success.

For most of us, money tends to rank high as an indicator of success. Wealth is the most common way of measuring one's accomplishments, and in general the more money you have, the more power, prestige, and admiration others offer you.

In addition to financial wealth, many people seek status. Sometimes this is limited to status within your field, and other times people seek worldwide fame. Many have come to associate fame and its resulting attention with love and admiration, so they strive to "gain followers" in order to feel important and accomplished. Being seen as an expert is another goal that some pursue, as being "the best" can also bring special status and privileges.

Even if you're not pursuing fame or a specific title, most of us want to be viewed as hardworking. Being incredibly busy is now its own sort of status, as it implies that what you do is critically important. Our culture tends to offer more admiration for those who've earned their wealth rather than inherited it. Because we live in a society that values the hardworking individual, nearly everyone believes that they have to "earn" wealth and success through their hard work. So it may surprise you to learn that your spirit is more triumphant when you figure out how to attract your desired results rather than work hard to earn them bit by bit.

YOUR SPIRIT'S CONCEPT OF SUCCESS

As you've probably guessed, your spirit has very different career goals than the ones your ego-mind holds. Our spirits measure success not by our list of accomplishments or the amount of money we earn, but by the number of powerful lessons we've had, the loving connections we've made, and the personal growth we've embraced. Your spirit's not tracking your savings account or how many times you've switched careers. Instead, the focus is on how your understanding of love, compassion, and forgiveness grows each year. Your ego-mind may feel excited when you receive a raise at work, but your spirit's pleasure comes from you pursuing personal healing, forgiving a loved one, advocating for yourself, and examining feelings of vulnerability.

In a world driven by success, sometimes this concept makes my clients worry that their spirit doesn't support their dreams of prosperity. But don't worry—there's good news.

There's another facet of your spirit's goals that can help you achieve all manner of abundance. Your spirit loves to demonstrate that the Universe's bounty is always available to you. Believe it or not, one of the reasons we incarnate is to have fun as creators, deciding what we want and then making those things happen. So how do you utilize the desires of your ego-mind to tap into this reservoir of magical manifestations? Playful collaborations with your spirit are in order! Here's how to enlist your spirit's help.

If you're reading this book, you've probably heard of the law of attraction, which states that things vibrating at similar frequencies are drawn to each other. Teachers of this principle promise that if you make yourself a vibrational match to your desire, it can't help but manifest into your experience. But I've had clients working diligently to hold themselves into vibrational alignment with their dream house or job or relationship for months with no results, so we've realized that things may not be that simple. *It turns out that your spirit must also align/agree that the item, relationship, or event is in your best interest.* Think of this as a sort of veto power your spirit holds if your desired outcome doesn't serve your present growth. While clients may initially view this as their spirit having too much power, once they realize that they ultimately tend to obtain the growth *and* the desired object or relationship (or something better), they usually change their minds.

I want to assure you that your spirit places great importance on your ability to learn and create what you desire and is enthusiastic about helping you manifest your dreams. Allow me to share a formula that I've been offering to my clients for over twenty years, helping them effectively manifest their heartfelt desires.

1. Identify what you want—the promotion, the raise, a new job, etc.
2. Journal about why you want it. This may seem obvious to you, but it's an important step because your spirit may have an even better idea or an easier way to get you what you desire than the path that you're imagining.
3. Sit in meditation and let your spirit know what you want and why you want it. I recommend also saying something like "This or something even better." This acknowledges that you may not always know what will make you the happiest, so you're presenting the best thing you can come up with currently.
4. Then ask your spirit for feedback. Your spirit may let you know that your desired result is on its way or that something better is being arranged and will arrive in the future.
5. I usually conclude such meditations with a statement like this one: "I trust the Universe's ability to deliver abundance to me, and I trust the Universe's timing. Spirit, I would like to receive _____; is there any action that you suggest I take now toward this goal?"

These steps can yield results that prove it's possible to tap into the never-ending abundance of the Universe. Once I learned to work in partnership with my spirit in this way, I began creating amazing relationships, work opportunities, and the ideal house and garden. You're going to love seeing how your spirit can wow you!

Before we go further, I want to clarify something that confuses nearly every one of my clients. It's a concept you've likely been taught to value that your spirit doesn't fret about: completion. We live in a culture that teaches "Don't be a quitter!" While it might be helpful to encourage children to stay in the game, this principle is often stretched far beyond sportsmanship (and childhood) to prioritize finishing *everything* we start. Our spirit knows that we can lose track of whether a pursuit is still right for us once we become determined to "check all the boxes" or "cross the finish line."

Just as you enjoy the phases of a character's journey in a movie, your spirit appreciates moments when something reaches its natural end for you, whether it's a job, a specific work project, or an entrepreneurial business venture. This is different from "seeing something through till the end," which involves sticking to a predetermined plan no matter what happens. Your spirit wants you to pay attention to how something feels emotionally and honor when something no longer excites you. When you notice that feeling of "I think I'm done here," I recommend that you follow it and see what feels like the next natural step for you. Your spirit won't see it as quitting but as noticing—and accepting—an invitation to the next chapter.

So how do you recognize when you've completed something and it's time to move on? First, give yourself permission to feel if a job or a project within your business feels flat and uninspiring to you. Second, notice when you stop learning and growing in that area. It's possible you may feel called to stretch into deeper learning, or to teach what you've learned to others, or to simply move on. As you learn to honor when each chapter of your work life feels complete, your career will feel more purposeful and synchronistic.

Now that you understand completion from your spirit's point of view, let's move on to the good stuff. Given that you and your spirit may have different ideas about your career trajectory, how should you ask your spirit for advice in this area? If you're unhappy in your current job, I recommend asking your spirit for help in understanding why—the answers may surprise you. You can also ask how your current job serves your spirit's broader purposes. This question shows you understand that how you show up in your job each day is more important to your spirit than the salary or work product you create. Here are sample questions that you may want to ask your spirit:

1. Why do I have such communication challenges with _____ in my office?

2. What is there for me to learn from my issues with how this company is run/how I'm being managed?

3. I sense that _____ and I push each other's buttons. Can you help me see how to diffuse this tendency so that we can work together amicably?

4. How does my current job serve my broader purpose? (This can be a fruitful question because the answers can illuminate what your spirit is wanting you to experience in this chapter of your life.)

5. I'm grateful for the income from this job, as it gives me a nice quality of life, but I don't understand why I'm still at this position. Can you help me understand my next best steps? (It's helpful to ask your spirit for the next recommended step rather than the end goal, which can change as you evolve.)

This idea of asking your spirit for the next recommended step is an important one. Sometimes your spirit simply wants you to take one step, observe something, and then be done. It's natural to assume that when we feel the nudge to "go for it!" we're meant to realize the goal. But remember that your spirit is seeking out experiences for you, not instant achievements. So check in frequently to see if you're still feeling drawn to continue forward.

Here's a story about a client who spent months feeling very confused by her spirit's career choices.

When Keavy booked a session online, she wrote on her client intake form that she was "in a career spiral." Curious to hear more, I logged on and smiled at the auburn-haired woman looking back at me. Her green eyes looked troubled, so I jumped right in, asking, "What do you want to focus on during this session?"

Her thick Irish accent was beautiful, but her sadness was unmistakable. "I'm quite spiritual, and I've been a seeker for some time now. I've been praying and meditating to try and create a role for myself in the publishing industry here in the US. I truly felt the guidance to come to New York City for this job, but now that I'm here I see that it was a big mistake. I'm miserable and now I'm stuck here."

"Why are you stuck there?" I asked softly.

"It's a long story, but this publishing company sponsored me for my work Visa and paid me a year's salary up front. So now I'm legally obligated to stay for another nine months. And not only is it an awful job, but it's a position far below what I was doing back in Ireland. It feels like self-inflicted career suicide."

I connected to Keavy's spirit, and the first thing she told me was that Keavy's intuition was accurate—she *had* felt her spirit nudge her to accept the job in the US.

"But why?!? Why would my spirit tell me to step toward a thing that would make me so miserable?"

I returned to my conversation with Keavy's spirit, hoping that I'd be given answers that would reassure her. "Your spirit tells me that the primary reason for your unhappiness at this job is your coworker. He seems very arrogant and dismissive of you."

Keavy nodded her head. "Aye, you have his number alright! Thomas is his given name, but I refer to him as the Big Arse when I'm not at work. He thinks he's smarter than everyone, especially me. I can't stand his cockiness, and I don't think he cares much for me either."

Curious as to why Keavy was steered toward working with someone so unappealing, I reconnected to her spirit, who said, "Working with Thomas is trying, but this job is good for you even though initially it might not appear so. You have learned your way around a new city and a new country, and you've made great friends outside of work."

Keavy frowned. "Aye, but c'mon! There have to be good people for me to meet in other places where my career doesn't look like it's going in reverse!"

Her spirit radiated comforting energy as she said, "There are many reasons why this is the best place for you right now. I'm going to ask you to have faith and trust that your initial feeling was accurate—this *is* where you're meant to be."

I heard from Keavy again three months later. She reached out asking for help with back pain, so I expected to see her in discomfort; what I didn't expect was to see her covered in mud.

"Hi there, please forgive my appearance—I'm in Santa Barbara helping to clean up after the mudslides here."

I'd watched the news and knew that Santa Barbara had first suffered devastating wildfires and then massive mudslides when the winter rains came.

Keavy continued, "My grandparents lived here and they're quite old and fragile. They're certainly not able to shovel mud, and it flowed right into their living room! My boss was very understanding, and he gave me time off to come help them and even paid for my ticket to fly to California!"

"Wow! I'm glad that he was so compassionate, and now I understand why you're having back pain."

"Aye, this work is a far cry from sitting at a desk all day! But you want to hear something wild? Thomas is here!"

"Oh dear," I said. "Does he have relatives there as well?"

"Apparently his whole family is from here—he and his brother moved to New York City, but everyone else is still here. So he traveled out here on the same flight I did. At first I was exasperated, thinking, 'I can't get away from this guy!' But on the third day, he showed up at my grandparents' house! He said that his family was doing okay, and he wanted to help me take care of my grandparents. We've been working really well together; by the evening we're exhausted, but he never complains."

My eyes were wide. "Well, that's certainly surprising to hear! Thomas sounded rather arrogant and self-absorbed when we talked last time."

"He was! That's how he came across at work for sure. But once we started working together, he started telling me about his family. He said his dad was really hard on him and his brother growing up. It led both boys to be very driven, but I guess it led to Thomas being defensive and coming across as arrogant and selfish."

I grinned. "I love that you're seeing this other, softer side of him."

Keavy had more to share. "Two nights ago we went out for dinner after working hard all day. We each had two drinks, and I guess they softened him up even more. He apologized for how he treated me at work and admitted that he felt threatened by me. We had a really good talk, and I told him that he tries too hard to convince everyone that he's better than they are. It alienates him and will hurt his career. I felt like I was giving advice to my younger brother. It felt like he heard me! He's really trying to make changes."

At this point Keavy's spirit jumped in to say, "Keavy, you've had a past lifetime with Thomas, one where you were fellow business owners who helped each other. You had a karmic agreement to connect with him in this lifetime if possible and help him see the power in being humbler and more vulnerable."

Keavy's eyes opened wide. "Wow! Maybe that explains why I had such a strong reaction to him when we first met. Like a bit of dread because I felt this connection as though he was going to be in my life for a while."

Keavy's spirit nodded her head and said, "Yes, it's not uncommon to feel a type of soul recognition when you encounter someone you've had past lifetimes with. And now that you've helped Thomas shift, your karmic debt to him is satisfied."

"What does that mean?" Keavy asked.

"It means that you can continue your relationship with him or not—whatever you choose. And now the next chapter can unfold for you."

"Well, that makes me nervous," Keavy said with a chuckle. "This chapter wasn't exactly easy."

"But it's been powerful—for both you and Thomas," I said.

Keavy sighed. "Agreed. Still, it's all been a bit daunting. And a pain in my back, literally—ha!"

I had Keavy lie down on the floor so that I could see her and use energy to adjust her back similar to how a chiropractor might. Within ten minutes I'd adjusted the two vertebrae that were out of place and recentered her hips. When she stood back up and moved around, she was astonished.

"Holy cow! I'd say that the pain is 90 percent better! That's incredible!"

I explained that the remaining pain was from the inflammation and that an over-the-counter anti-inflammatory should resolve that.

Two months later Keavy made another appointment, and I was pleased to see that she signed into our session mud-free. This time she wanted help with a knee injury and some relationship struggles between her and her mother. But she led off the session with her exciting news.

"Ready for my great news? The last day that I was helping my grandparents in Santa Barbara, Thomas's brother came by to pick him up. We all grabbed lunch and Kevin—that's the brother—told me that he's in the publishing industry too. Thomas started telling his brother how good I am at my job and that my talents are wasted in the role I'm in now, and Kevin offered me a job! I was able to negotiate with my former company and return some of the up-front salary they'd paid me, and now I work in my dream job! Can you believe it?"

My smile was huge. "Yes! I can believe it—and I love when

the Universe's plans reveal themselves quickly enough that we can see the perfection at work. I'm so happy for you. Is Thomas still at the other company?"

"Yes, he said that he couldn't work for his brother—they'd kill each other. But I still talk to Thomas every week and give him grief if he's going back to his old ways of being closed down and obnoxious."

My relationship with Keavy has continued, and I've loved seeing her career soar in the publishing industry. Her spirit understood Keavy's career goals but was willing to take a circuitous route to get there so that she could help a friend from a past lifetime learn how to open his heart. Now Keavy can agree that her spirit had a wise plan when she nudged her to accept her first job in New York City.

Hopefully you're now feeling prepared to ask your spirit questions about your health, your career, and the people you work with. What's left to explore? Maybe you're curious about your pets, family members, or even celebrities and acquaintances. In the next chapter, I'll provide additional insights on how to seek guidance from your spirit regarding these scenarios, including the furry ones.

CHAPTER 25

ASKING YOUR SPIRIT ABOUT OTHER PEOPLE & PETS

This is good stuff! You've taken a monumental step in personal growth and connected with your spirit. Then you explored questions about your health, your relationships, and even your work. This relationship with your spirit allowed you to develop your elevated intelligence, which guides you to behave more intuitively every day. But I know that you won't want to stop there, as there are so many other aspects of your life that your spirit can advise you on. This chapter can help guide you through some of those subjects. Let's begin with how to ask your spirit questions about your loved ones.

QUESTIONS ABOUT OTHER PEOPLE

One difficulty in asking your spirit for information about other people (especially those you care about) is that you're usually very invested in the answer. Remember how challenging it was to be fully open to any possible details that your spirit might give you regarding your health or your romantic relationship? It can be just as difficult to get our ego-mind's fears and assumptions out of the way when asking about our family members and friends. Because we love these people, we naturally hope to "hear good news," so it's very important to apply the Expectation Eraser before sitting down to connect with your spirit. (For quick reference, the Expectation Eraser is detailed on page 20.)

If you've used the Expectation Eraser and still can't hear any messages from your spirit regarding your loved one, there's an important question for you to ask before you go any further: *"May I have this information?"*

Over the years I've learned that there are some questions our spirits can't answer for several reasons.

The first reason is that you're "not allowed" to know the answer. This might be because it's really not your business to know if your friend is cheating on her taxes—or on her spouse! It may also not serve you to know something before your loved one knows it. I've seen this type of "information block" happen when my clients have asked their spirit if their daughter was pregnant (before the daughter knows), happy at her job, or if she's gay. There are pieces of information and realizations that should occur first to your loved one, not necessarily to you. So asking if you may have the information keeps your curiosity in check so that you don't trample over other people's boundaries.

The second reason your spirit may not answer a question is because you're either asking the wrong question or the answer is beyond what you can comprehend. Here's an example of asking the wrong question: one of my advanced students, who was proficient at hearing her spirit, asked in meditation if her new Siamese kitten would mature into a cat who'd deliver healthy kittens if she chose to breed her. Her spirit kept fading away, signaling that she couldn't have the answer. Out of frustration, she took the kitten to the vet and discovered that the "female kitten" she bought was actually a male! Her spirit couldn't accurately and fully answer the question, so she declined to answer.

I've also had spirits refuse to address a question when the answer involves information that we, as a species, have not yet discovered, or that I myself cannot understand. (If the answer involves engineering and advanced mathematics, I can get lost quickly.) If you try several times to ask your spirit a question and don't receive an answer, try asking if you may have the information and/or if you need to frame your question differently.

Here are some questions that you can use when asking for insights about your family and friends. For these questions, let's assume your sister's name is Beth.

1. What can you tell me about Beth's current situation?
2. What is the best way for me to support Beth right now?
3. Do I have a role to play in Beth's recovery/process?
4. Am I in the way with how I'm helping Beth now?
5. Are there resources that I can help Beth find that will assist her?

QUESTIONS ABOUT YOUR CHILDREN

Asking questions about your children is another area that can get tricky. Now that you've developed your elevated intelligence, you may begin sensing things about your child's emotional and intellectual growth and be curious to ask your spirit for more details. And it's also natural to want to know how to help our children move through difficult situations. But sometimes your child's spirit may ask your spirit to withhold information so that your child can finish having a particular experience. Even painful events can be very powerful teachers for our children, and as parents we can struggle with wanting to honor their growth process but hating to see them unhappy. Again, I recommend asking your spirit if it's advisable for you to have information on the current situation with your child.

Here are questions that you can use when asking your spirit about your young children:

1. Is my child having difficulties that I'm not noticing?
2. Are there ways I'm parenting that are confusing or diminishing for my child?
3. How can I correct this unwanted behavior without shaming my child?
4. What are ways that I can boost my child's health?
5. How can I support my child's development of compassion (or forgiveness)?

As your children become teenagers and adults, the boundaries will change regarding what your spirit will tell you about their personal details. Remember that our first goal in asking the spirit world for information on our loved ones is to improve their lives; if they feel that their privacy has been violated, then we've detracted from their experience. I try to respect the autonomy of any child over the age of twelve or thirteen, asking them if I may please be of service by asking the spirit world for helpful information. Sometimes they may refuse the help, but I trust that eventually their curiosity will tempt them to ask for advice from the spirit world. Often when I work with teens, I find that their biggest stressors may not be the things their parents think are stressing them. So I usually start a session with a teen by asking, "If you could change one thing about your life (not your appearance but your life), what would that be?" Their answer is then our starting point for questions.

Here are questions that you may want to ask your spirit when you want to support your teenager (let's call him Brian for these questions):

1. What do you see as the biggest challenge that Brian has currently?
2. How can I help Brian feel more loved?
3. Are there steps that Brian can take to thrive in his life?
4. How can I support Brian's health?
5. Are there areas where Brian needs to feel more supported by me?
6. Is there something that would be soothing for Brian that he's not aware of?

QUESTIONS ABOUT STRANGERS

What about people who are complete strangers? It can be easier to accurately receive information on them because you typically are less invested in the answer. But there may still be a block— your spirit's respect for another person's privacy.

In general, I find that if someone is a celebrity, then our spirits are willing to answer some questions about their life because such people have chosen to be public figures. But even with celebrities, I find that the spirit world is hesitant to indulge in gossip simply because you're curious about, say, the faithfulness of a pro athlete or the income of your favorite celebrity chef. If the person you have questions about is unknown to you, your spirit will generally not reveal much about that person's personal life.

What if you want to know how much your boss earned last year? Or if your coworker got a bigger bonus than you did? It's very unlikely that your spirit will answer these questions, as they fall outside of the realm of your personal health and spiritual development.

QUESTIONS ABOUT YOUR PETS

One area of great curiosity and delight for my clients is asking questions about their animal companions. Have you ever seen those photo collections of people who look like their pets? Those similarities might run deeper than just surface appearance. In fact, our pets can play a certain role in mirroring aspects of ourselves that we may not be aware of. So while the bulldog who looks like his owner makes us grin, there is occasionally something else that's happening between their spirits that you might want to know about. Let me explain with a client's story.

A few years ago, a client named Sally contacted me for a session. When she arrived, she looked guilty, which piqued my curiosity. As she settled onto the sofa in my treatment room, she cast her large hazel eyes downward and nervously twisted her long brown ponytail.

She took a breath, exhaled, and said in a rush, "I'm not here to ask about myself—I want to ask about my dog, Bart. I know that you're a medical intuitive for people, and your website doesn't mention pets, but I'm hoping that if I show you a video of him, you'll pick up on what's wrong with him!" At this point she teared up and began quietly crying.

I handed her a tissue and said, "No problem—I'm happy to help if I can. Tell me about Bart and his symptoms."

Sally blew her nose and looked at me hopefully. "This dog is the longest relationship I've ever had! I've had him for nine years, and he's been such a love muffin. He's moved with me several times, and he's seen me through my brief disaster of a marriage. And now he's limping and the vets can't figure out why. He's been to two specialists and had every X-ray and scan that they could think of, but we have no answers."

"When did his symptoms start?" I asked.

"Four months ago. I hate that he's in pain and I can't fix it," Sally said, fresh tears filling her eyes.

"What else was happening around that time?" I asked. "Did anything in your life change?"

She thought for a moment. "Work has actually been pretty calm this year... Oh, I know! Four months ago was when Scott asked me to move in with him! But that can't be it, right? I mean, Bart came with me when I moved into Scott's place, so it's not like he was left behind, even for a day."

I could see Sally's spirit over her right shoulder, and she held up her finger to pause us at this point. I immediately connected to her spirit to ask why the move was relevant to the dog's symptoms. Her spirit suggested that I ask Sally to describe her relationship with Scott.

"He's a good guy, he really is," Sally insisted, "but he can get intense and worried about me..."

Hmmm, that response felt very carefully worded. "What happens when Scott gets intense and worried about you?" I asked.

Sally looked self-conscious. "He worries if I go to art classes and poetry readings at night 'cause we live on a fairly dark road. And he also worries if he thinks I'm spending too much time with my family, and I guess they can be a bit much."

I hesitated and then repeated what Sally's spirit said to me: "Scott describes himself as worrying, but he's actually using that word to coerce Sally into limiting the activities that he doesn't like."

Sally opened her mouth to object, then closed it. "I want to argue with you and my spirit, but I guess it's kinda true. Is she saying that Scott is bad for me, and I should break up with him?"

I smiled reassuringly. "No, she's not saying that you should end the relationship—spirits rarely give that definitive an answer about relationships. But she is asking you to more accurately notice what's happening. Your spirit says that after your marriage ended, you had the fear that you'd never find another partner. So when you met Scott and enjoyed his company, you were thrilled when he asked you to move in with him. But you choose to minimize how controlling his behavior can be. He, in effect, hobbles your movements. And your beloved dog is mirroring this for you."

Sally's eyes opened wide. "You're kidding me! Bart is trying to show me how this relationship hobbles me? But he's a dog! No offense to Bart, but he can't figure out how to get his tennis ball out from under the coffee table! How is he able to assess my relationship and give me relationship advice?"

"That's a great question, which leads to an important distinction. Your dog's conscious mind is limited in its capacity to understand concepts—like the physics of getting a ball unstuck. But your dog's *soul* incarnated with the purpose of being your companion and your mirror."

"My mirror?" Sally queried.

"Yes. All pets come to us for the companionship and the loving connection that we have with them. But some pets also come to mirror things for us—things that we might have trouble seeing for ourselves. Your spirit is telling me that Bart had digestive issues during your divorce—do you remember that?"

Sally leaned forward. "Yes! I was constantly cleaning up dog barf even though he was eating the same food he'd always had. It did not help my stress levels at the time, let me tell you."

I grinned. "I'm sure. But your spirit says that you were having trouble digesting your life at that time, especially how you saw yourself—as a woman who was cheated on."

Sally grimaced. "Ugh, yeah. I was so determined not to be cheated on like my sister was, and yet there I was, dealing with the same damn situation! I couldn't believe that it was happening to me."

"Well, your spirit is confirming that Bart was feeling the upset that you were feeling and displaying it in a way that was hard to miss."

Sally looked confused. "So what do I do now? If I stay with Scott, then Bart will remain in pain?"

I wanted to reassure her. "I'm confident that your dog's symptoms are not meant to force you to act in any particular way. Let's start with preparing you to have a conversation with Scott where you tell him that you don't want to feel manipulated into avoiding your friends and your family."

The remainder of the session was spent helping Sally get clarity about her relationship so that she could speak confidently about the aspects of it that she wanted to change. Then I sent healing energy to Bart to help his leg and hip pain.

Two weeks later Sally came back for another session. Her step was lighter, but I could tell from her energy that she was still conflicted.

"Well, Bart's doing better..." Sally began. "But I'm still not sure what to do. That little bugger is really holding my feet to the fire!"

I smiled and asked, "What do you mean?"

"Two nights after our session I spoke to Scott. The conversation went badly. Like, really badly—with me crying and Scott yelling. I ended up packing an overnight bag and going to my friend Darla's house. Of course I took Bart with me, and do you know that as soon as we got to Darla's house, he stopped limping? I mean, c'mon! You can't make this shit up."

"Then what happened?" I asked.

"Well, that got my attention! But I also remembered you saying in our session that he wasn't trying to force me to leave Scott, just notice things. So I accepted Darla's invitation to stay with her for a week. And I paid attention to how I felt instead of just telling myself that everything was 'fine.'" Sally held up her fingers to signal air quotes, and I realized that she was seeing her pattern of suppressing what she wanted in order to keep her partner happy.

Sally looked somber. "Bart and I went back to the house to get more clothes, and he didn't limp at first, but when Scott started guilting me about how lonely he felt with me gone, Bart walked to the kitchen limping. That made me realize that I was once again focusing on soothing Scott and ignoring what I wanted!"

I grinned. "It sounds like Bart's spirit is very wise and attentive to you. What are you feeling now about your relationship?"

Sally's energy looked heavy but felt determined. She said,
"I'm staying at Darla's place for a while. I'm going to go back to
dating Scott and see if we can remodel this relationship so that
it's not so focused on what he wants. And Bart seems totally
fine! I really can't believe how he has been trying to help me this
whole time."

I wasn't surprised six months later when Sally told me that
she had ended her relationship with Scott and that Bart was now
healthy, happy, and no longer limping. Sally had also met a new
man at the dog park, and so far the relationship felt very healthy
and nurturing.

Please know that every time your beloved pet has a physical
symptom *it is not necessarily a message for you.* I shared this story
to give you a memorable way of introducing the concept that
our pets can mirror things for us—patterns of behavior, emotions, etc. So this concept should be included in your questions
when you ask your spirit for help with a sick or injured pet.

Here are some other ways that my clients' pets have mir-
rored things for them:

- Juliana's cat had an autoimmune illness that went into
  remission when she left the grad school program that
  was toxic for her.
- Roberta had been dealing with anxiety her whole life,
  but when her newly adopted dog developed anxiety, she
  realized how much her fears compromised her daily life.
- George couldn't figure out why his saltwater aquarium
  was constantly cloudy. In meditation his spirit asked

him, "Who is poisoning the environment in your office?" George investigated and discovered that one employee was sexually harassing a newly hired woman.

As I mentioned above, when one of your pets is having an issue, I do not recommend jumping to the conclusion that it's a message for you. But when a pet's issue persists after standard medical care, I do suggest asking your spirit if your pet's symptoms contain a message for you. You can start by asking your spirit, "Is this symptom a message for me, or a mirroring of something I'm not noticing?"

If your spirit signals to you that your pet's symptom is a type of mirror or message for you, then it's helpful to not look too literally at the pet's symptom. Try thinking of the symptom as a metaphor and notice how you feel about the solutions that your spirit suggests to you.

If you sense from your spirit that the answer is no (there is no message or mirroring in your pet's symptom), then you can proceed to ask questions such as:

1. What can I know about these symptoms?
2. Are these symptoms related to diet, behavioral issues, or a medical situation?
3. How can I best help my pet now?
4. Should I be looking for an additional practitioner, or is our vet the best option?

Because our children and pets are so dear to us, it can be extremely difficult to get peaceful and centered enough to connect with our spirit and ask for help when one of them is ill. I recommend getting the medical help you need from a doctor, and then once you're assured that there is no dire emergency, sit in meditation and ask what information you may have. Your spirit is happy to help shed light on physical symptoms whenever possible; I find that my challenge is being calm enough to hear the answers! But the information is available, and your spirit is understanding and will wait until you can meditate and connect.

As we near the end of your manual for having a powerful relationship with your spirit, I hope you feel ready to engage in enlightening discussions with your spirit that can enhance your health, wealth, and relationships. Connecting with our inner wisdom can truly transform the way we live our lives.

CHAPTER 26

PLEASE REMEMBER THIS

Could you have imagined—before reading this book—that you'd be able to tap into the spirit realm and receive wisdom directly from your spirit? How about explanations and details that seem to defy logic? It has been my pleasure to give you the mystical key to open a door that most people do not even believe exists. By this point you not only know that your spirit is delighted to give you information, but you've also hopefully experienced numerous conversations where you received helpful insights.

I truly believe that everything benefits from you having this connection with your spirit and cultivating your elevated intelligence. Everything! As your spirit helps you understand yourself better, you heal old wounds and remove limiting beliefs. You make connections between behaviors that confounded you and events from your past. You can now gain a better understanding of the triggers you have and how those "buttons" were created.

This power to facilitate your own healing and personal growth can be your own jet propulsion, sending you soaring in the direction of improved health, beautiful relationships, and work that feels meaningful to you. There's an unlimited number of topics that you may wish to ask your spirit about, and you have the rest of your life to pursue those questions.

For me, the most difficult part of learning to converse with my spirit was practicing patience. I am admittedly a very impatient person, and I'm still working on this virtue. More than once my spirit has had to remind me, "You're learning a new way of speaking and hearing in order to have this conversation. How long did it take you to learn to speak as a baby?" I know that this is a good analogy, but I'm still working on being forgiving of myself when I make mistakes and misunderstand the insight that my spirit offers. Please be gentle with yourself as you go down this path.

You've got this! I know that you can do it because I've trained so many others to receive information from their spirit. But I also want to remind you that developing your elevated intelligence takes practice, just like playing a musical instrument or learning a foreign language. The good news is that learning to communicate with your spirit generally happens faster than learning to do either of those other things! And once you begin infusing your spirit's wisdom into your decision-making processes, your reliance will shift away from making every decision from just your ego-mind. It will become more natural for you to pause and consider the larger perspective and seek your spirit's input, as you know the value of working from your elevated intelligence. This shift leads to a life that's more glorious every year!

Most of us who hear messages from our spirit develop a type of "shorthand," and you'll likely do this too. For instance, sometimes my spirit shows me an emerald stone when I ask her a question. Emeralds are very hard stones because they're composed of so many layers, and this visual is my spirit's way of telling me there are a lot of layers to my answer, so be patient. And if I smell cigarette smoke when I'm sending healing energy into someone's lungs, this is a signal to me that the client's lungs are compromised. Frequently these clients have never smoked, but this is a fast way for my spirit to tell me that the lungs need extra healing energy. I look forward to hearing all about the shorthand that you and your spirit develop.

When you can't seem to get an answer from your spirit on a particular topic, refer back to the corresponding chapter in this Relationship Manual for tips on reframing your question so that your spirit can give you guidance.

I'm so thrilled to walk beside you on this journey! I believe your life will become continuously easier, more meaningful, and more magical. Painful events will still occur, but now you know that in time your spirit will speak to you about them, helping to bring understanding and self-compassion to the situation. The difference that this makes in one's life is immeasurable. In fact, the comment that I receive most often from my advanced students is this:

"I live with less fear and more gratitude now. I see the 'why' behind so many things in my life, and it fills me with peace. Now I feel safe and well cared for by the Universe."

I cannot think of a more meaningful gift to leave you with than the ability to get answers to everything in your life that troubles or confuses you. Be well, and may your conversations with your spirit feel as mystical and powerful as you are.

APPENDIX

AREAS OF THE BODY WHERE WE TEND TO STORE STRESS

(and What Your Symptoms Might Mean)

Our bodies can be viewed as a sort of road map with particular areas representing different topics we may feel stressed about. When we shove this stress inside and don't process it, that particular "storage area" of the body may become weakened, and our spirit may then send us symptoms to alert us to this compromised area.

To help you understand this road map of the body, I've listed the most common areas for symptoms and the types of messages that get stored there. I've also included reflection questions for you to think about before you meditate and ask your spirit about your symptoms.

* Cautionary note: this reference tool is not intended to be used as a substitute for a medical diagnosis or medical advice.

** I urge you not to use this appendix as a way to limit what you're open to hearing from your spirit. This list suggests the types of stress that are *commonly* stored in each area of the body, but

it's by no means the case in every instance. Once you're familiar with the possible topics that your symptoms may be pointing
you toward, you'll need to push your conclusions aside with your
Expectation Eraser so that you can be open to receive all possible
messages about your particular symptoms.

Back—Upper—The upper back region is where we tend to
store stress related to how supported we feel in life.

QUESTIONS TO ASK YOURSELF:

1. How many people in my life feel supportive of me?
2. Do I make myself open to support and ask for it when
   needed?
3. How can I get more comfortable asking for the support that I need?

Back—Middle—In this area we can store stress tied to how we
relate to ourselves, how we speak to ourselves, and how we treat
ourselves. Soreness here points to a lack of self-valuing that is
calling out to you.

QUESTIONS TO ASK YOURSELF:

1. Where am I hard on myself?
2. Am I more compassionate of others than I am of
   myself? Why?
3. How can I have more compassion for myself?
4. When am I dismissive of myself and my desires?

Back—Low—This area is frequently the "storage bin" for all our
fears about money, sex, and power and how stressed we feel about

these subjects. Having lower back pain usually means that we're feeling disempowered and unsure how to resolve those feelings.

QUESTIONS TO ASK YOURSELF:

1. In which areas of my life do I feel the most powerless?
2. The topics that I have the most stress about are

   _____.

3. What would it take for me to feel empowered on these topics?

Back—Sacral Area—The area of our lower vertebrae and our tailbone can represent our foundation—our job, our family, our place to live, and our community of support. When there are issues in this region, clients are frequently experiencing things like a move, a breakup, or a job loss. When we feel that part of our foundation is crumbling, this lack of stability can register in our spine's foundation.

QUESTIONS TO ASK YOURSELF:

1. Who/what are the important components of my base of support?
2. How is my foundation weak?
3. What will I need to do to strengthen my foundational support?
4. How can I feel stable in the meantime?

Bladder—In this organ we can store stress related to our "unshed tears." We may not allow ourselves to cry because we believe that it's inappropriate or excessive, or because we've shut down our emotions.

QUESTIONS TO ASK YOURSELF:

1. When I cried in front of my parents, this is what happened _____.
2. What topics make me shut down/afraid to feel my feelings?
3. Which memories make me feel that if I start crying, I'll never stop?
4. Do I see crying as a sign of weakness?

Breasts—This is an area of the body where we may store stress that relates to how we are nourished and how we nourish others.

QUESTIONS TO ASK YOURSELF:

1. How often do I feel emotionally nourished at the end of the day or week?
2. Am I good at nourishing myself? (This is distinguished from indulging ourselves with food, shopping, alcohol, etc.)
3. Who in my life nourishes me? Do I enjoy reciprocating?

Ears—You may store fears here about what you're afraid to hear (bad news, rejection, etc.).

QUESTIONS TO ASK YOURSELF BEFORE MEDITATING:

1. What bad news am I afraid of hearing?
2. Who am I afraid to listen to?
3. What have I heard in the past that I'm afraid I can't face again?

Eyes—You may store fears here that relate to what you'll see next in your life.

QUESTIONS TO ASK YOUR YOURSELF BEFORE MEDITATING:

1. What am I afraid of seeing?
2. Is there something I'm starting to see that scares me?
3. What have I seen in the past that I'm afraid of experiencing again?

Heart—Stress that is stored in our heart area tends to be more current than the stress stored in our lungs. These stressors generally relate to how loved we feel by others and how loveable we feel in general.

QUESTIONS TO ASK YOURSELF:

1. Who do I feel loves the authentic version of me/who I really am?
2. How do I show love to myself? (What honoring and nurturing behaviors do I frequently use?)
3. What do I think would make me more loveable? Is this a reasonable standard for me to hold for myself?

Intestines—In this region we store stress that relates to our sense of control over our life. Constipation can result from holding on to power too tightly, clinging to the result that we think is perfect. Diarrhea can result from feeling out of control, like things are slipping through your fingers.

QUESTIONS TO ASK YOURSELF:

1. What aspects of my life am I striving for perfection in?
2. Where do I feel a complete lack of control?
3. What topics make me feel out of control?
4. Fill in the blank: If I don't keep a tight rein on _____, things will fall apart.

Knees—If there's a message for you within your knee pain, it likely relates to being more flexible in your thinking. Often, we don't even realize that we're holding a belief that there's only one way to achieve our goals, and we become rigid in our efforts to accomplish our desires.

QUESTIONS TO ASK YOURSELF:

1. What goals am I pursuing in a determined way?
2. How open am I to new approaches?
3. When was the last time I tried a different way of doing something?

Liver—The liver is where we tend to store anger, so issues with this organ ask us to consider how much anger we're carrying.

QUESTIONS TO ASK YOURSELF:

1. What are the top ten issues that I'm storing anger about?
2. What will it take for me to release this anger?
3. How much anger am I holding toward myself, and is there some way that it's helping me?

Lungs—This is an area of the body where we frequently store grief. If you have symptoms here, it's likely that you're storing grief you haven't fully processed.

QUESTIONS TO ASK YOURSELF BEFORE MEDITATING:

1. What are four painful episodes from my life that still feel raw to me?
2. Which parent do I feel hurt and/or disappointed me the most as a child?
3. My most painful childhood memory is _____.
4. What topic seems to be my biggest emotional trigger?

Neck and Shoulders—While the front of the neck can store stress regarding our ability to speak without fear of repercussions (throat issues), it can also house stress related to our responsibilities. Many of us carry the energy of our commitments and duties on our shoulders, and the result is a tightened neck area and sore shoulders.

QUESTIONS TO ASK YOURSELF:

1. Do I feel that I have too many responsibilities?
2. What would it take for me to pare down my commitments to a more reasonable, balanced load?
3. Am I good at delegating to others? What items could I ask others to handle?
4. How do I know when I have taken on too many responsibilities?

Stomach—This is the region of the body where we store stress about how we view ourselves and how we think others view us.

It's also where we hold tension for things that we're having trouble digesting in our lives.

QUESTIONS TO ASK YOURSELF:

1. What parts of my life am I having trouble digesting?
2. What aspects of myself am I having trouble accepting?
3. What judgments do I worry that others have of me?
4. What evidence do I look for that others are not approving of me?

Throat and Mouth—This area is where we store stress that has to do with speaking our truth. If you have issues in this area of the body, it may mean that you are afraid to speak your truth for fear of the repercussions.

QUESTIONS TO ASK YOURSELF BEFORE
MEDITATING:

1. As a child, what happened when I spoke up for myself?
2. Currently if I speak my truth, what tends to happen?
3. What's my biggest fear in speaking my truth—which repercussions are the most daunting?
4. What phrases do I find yourself "biting back" and holding inside?
5. Who's the person that I am most nervous to speak to honestly?

Uterus and Other Reproductive Organs—This is another area where we can store stress related to the subject of power, but we can also hold stress here that relates to our sexual energy and our fears around money.

QUESTIONS TO ASK YOURSELF:

1. What areas of my sexual energy make me uncomfortable?
2. How can I feel more empowered about sex?
3. What are my beliefs about money? Do I trust myself to earn it sufficiently and spend it wisely?

It's also worth noticing if your symptoms are predominantly on one side of your body. Here's why:

The right side of your body frequently relates to worries about your future.

The left side of your body frequently relates to an upset (or multiple) that happened in the past that still plagues you.

An occasional injury or symptom on one side of the body should not make you concerned that you're worrying too much about your future or your past. But if you notice that your injuries or symptoms are predominantly on one side of your body, this is worth considering.

QUESTIONS TO ASK YOURSELF:

1. How much do I worry about my future?
2. Do I have fears/hesitation about stepping into my future?
3. Do I unconsciously block myself from my next steps?
4. How often do I feel frustrated over past events (versus moving on)?
5. Do I believe that my past will limit me?
6. Does my past limit me more than other people's history limits them?

There are some common conditions that, while not associated with one region of the body, frequently contain common themes or patterns of thinking.

Here are the ones I see most often:

Adrenal Issues—Many of my clients have discovered that their adrenal issues are alerting them to their pattern of racing. Often, they're racing toward a finish line that moves as soon as they get close to it! And after a while the racing behavior becomes a habit.

QUESTIONS TO ASK YOURSELF:
1. How do I define success for myself?
2. How will I know when I've attained success?
3. During my childhood, who modeled my current pattern of "hustling"?

Anemia—I see this condition arise when clients feel overwhelmed and not strong enough to handle what is being asked of them.

QUESTIONS TO ASK YOURSELF:
1. Who set high goals for me as a child?
2. Have I internalized this inner critic's voice in my head?
3. Which responsibilities would I say weigh most heavily on me?

Arthritis—Our joints tend to be a gathering place for negative thoughts and emotions. Studies have shown that people who describe themselves as more pessimistic in nature tend to suffer from more arthritis.

QUESTIONS TO ASK YOURSELF:

1. Do I tend to look for what's right or wrong in a situation?
2. Who are the people in my life that encourage my worries, pessimism, etc.?
3. How can I notice and release my frustrations throughout the day?

High Blood Pressure—Most of my clients have found that their high blood pressure was a physical manifestation of feeling distrustful about how safe the world is for them.

QUESTIONS TO ASK YOURSELF:

1. How safe do I feel in the world?
2. Do I feel like I always have to stay on high alert/vigilant?
3. Who's responsible for making sure that things are "done right"?

Inflammation—My spirit has told me that every time we think an inflamed thought, we create inflammation in the body. An inflamed thought is any sentence or question that would end with an exclamation point. We each have many of them every day, of course, but chronic inflammation invites us to notice how often we have thoughts of alarm or upset.

QUESTIONS TO ASK YOURSELF:

1. How often do I make exclamations?

2. Do I think that my life has too much drama?

3. How often do really terrible things happen to me that have no upside?

Low Blood Pressure—When we feel defeated and powerless, it can result in feelings of exhaustion, as well as low blood pressure. I think of low blood pressure as a hesitancy to "jump into the rat race."

QUESTIONS TO ASK YOURSELF:

1. How do I feel that "the game is rigged against me"?

2. How often do I feel like "the unimportant/insignificant one"?

3. Where do I feel empowered in my life?

Skin Issues—As the largest organ of your body, the skin is frequently used to flush out unwanted chemicals. This might be a substance that you've produced internally such as adrenaline or histamine (which can result in hives or a rash) or a chemical that you've been exposed to such as a virus or a lotion that irritates your skin. Your skin is also a great barometer of when something has "gotten under your skin." I frequently see clients with "mysterious rashes" who have not given themselves permission to admit how another's behavior is irritating them. In such cases, their skin "speaks for them," displaying their irritation in a hard-to-miss form.

QUESTIONS TO ASK YOURSELF:

1. What situation has made me feel irritated recently?

2. Has anyone gotten under my skin?
3. Do I have concerns about getting angry at certain people?
4. What fears do I have about acknowledging my irritation?

ACKNOWLEDGMENTS

I am profoundly grateful to my spirit and all of the teachers in the spirit realm who have patiently answered my questions for nearly thirty years. Thank you for your guidance on this journey, for blessing me with wisdom and abilities, and for helping me to utilize the healing energies the Universe has blessed me with. May the teachings in this book accurately reflect your enlightenment and love.

As I wrote this book, I held in my heart the beautiful clients who have shared their journeys with me, entrusting me with their truths and their healing. Your courage to seek answers is reflected throughout this book, and it has been my privilege to learn from each of your spirits. I hope these stories accurately reflect your transformative experiences and contribute to the collective healing we are all seeking.

Deep gratitude for my friend, collaborator, and "story excavator" Crystaline Randazzo. From you I learned to tell my client stories in a way that allows others to feel the profound nature of a conversation with the spirit world. This book is so much better because you have blessed it with your talent.

My heartfelt thanks to my literary agent, Bonnie Solow, whose intuition helped steer this book's journey. Thank you for knowing when to push because there was more to be achieved. And to Marci Shimoff, who trusted her own intuitive nudges when she introduced me to Bonnie and other brilliant people making a difference in this world. My thanks to Diana Ventimiglia, my editor at Hachette Book Group, for reading this book and experiencing an absolute knowing of its potential to transform lives. Thank you for trusting your own elevated intelligence, Diana.

To my husband, Steven: Your unwavering love shines on me like sunbeams and moonlight spun together, and I'm eternally grateful for how clearly you see me and support my work.

To my beloved family and friends, who have held me through this work's highs and lows, thank you for your continual love and encouragement. I am supported by my wonderful team, who works tirelessly to help me spread these teachings around the world, and I thank you for your dedication, support, and incredible efforts to meet the needs of an ever-growing list of people seeking answers.

Finally, to you, my reader. This book exists *for you and because of you*; my spirit tells me that this book was "summoned" by your requests of the Universe. May its pages bring you the clarity, peace, and healing that your heart deserves. Thank you for having the courage to explore new possibilities with me and forge a profound relationship with your spirit.

ABOUT THE AUTHOR

Christine Lang is a trusted spirit channel, medical intuitive, and energy healer renowned for her ability to bridge the spiritual and practical worlds in her private sessions, channeling workshops, and guest-expert appearances. Internationally renowned, she works with a diverse range of clients, including C-suite executives, professional athletes, television writers and actors, and medical professionals.

As a former attorney, Christine combines her sharp analytical skills with her intuitive gifts to deliver actionable answers and guidance that yield clarity, personal transformation, and professional growth. Her clients report profound improvements in physical and emotional well-being, as well as breakthroughs in their careers, relationships, and creative pursuits.

Christine lives in the college town of Chapel Hill, North Carolina, with her husband and their two spoiled cats. When not guiding clients or teaching, she enjoys gardening, riding horses, training dogs, and attempting to train her cats.

To see her latest offerings, visit her website at www.Chris tineLang.org.